THE KING OF SUNLIGHT

THE KING OF SUNLIGHT

HOW WILLIAM LEVER CLEANED UP THE WORLD

ADAM MACQUEEN

BANTAM PRESS

LONDON · NEW YORK · TORONTO · SYDNEY · AUCKLAND

TRANSWORLD PUBLISHERS
61–63 Uxbridge Road, London W5 5SA
a division of The Random House Group Ltd

RANDOM HOUSE AUSTRALIA (PTY) LTD
20 Alfred Street, Milsons Point, Sydney,
New South Wales 2061, Australia

RANDOM HOUSE NEW ZEALAND LTD
18 Poland Road, Glenfield, Auckland 10, New Zealand

RANDOM HOUSE SOUTH AFRICA (PTY) LTD
Endulini, 5a Jubilee Road, Parktown 2193, South Africa

Published 2004 by Bantam Press
a division of Transworld Publishers

Copyright © Adam Macqueen 2004

A catalogue record for this book is available from the British Library.
ISBN 0593 051858

Typeset in 12/14pt Ehrhardt by
Falcon Oast Graphic Art Ltd.

Printed in Great Britain by
Mackays of Chatham plc, Chatham, Kent

1 3 5 7 9 10 8 6 4 2

Papers used by Transworld Publishers are natural, recyclable products made from
wood grown in sustainable forests. The manufacturing processes conform to the
environmental regulations of the country of origin.

For Aunt Helen, for giving us all a space to think

CONTENTS

CONTENTS

Prologue

THE BALLROOM ON THE MOOR

HOWEVER FIT YOU ARE, RIVINGTON PIKE IS THE SORT OF climb that makes you realize you're not as fit as you used to be. The coach-trippers are content to mill around at the bottom, taking advantage of the tea-rooms and maybe stretching their legs on one of the formal avenues that criss-cross Lever Park and lead you down to the reservoir. Only the hard-core ramblers press on past Rivington Hall and the headquarters of the local Rotary Club, and follow the grass-pocked macadam road across the fields behind, a stumbling parabola up into the woods that cling to the side of the hill.

It's only when you reach the shade of the trees that you realize they are not what they seem; though the branches are as gnarled and intertwined as the spookiest of fairy-tale forests, this woodland is barely a century old. It's the rhododendrons that give it away. Nineteenth-century British landowners planted them like tom-cats laying down scent: you are now entering our territory, beware, Big House ahead. But money comes and money goes, while plants that were built to survive the snowstorms of the

1

Himalayas prosper, and these rich green bushes have long since spread and multiplied across the hillside, swamping paths and bridges and summerhouses on their way. For beneath the rhododendrons, the leaf-mould and bracken and the detritus of eighty years of neglect, there is a formal garden here. A series of terraces is etched into the sandstone like the levels of Dante's inferno, their once formal planting sprawling out and spilling between levels in the darkness beneath the trees. A flight of 365 steps snakes steeply between them; one for each day of the year, bisected by four paths which were built to represent the seasons but have long since mulched down into a year-long autumn twilight. The upward path is treacherous; the steps irregular and slippery underfoot. You're exhausted before you've even made it up the first month's worth.

A hundred years ago, there were lions round here. And zebras, and emus, and buffalo and yak in specially built paddocks, not to mention the flock of flamingos that lived on the Japanese pond further up the hill, laid out with ornamental lamps and pagodas as a living copy of the willow-pattern plate. There was every intention of stocking the caves that had been specially bored into the hillside with bears, too, but somehow it never quite happened. The man behind this fantasy made real, this other Eden in Lancashire, had moved on to another project by then – reading a book about the history of Liverpool Castle and its ruination by Cromwell's armies, he had been seized by the similarity between its site and the banks of the reservoir below, and decided to build a full-size, pre-ruined replica of it instead. Like you do.

At the top of the steps there is a bridge. It spans a narrow gorge above a road, a distance of perhaps forty feet. It could quite easily be traversed by a single arch, but the man whose estate this was wanted seven. Three hundred and sixty-five steps, four paths – so, obviously, seven arches, as he patiently explained to his chief stonemason. But it's too narrow, the man objected. Right, pack a suitcase, he was told. We're going on a trip. As the legend tells it, the next morning the stonemason found himself on board an Imperial Airways flight to Nigeria; a short drive through Lagos left them standing beneath an extraordinary bridge with one central arch and six smaller, decorative ones above it. Like that, his boss said, and handed him a sketchbook.

The bridge rises at a steep angle and leads on to the lawns – the terracing here is wider, with great flat spaces created by simply slicing off great chunks of the hillside. A vast rock has been left in the middle of the largest lawn to show the original height of the ground: it stands some seven feet high, though now even this is all but lost in a riot of brambles which have swamped the immaculate turf, once specially imported from the mountains of Scotland. A flight of semi-circular stairs leads up from the great lawn to another plateau, this one at 1,000 feet above sea-level, almost the very pinnacle of Rivington Pike. From here you can see for ever. And in the grass, amid the bracken and brambles, you can make out the ghost of a house, its foundations protruding from the thick vegetation. An extraordinary house, one that stood low but long, laid out in the shape of two interlocked capital Ls: LL, for the man who created all this, the man whose home it was, William Lever, Lord Leverhulme.

The northernmost wing of this house – 'The Bungalow', he called it, though it had its own ballroom, domestic staff, gatehouses and forty-five acres of grounds – was left unglazed, the winds rushing in unimpeded across the Lancashire moors and whistling through the pillared cloisters, the rain crashing down into the inner rooms which were left unroofed. These were the conditions in which Lord Leverhulme, a millionaire with four luxurious homes, one of them a castle, liked to sleep. He would lie in bed beneath a few blankets and a thin counterpane, and let nature do its worst. He slept like a baby. Neither shower nor storm could stir him. It was not unknown for him to wake up beneath a covering of snow, which he would shake off before plunging with vigour into a freezing cold bath at dawn. It was, he insisted, the only possible way to rest.

I took out a plan of the house from the 1920s, and smoothed it out flat on the ground, trying to protect it from the biting wind. Here were the winter gardens, a glazed walkway where flowers, vines and tropical ferns thrived in the heat pumped out by the bungalow's boilers, and tank after tank of goldfish gazed myopically out at the moors beyond. This must have been the inner hall, where once a tiger-skin rug had lain guard over Lord Leverhulme's priceless collection of art and antiques. And here was the dining-room, where once you could lean back and study the constellations of the northern hemisphere picked out in gold on the panelled ceiling.

Here and there were patches of black and white tiles, their incongruous chequerboard pattern peeping through a covering of green. I knelt and began to pull away handfuls of moss: it came away clean, exposing more and more of the ornate floor beneath, perfectly preserved. Before long a whole room was visible: a triangular alcove, its curved hypotenuse following the edge of the ballroom that Leverhulme had installed when he discovered a passion for dancing in his seventies. 'I like to have a few young friends about me against whom I can chaff; it keeps my mind young and prevents me from becoming dull and heavy,' declared the old man. The dance-floor was forty-five feet in diameter, and the room had its own minstrels' gallery above the door, designed to amplify the sound of a band already instructed to play uncomfortably loud. He was deaf as a post, and couldn't even hear the music. Sometimes he carried on dancing after everyone else had stopped, twirling an embarrassed partner round the floor as the others were busy applauding the orchestra. But he found an ingenious solution to this problem too: one instrumentalist was employed to switch on a blue light in the ceiling as each tune came to an end, and Lever caught the reflection in his specially polished patent leather shoes.

This was not a man who let such trifling things as disability, the weather or mountains stand in his way. As one baffled interviewer put it in 1910, 'Mr Lever seldom does anything like other people.'

1

BOLTON BOYS

LATER IN LIFE, WHEN HIS NAME WAS KNOWN AND PRAISED throughout the British empire, when workmen from the Mersey to the Congo called him Chief, when he counted kings and prime ministers among his personal acquaintance, had a seat in the House of Lords and owned four stately homes scattered the length of the country, William Lever was fond of telling anyone who would listen that he had come from poor beginnings.

He was born on 19 September 1851 in Bolton, a town described seven years earlier as 'one of the worst' in Britain by no less an authority than Friedrich Engels. Bolton was 'badly and irregularly built, with foul courts, lanes and back-alleys', he wrote in his book *The Condition of the Working Class in England*, a scientific inquiry into whether it really was Grim Up North which the mill-owner's son penned a year before teaming up with Karl Marx to try to change the world. Engels found that Bolton had 'but one main street, Deansgate, a very dirty one, which serves as a market and is even in the finest weather a dark, unattractive hole'. Smoke belched from the dozens of chimneys that stabbed into the sky above the town, and settled on the ramshackle homes, dank cellars and jerry-built terraces that housed the town's 60,000 inhabitants. Through the daylight hours men, women and children alike toiled in the deafening racket of the cotton mills, the heat and fug of the steel forges, or the shifting, crumbling darkness of the fifty or so mines that wound beneath the surface of the city. And by night they drank themselves into lairy oblivion in the hundreds of beer-houses and illegal spirit shops that sprawled through every street and made certain quarters no-go areas even for the town's newly formed police force.

But William Lever wasn't part of this. His family home at 16 Wood Street may have only been 100 yards from the 'dark hole' of Deansgate, but it was like another world, an enclave of middle-class sobriety and professionalism where every house came with at least one servant attached. It's almost unchanged today: head up Bradshawgate from the station past World of Leather, the pawnbrokers and the pay-and-display car parks that always seem to proliferate in the less salubrious parts of town, turn right just before the Yates' Wine Lodge and you step back 150 years. A little-used cul-de-sac which terminates at a pretty private garden, Wood Street had already fallen behind on the council's road replacement programme before they noticed in 1970 that the cobbles looked quite nice after all and designated it as a conservation area. The Georgian terraces on either side are occupied by brass-plated solicitors and chartered accountants: it's so posh Pizza Express have opened a branch in the old bank three doors up from number 16.

When William Lever's son visited his father's birthplace in 1927, he was amused to find it had become the headquarters of the Bolton Socialist Club: 'Strange indeed are the chances and changes in the whirligig of time,' he mused. Time, it would seem, is still whirligigging today, because despite New Labour's best efforts to stamp their kind out, the Socialists are still in residence, and, like most socialists, they've not got much cash for home improvements, which means the building is virtually unchanged. A smart bow window and pedimented door were added to the front not long after the Levers moved out, but head through the ginnel at the side of the house to stand among the bins and you can see a scene that could have come straight out of Dickens. A dank yard is overlooked by the one remaining original window, now half bricked up, its frame rotting away, covered by thick iron bars. Perhaps this is the family nursery where little James Lever, unwatched by the maid and playing too close to the fire, went up in flames and had to be saved by seven-year-old William. He rolled the toddler up in the hearthrug, earning praise from his parents for his 'great promptitude' and eternal gratitude from his younger brother.

Despite James's flammable tendencies, the Levers only lost one of their ten children, their eldest daughter, who died at the age of nine. This was no mean feat in Bolton in the 1850s: the high rate of infant mortality dragged the average life expectancy among the working classes down to a pathetic eighteen, and the tradesman class to which the Levers belonged fared little better with an average of just twenty-three. Eight out of their ten were girls, which according to their cheerful father James was 'all right to me', but his wife Eliza admitted to a sense of relief when William and the younger James turned up as numbers seven and eight.

Ever mindful of the business that had provided for this amount of Leverage, James paid a double tribute with the name he gave to his firstborn son. William's middle name, Hesketh, served as a dual tribute to his mother's family and the (unrelated) wholesale grocers Stones and Hesketh who had taken on his father as a partner in 1841. Little James did even better: proud of a family title that resonated throughout the place names of the area and which could be traced back to the fifteenth century, his father saddled him with the middle name Darcy after the village of Darcy Lever a few miles south of Bolton. It could have been worse – the villages on either side were called Great and Little Lever. And they weren't all that far from Nob End.

James senior looked exactly like Victorian patriarchs ought to, his long face framed by two great mutton-chops that stretched from temple to jowl but failed to meet at either the top or the bottom. A devout Congregationalist churchman, he frowned on smoking and drinking, but having converted late in life from the less strict C of E, he got his kicks vicariously by permitting his children to play cards in the house as long as they a) didn't play for money, and b) let him watch. Unlike many of Bolton's religious men, he didn't condemn the theatre, and while the family avoided the boozy music halls favoured by the drinking and fighting classes, they were quite happy to take in the pantomimes at the Theatre Royal, which stretched the traditional storylines to include the very latest in spectacular special effects – 1859's *Babes in the Wood* managed to shoehorn in a scene onboard 'the deck of a man of war, manned by sixty children' as well as a cameo from the 'original man monkey'. Just as spectacular was the New Year Fair, which featured presentations such as 'the most wonderful and vastly astonishing views of the battle of Vaterloo' and 'Guy Faux a-goin' to blow up the Houses of Parliament' as well as pasty-eating competitions, fortune-telling, stalls selling ice cream, oysters or hot potatoes, and the music of competing barrel organs and fiddlers ringing out till the small hours across the Market Square. For the most part, however, the Lever children spent their evenings 'at home in quiet occupation', something at which William excelled.

He was a precocious child. Before he could even walk, let alone read, William had rearranged the family's library by height order, a 'systematizing' which he later recalled 'used to give me such intense delight when I could only crawl to the bookshelf'. With his family's own shelves ordered to his satisfaction, he became an enthusiastic patron of the Bolton lending library, opened in 1853 to, as the mayor put it, 'turn a man's habits from being of a degraded and sensual nature to being of an educated and intellectual character', though he preferred the factual works in the reference section to the classics of children's literature that suddenly started popping up like mushrooms in the 1850s (*The Rose and the Ring*, *Tom Brown's Schooldays*, *The Water Babies* and *Alice in Wonderland* were all published during the first fourteen years of William's life). While some children might have regarded the rabbits his parents kept in the back yard as pets, William saw them as a chance to design a self-sufficient ecosystem, growing trays of grass on the roofs of the hutches to serve both as insulation and food, fattening the beasts up effectively for the household pot. With the family dog, a black and white collie by the name of Guess, he roamed the moors above Bolton. Boy and dog wandered as far afield as Rivington Pike and the model factory communities north of the town at Barrow Bridge and Eagley, which Quaker boss Henry Ashworth had provided with schools, reading rooms and gardens, luxuries unheard of back in town. He would return home with samples of plants and insects he had found on the moors and study them through his microscope, a gift from his father, making careful notes of his findings.

From the age of six, William attended a private school conducted by two spinsters by the splendid name of the Misses Aspinwall. Here he received the peculiarly un-balanced basics of Victorian education; children were expected to be able to add and subtract four-figure sums by the age of six, but only to master single-syllable words, which enabled them to read primers that told them 'Ben has a nag and a gig, the nag is fat and big', but nothing that actually meant anything. If they were good, after that they were allowed to tackle 'words of two syllables accented on the first', which in one 1872 textbook included such every-day kiddiespeak as 'doom–ed', 'e–dict', 'eth–ic', and 'fu–tile'.

He didn't have far to go – the school was in a house on the opposite side of Wood Street. Two of his classmates were to play a huge part in his life – a boy called Jonathan Simpson, who shared Lever's voracious appetite for read-ing, and a girl called Elizabeth Ellen Hulme, the daughter of a local draper, who was best friends with his sister Alice and whom he admired during games of tig for being 'the best runner away of any of us'. The children at the Misses Aspinwalls were a privileged lot: primary schooling did not become compulsory until the 1870s, when the under-nines were officially banned from employment in factories, though in reality children risked life and limb crawling between the spinning-mules in the factories that surrounded the genteel oasis of Wood Street for years after that. At thirteen both William and Jonathan Simpson were enrolled at the local Church Institute, just a couple of streets away. This gothic pile is now a church hall, surrounded by other more modern buildings and stranded in the middle of a car park, but contemporary photographs show it standing splendidly aloof in the midst of a vast, scorched-earth playground patrolled by a bearded school-master complete with mortar-board and gown. The pupils wore long breeches and boaters; they worked at long communal desks beneath vast windows, but their light never seemed to penetrate the dingy classrooms.

> A long room, with three long rows of desks, and six of forms, and bristling all around with pegs for hats and slates. Scraps of old copybooks and exercises litter the dirty floor. Some silkworms' houses, made of the same materials, are scattered over the desks . . . There is a strange unwholesome smell upon the room, like mildewed corduroys, sweet apples wanting air, and rotten books. There could not well be more ink splashed about, if it had been roofless from its first construction, and the skies had rained, snowed, hailed, and blown ink through the varying seasons of the year.

William would have recognized that schoolroom from the novel that remained his favourite throughout his life, Dickens's *David Copperfield*, published in 1850. While he never, like the unfortunate David, had to wear a placard warning of his evil behaviour ('Take care of him! He bites!'), he was an unexceptional pupil, plodding through his studies competently, learning by rote such vital inform-ation as the names and order of the capes and bays round the coastline of Britain, the dates of England's kings and queens, and vast swathes of the King James Bible which was the standard text in all schools. While he failed to excel on the sports field, he was a good swimmer, maintaining his *mens sana in corpore sano* with obsessively measured-out lengths in the town's chilly swimming baths.

Why did James Lever, a firm Congregationalist, send his sons to a school run by the rival Church of England? Partly it was down to the reputation of the master, Mr Mason, as a man who brooked no nonsense from the boys in his care and could beat Latin grammar into even the most recalcitrant mind. But some of it must have been down to pride in the family tree: the Church Institute existed largely thanks to the generosity of Robert Lever, a philanthropically minded Boltonian who died the year before the Civil War broke out, and to whom the Wood Street Levers claimed a direct link.

Naturally, his school studies were not enough to keep William busy, and he fitted lessons in French and shorthand into his spare time. His son put it this way: 'he cultivated the habit of reckoning out almost each hour of the day and spending it to advantage, making his life a voyage westward with those extra minutes gained each day which are non-existent to him who stands still'. His extra-curricular activities would put even the pushiest of today's parents to shame. He and Simpson started up their own reading circle, with works by Shakespeare and Dickens on a cycle alongside the Bible, which William dipped into daily and regarded as 'a book of practical advice'. Subscribers to Dickens's *Household Words* magazine, they heard the man himself read from *The Pickwick Papers* when one of his endless public reading tours stopped off in Bolton, and travelled to Manchester to see various Shakespearean productions at the Princes' Theatre on the cheap, standing in the pit with, as the thrifty William put it, 'an excellent view for a shilling'. He was less keen on the sort of entertainments his sisters dragged him along to – 'Mary, Jane, Alice and I went to Mrs Tillotson's party and enjoyed it very much but I should have liked it better if they had not danced all night,' he moaned to a friend at thirteen, though, he was chuffed to admit, 'we did not come home till 3 o'clock in the morning!' For Mary, the night was more of a success, since she ended up marrying Mrs Tillotson's eldest son. A family holiday the same year was met with more enthusiasm – 'The day before Good Friday Mamma, James and I went to Blackpool and Papa came on Friday morning. On Friday we had a sail on a steamer, and I thought that it would be very nice sailing to Egypt if there were not such a thing as sea-sickness!' In 1865 he solemnly noted the assassination of Abraham Lincoln in another letter: 'these events have caused a great sensation in Bolton'.

The most significant event in William's teenage years, however, came on his sixteenth birthday, when his father presented him with a copy of *Self Help* by Samuel Smiles. 'It is impossible for me to say how much I owe to the fact that in my early youth I obtained a copy,' he repeated end-lessly when asked the secret of his success, and he almost single-handedly kept the book on the best-seller lists for fifty years by presenting an inscribed copy of it to any adolescent who happened to cross his path. A kind of nineteenth-century *Men Are from Mars, Women Are Best Not Thought About at All*, Smiles's best-seller was a series of brief lives of Great Men who had tugged themselves up by their own bootstraps. It chimed perfectly with the mood of the times – Andrew Johnson had risen from humble tailor all the way to US president, and countless British boys made good on the back of the industrial revolution were busy blowing the dust from the ancient ranks of the peerage. But Smiles's book resonates beyond the 1850s: this is the book that other grocer's child, Margaret Thatcher, had in mind when she banged on about Victorian Values. Its pages of practical advice remain relevant: you can easily imagine advice addict Bridget Jones agonizing over such homilies as 'we must be satisfied to advance in life as we walk, step by step', or vowing to follow his instructions about 'writing down thoughts and facts for the purpose of holding them fast and preventing their escape into the dim region of forgetfulness'. To William, of course, all this came as second nature. 'With perseverance, the very odds and ends of time may be worked up into results of the greatest value – an hour in every day withdrawn from frivolous pursuits would, if profitably employed, enable a person of ordinary capacity to go far towards mastering a science,' wrote Smiles, in a single stroke validating the last sixteen years of the boy's spare time.

Lever would have read with particular interest Smiles's potted biographies of Shakespeare, Michael Faraday and Cardinal Wolsey, three figures who he claimed had started out in life behind the counters of shops. For in 1867, not long after his sixteenth birthday, William started work. His mother had always hoped he would train as a doctor, like their most respectable neighbours in Wood Street. But his father never had any doubt that his eldest son would follow in his own footsteps. 'I was never asked if I wanted to go into the grocery business,' recalled Lever, 'and it was perhaps a good thing that I was not. My father told me, one day, that I had better get ready to come into the family grocery business, and as the holidays were nearly over, I thought I might as well begin next morning, and I did.'

2

TODAY WIGAN, TOMORROW THE WORLD

MRS HESKETH WAS A MERRY WIDOW WHO BROUGHT JOHN
Stones in to help her run her wholesale grocery business in
Bolton's Manor Street after her husband dropped dead, and
wasted no time in letting him have a share of her home life
as well. Despite an age-gap of some twenty years, they
married, and James Lever, William's father, was brought
into partnership to look after the retail side of the business
while the odd couple ran the warehouse next door and dealt
with the orders that came in from grocers throughout the
local area. Known as the Lower Blackamoor after the sign
James Lever displayed in the window for the benefit of
illiterate customers, the shop was popular, but when his
partners retired in 1864 and James took over the whole
of the business, he shut it down to concentrate on
the more profitable wholesale side of the company. It was a
shrewd move. Small grocery shops always teetered on the
edge of bankruptcy: customers tended to abandon them in
favour of the markets with their more negotiable prices
when times were hard, while the richer patrons took

16

everything on account and needed much prompting before settling up, a privilege that was not extended by the suppliers at the other end of the food chain. Within a decade the independents would start to be forced off the streets by 'multiples' like Liptons, Boots and J. Sainsbury: shops like the Lower Blackamoor would soon be a thing of the past.

As an apprentice William was shown few favours by his father. James had inherited a long-serving and loyal staff along with the business, and he had continued to cultivate them – in William's words, 'the methods he had always adopted of taking a personal interest in all his staff, in their health and family circles, established a relationship between them that was outside the usual limitations of business'. He always recalled one of his father's assistants, a man with a wife and children to support, offering to take a pay cut when the business was going through a bad patch. The last thing James needed was to put their noses out of joint by over-promoting his son in their midst. William's apprenticeship was under the same terms as anyone else's. His day began at seven; first in, he took down the shutters and swept and tidied the warehouse ready for the arrival of his father half an hour later. At least he did not have far to go – the family had moved 'over the shop' when James took over the business, and in the absence of Eliza, Mary and Jane, who had all been successfully married off, they had just as much room as they had been used to in Wood Street. The day was spent preparing orders for the various shops the business supplied. The salesmen returned from their rounds with orders for the products Lever's specialized in – potted meat, mustard, soap, starch, black lead, milk, butter and eggs – and gave them to the clerks, who totted them up and passed them down to the warehousemen to be made up. One of the last links in the chain was William, who was put in charge of preparing sugar and soap. Both products arrived in large, solid bars more than a foot long, which had to be sliced down into manageable quantities and individually wrapped in greaseproof paper. It was tedious and tiring work, and William, ever the improver, couldn't help thinking there had to be a better way.

He stuck at it, however, and before too long his father had moved him to a department that better suited his talents. Ensconced in the office, his soap duties taken over by a younger apprentice, William set about sorting out the company's accounts. The company relied on a haphazard system left over from the days of Widow Hesketh: William put his mind to creating an alternative, more efficient method of book-keeping. Knowing his father's natural conservatism all too well, William wisely got his fellow clerks on-side before attempting to sell the idea to the old man, but the success of his modernized system granted the son new respect and an increased voice in the company.

Business was good, and James Lever was soon able to swap the Manor Street warehouse for bigger and better premises on Victoria Square, slap-bang in the centre of town. The square had recently become one of the city's most desirable addresses thanks to the sweeping away of the market stalls that had filled it for centuries to make way for the brand-new Town Hall. One of those extraordinary explosions of municipal grandeur that the Victorians specialized in, the building mingles bits and pieces of church, palace and Greek temple in a glorious mish-mash of which William would have definitely approved. It was opened by the Prince and Princess of Wales in 1873: 150,000 people turned out to line the streets and were soaked by the rain that poured down throughout the ceremony. The Levers and their staff, however, remained dry, with a prime view from the upper windows of the new warehouse as Prince Edward climbed the steps of the new building and unlocked the great doors with a ceremonial silver key.

The Town Hall is all that remains of the square from Lever's time. The building where the Levers worked is long gone, swept away along with all its neighbours in the early 1960s and replaced with a featureless shopping arcade which glories in the title of the Concrete Society's Best Concrete Landscape in the Country 1977. It's just as depressing as it sounds.

William had no desire to hang around in Victoria Square. When a vacancy came up on the sales staff, all his persuasive powers were called into play. James was at first unwilling to let his son take the job, claiming he needed him on the premises, but simple economics won out. William pointed out that good salesmen got £4 a week in salary: he would do the job on the same terms as he had taken his apprenticeship, bed and board plus pocket money of a shilling a week and a little extra for special occasions – even with the thirty shillings that would be needed to pay the clerk brought in to do his current job, that meant savings by any accounting system. Besides, his younger brother James had turned sixteen and was ready to come into the warehouse, so his father would actually be getting two sons for the price of one.

Years later, William would remember the time he spent driving his one-horse gig through the countryside around Bolton as some of the most enjoyable work he had ever done. He was a natural salesman, never happier than when setting targets for himself and then striving to exceed them, unfailingly charming, and willing to venture into even the roughest neighbourhoods, sighing to himself that 'there are men like this, but they have to buy goods'. 'To be an ideal commercial a man must have all the qualities of a Prime Minister, a Chancellor of the Exchequer, a French Ambassador and a leading King's Counsel,' he lectured his own sales force forty years later. He didn't often find himself lacking the necessary skills, though one incident stuck in his mind.

I remember on one occasion, I was travelling in that part of the world somewhere between Upholland and Skelmersdale, and I pulled up in my gig at a customer's as usual one morning about eleven o'clock and jumped out. The lady who was usually in the shop was absent on this occasion, and the strange lady who was in the shop and whom I had never seen before, said, 'Will you come this way?' When I got through the shop the lady began leading the way upstairs, and I said, 'I think you must be mistaken, madam', whereupon she said, 'You are the doctor aren't you?' 'No,' I replied, 'I am the grocery traveller, and I have come for the grocery order.' 'Oh,' said the lady, 'my sister is upstairs expecting a baby, and I thought you were the doctor.' You see what a narrow escape I had?

William's work was not his only reason for travelling. Following the death of her father when she was eleven, his young playmate Elizabeth Hulme had moved to Southport to be nearer her mother's family. She and Alice Lever had remained friends, and William often offered to chaperon his sister during her visits. It was not an entirely disinterested gesture. The boy who had found girls tiresome and dancing-fixated at thirteen had decided he quite liked them after all, and Elizabeth in particular. Fortunately she was less inclined to run away from him by this time, and agreed to join him on a series of picnics on the moors above Bolton. Their favourite spot was a remote and steep hillside with extraordinary views across the surrounding areas, 1,000 feet above sea level on Rivington Pike.

In 1872, when William and Elizabeth were twenty-one, they announced their engagement. His best friend, Jonathan Simpson, who had been articled to an architect at sixteen, announced his own betrothal to one of Elizabeth's best friends, Mary Lomax, at the same time. So delighted were the Levers with the match that James announced he was taking his son into partnership in the family business, with a consequent jump in his earnings to the princely sum of £800 a year.

William and Elizabeth were married two years later at the Congregational Church on St George's Road, Bolton. These days it shares its name with another Saint (Andrew shacked up with George in 1979) and its building with a new-agey charity shop, but it is doing better than the C of E across the road, which is now a craft market, and the Methodist chapel further along, which has become a casino, which neither John Wesley nor God would be too chuffed about.

Elizabeth was no beauty – there is a wonderful portrait of her in her fifties where she looks almost identical to the pet bulldog sitting by her chair – but then William, a short man whose eyes stuck out and gave him a permanently startled look, was hardly a catch either. She had a kind face and an infectious smile, and, more to the point, she loved William and supported him to the point of indulgence. According to their son, 'her contribution was sympathy and understanding – an unquestioning belief in the rightness of all that her husband undertook. She never asked for any altered mode of life which might have distracted him from the work he had in hand,' but he also conceded that 'my mother influenced his life's achievements in a way not easily to be explained to those who did not know her intimately'. Certainly her mark was upon many of Lever's subsequent schemes, a homely practicality that served to fill in the blind spots in his grand visions and ensure they survived the addition of real living people to the equation. And the couple were utterly devoted to one another. As their son put it years later, 'my parents used to say that they never remembered a world without each other in it'.

William's pay rise enabled the young couple to move up in the world. Their first married home, number 2 Park Street, was a distinct shift towards the posh end of town. The Chorley New Road stretched out from Bolton through the suburbs of Heaton and Victory, and on into open countryside, flanked by the vast villas of the mill-owners, built on cotton and stinking of cash. Park Street was at the town end, but number 2 was a solid hulk of semi-detached respectability, complete with a set of bay windows meant as much for looking at as out of. The dingy yard at the back was transformed into a mini-rain forest: 'I have always been a lover of ferns, and at Park Street I built a fernery out of old bacon boxes in the back-yard, covered the inside with virgin cork and had ferns growing luxuriously.'

Lever got to indulge another hobby in the new house too: his passion for amateur architecture, as cultivated vicariously through Jonathan Simpson's training. Park Street didn't have much in the way of features, but it did have plenty of doors and fireplaces, which Lever quickly ripped out and replaced with fancier versions that were more to his taste. He mixed and matched periods in a way that irritated both Simpson, who thought he should choose a style and stick to it, and his parents, who disapproved of his 'needless extravagance'. However, since it was the cash William had brought into the business that was paying for both his and their little luxuries, they didn't complain too loudly.

For William had transformed his father's company. Not by introducing anything revolutionary, but simply by carrying on doing what was being done anyway – only better. 'There is a general impression that in making money you have to do something very wonderful, but believe me, there is much more money made in doing something better than ever it was done before than in doing something new – far more,' he said in a 'secrets of my success' speech in 1915. Certainly he was a better salesman than those that had done the job before him – he realized early on that women were more inclined to try new products than their husbands, and from that point on, he never forgot the name of a child on his rounds, so that he could impress their mothers by asking after their progress and segue neatly into a special offer on butter. So effective was his patter that he found himself in the village of Hindley, the end of his round, by half-past three one spring afternoon, with a bulging order book, and nothing but a long ride back into town ahead of him. Where others would have sloped off for a crafty pint in the sun, Lever directed his horse towards Wigan, stopped at the first grocery shop he came to in a village called Ince, and introduced himself.

I can still see the shop. I can still see four or five baskets of French butter in it, I can still see where they had the cheese on the counter, and I can still see where they had the sugar wrapped up on the shelves ... I got an order for three-quarters of a hundredweight of sugar wrapped up in pounds. I went to another man and got an order from him. Then I went to another and got an order from

him. Altogether I did five or six calls in that hour-and-a-half, in
addition to the driving.

Forty years on, his recollections were so clear because he
traced all his subsequent success to that moment. 'If I had
not had an insatiable thirst for expansion and for the trial of
novel methods, if I had felt at 3.30 that merely because the
usual day's work was completed I could return home and do
nothing more for the remainder of the day, the present
business could never have been built up.' If he had been
able to consult his father, he would have undoubtedly
been told not to bother. The next town was another world,
with its own ways and wholesalers, unknown territory. The
wise businessman should stick to what and where he knew
best. But then that was why James Lever never became a
millionaire, and his son did.

Before long the shopkeepers of Ince had been
permanently added to his rounds.

I found that on each successive journey I was doing a little more
and a little more, getting away for Hindley earlier and earlier, and
getting more customers – in fact, I made a regular journey of it
and had to alter the arrangements and take a whole day for Ince.
Then, when I took a whole day for Ince, I began travelling beyond
Ince into Wigan, and I gradually got some customers at Wigan,
until I thought, 'well, this is very foolish – here we are paying
three-quarters of a ton extra railway carriage from Liverpool to
Bolton through Wigan, then having to cart it back again to Wigan
at five shillings more. We had better have a place in Wigan.'

Even his cautious father could see the sense in this. They
bought up Ormerod and Company, a wholesale business
charitably described as 'ailing' (partly because the Levers

had taken all their trade away), and the eldest son was installed as manager. Just three years into their marriage, Elizabeth and William were separated. The idea of spending several hours a day simply commuting back and forth when he could be doing something useful was more than William could bear. Instead he rented a house in Upper Dicconson Street in which he lived during the week, returning to his young bride each weekend. He made some home improvements here as well, and it was soon the only house in the 'plain, monotonous' road to feature a Robert Adamstyle moulded ceiling and decorative frieze. Even more spectacular was the couple's new Bolton home, way up the Chorley New Road, which Jonathan Simpson designed for them complete with fancy parquetry, ornamental ceilings and a plethora of differently shaped windows. His parents, meanwhile, went even more upmarket, with a move to Harwood Lodge, a Jacobean pile two miles outside town. Always respectable, the Lever family had finally made the jump into the big-money league.

With his sixty-six-year-old father in semi-retirement, William was allowed more of a free rein in the running of the company. His brother and co-partner James was as cautious as their father, but infinitely more persuadable. The brothers could not have been more different. James junior was a timid man who agonized over every possible outcome of each decision; William thought only in straight lines and simply forged boldly forwards through anything that came up in his path. William took to his position as boss as if it was divinely ordained; James was so worried about upsetting staff that he would often do a job himself rather than order someone else to do it.

Nevertheless, both brothers put their all into the family business. Their father had had to rely on local suppliers for

his fresh produce: these days the railways could bring anything from anywhere in under a day. The best butter and
eggs came from Ireland, so William and James went there
with a sheaf of blank contracts and came back with a new
supply. Too many of the eggs arrived broken from Dublin,
so they designed a special kind of crate that would hold
them separately and stop them cracking in transit. Pleased
with their new idea, William headed down to the patent
office to safeguard it; while he was there he registered the
name 'Lever's Pure Honey' and started stamping it on bars
of yellow soap which he sold for a higher price than usual.
Orders went up, so he tried the same trick with their butter,
christening it 'Ulster Fresh Lumps' and placing advertisements in the *Bolton Evening News* and the *Weekly Journal* to
announce just how fresh and lumpy it was. They got the ads
at a knock-down rate, courtesy of publisher W. F. Tillotson,
who happened to be their brother-in-law, that same boy
who had danced with Mary at the ball all those years ago. In
return, Tillotson gave them cut rates on articles from the
syndication service he ran between Britain and America,
which were printed in the *Lancashire Grocer*, a monthly
'house organ' which the Levers supplied to all their clients.
The American material helped liven up what was otherwise
a fairly dull read, consisting of 'price lists, principal brands,
and items of interest to the trade, as well as articles of an
educational nature for retail grocers and their assistants'. It
was typical William – not just making sure his clients got
their money's worth, but trying to make their lives just a
little more worthwhile at the same time.

Every single experiment paid off. In less than twenty
years, William had gone from a shilling-a-week apprentice
to the dominant partner in a thriving business, with a
turnover of tens of thousands every year. He had done so

with barely a break, but in 1884 Jonathan Simpson managed to persuade him to take a few weeks off and bring Elizabeth to join him and his wife on a cruise round the Scottish islands.

As the boat chugged up the west coast past Islay and the Mull of Kintyre, some of Lever's characteristic intensity seemed to ebb away. His shoulders dropped, his gait on his daily perambulations around the deck slowed, and he turned his face to the August sun that shone strongly down on the holidaymakers. At Stornoway on the Isle of Lewis they disembarked for a few hours, and wandered the streets of the pretty town, where Lever was delighted by the 'natural beauty and variety of scenery, its wonderful healthiness of climate and the charm and attraction of its people'. It was here that he announced a decision to his old friend. At thirty-three, he had had enough. He was going to retire.

3

SUDS LAW

DO YOU KNOW WHAT SOAP IS MADE OF? HOPEFULLY YOU USE it every day, but do you know what that stuff you slather over yourself actually contains? Answers on page 33. And don't go running off to the bathroom to check, that's cheating.

William Lever didn't know a lot about the stuff when he founded his fortune on it either – he was, he claimed, 'as ignorant of soap-making as a baby in arms'. All he knew, from his years dispatching the stuff to customers, was that it was popular, and getting more so. Britain became significantly less smelly in the nineteenth century. In 1801 the average Briton used just 3.6lb of soap a year on both their clothes and themselves. By 1861 this had shot up to a considerably more hygienic 8lb per annum, and it would more than double again by the end of the century. Part of this was simply down to more dirt: the industrial revolution had left every town in Britain under a permanent thick chemical fog: factory chimneys belched out black smuts which coated clothes and skin alike, while the work that went on beneath them was strenuous and often undertaken in sweltering conditions, on badly ventilated shop floors crowded with constantly moving machinery.

For the less-sweaty classes, fashion played a part. The Duke of Wellington might have hammered Napoleon and served as prime minister, but his other legacies were his famous boots and his habit of taking a bath every day, a trend which caught on with his better-off contemporaries. The wash-hand-stand familiar from innumerable antique shops, complete with its basin, jug and soap dish, was a Victorian innovation. Godliness was very much to be hoped for, but cleanliness had become in easy reach of all, especially after Gladstone abolished the soap tax in 1853. Now the stinky really had no excuse.

All this passed through the mind of William Lever during his 1884 cruise. His retirement announcement turned out to be not much more than the fantasy most of us indulge in after a couple of weeks away from the office. Jonathan Simpson would soon get used to these periodical bouts of pension envy – 'more than once, your father has talked to me about retiring from business, but I have always looked upon these announcements as being a prelude not to retirement, but to some further burst of activity', he advised Lever's son on one occasion, warning him not to anticipate an early legacy. While he was determined to move away from the grocery business, which was in rude enough health to keep him till the end of his days, thirty-three-year-old William could hardly have stuck doing nothing for forty years or more. As the boat sailed on round Orkney and down the east coast of Scotland, he cast his mind back to his first days in his father's warehouse, and remembered the tedium of soap-chopping. And he mused on the success of 'Lever's Pure Honey', the own-brand soap he had patented, which had proved such a hit that several other wholesalers had leapt into the market with impurer Honeys of their own.

Pure Honey had been born in the patent office in Liverpool, and it was there that Lever headed almost as soon as he and Elizabeth had unpacked after their return from Scotland. Patenting was a new art, introduced by government act less than a decade before, but many businessmen had been quick to see the advantages of registering their ideas. Cash could be reaped not only from the products themselves, but also in the law courts if their competitors' packaging strayed too close to their own. The Liverpool patent office was run by W. P. Thompson, a helpful chap who devoted most of an afternoon to coming up with something that would please his client. Thompson made several suggestions himself, and even jotted them down on a sheet of paper so that they could imagine how they would look on packaging. But nothing quite rang a bell with Lever. 'Really, at first blush, none of those names appealed to me. I had big ideas of some sort of name – I did not know what, but it was going to be such a marvel, and when I saw it written down in cold ink, the names that were possible, names that you could register and fight for, names that did not describe the article, that were neither geographical or descriptive, that didn't refer to quality, and got over all the obstacles that the trade marks law has very properly put in front of us, none of them appealed to me. I put the list in my pocket and went away feeling disappointed.'

During the next few days he carted Thompson's list around with him in his waistcoat pocket, taking it out whenever he had a spare moment at the office, sketching out the names on it in capitals and then again in lower-case, doodling around them and generally dithering, but no blinding light of inspiration appeared. It was only after the best part of a week had gone by that one suddenly jumped out at him, and he was filled with such a suffocating paranoia that someone else might have registered it in the meantime that he immediately rushed back to Thompson's office in person to stake his claim. And so Sunlight came into being.

All that was left now was to actually find a soap to stamp it on. Lever's original plan was to buy in a range of the better soaps from a variety of manufacturers, and simply market them all under the new name, to 'present a uniformity of quality under "Sunlight" brand, obtainable from no individual maker in the United Kingdom'. But one of the soaps that William and James, who tagged along in this enterprise as he had with all his brother's schemes, bought in for comparison stood out from the rest. It was sweeter-smelling than the others, with an air of freshness that they lacked, and it lathered beautifully – something that was essential, since it would mostly be used for washing clothes, a process that was back-breaking and time-consuming enough in those pre-machine days without having to spend extra time getting a decent froth on the soap. In fact, so latherable was it that Lever decided it deserved the title of 'Sunlight Self-Washer, for I claimed that it could wash of itself'. The stuff practically wrote its own advertising copy. There was no competition.

Unfortunately the makers of the soap in question also recognized a good thing, and promptly jacked up the price they were going to charge Lever when they realized they were talking about an exclusive deal. They would hold all the cards in any future negotiations if the soap proved a success – they could simply demand even more to carry on producing. The Levers would effectively be putting their own reputation on the line in order to make more cash for some soap makers who had never bothered to take advantage of their product themselves. It would make far more sense to rethink the business plan and for the brothers to simply buy the recipe and produce the stuff themselves. But that required capital. And getting capital out of the business involved getting permission from their father.

'The father seldom encouraged the son's expansiveness, although he was the first to applaud it when success came,' was how Lever's own son diplomatically described his grandfather. It must have taken all William's powers of persuasion to bring his father behind the soap business. At first the old man would only repeat one of his favourite sayings, 'a cobbler should stick to his last', and bang on about how he had seven daughters to provide for. In fact, the family managed to marry off all but three of William's sisters, and the spinsters who were left over almost certainly saved them a fortune in servants' wages around the house. Besides, as his more indulgent wife may have gently pointed out to him, they wouldn't be living in luxury at Harwood Lodge if it wasn't for William and his expansive tendencies.

Eventually, with much huffing and puffing, James Lever withdrew £4,000 from the grocery business and handed it over to his eldest son to do his worst with. He rather more quietly handed over a substantial personal loan as well, and from various other sources William and his brother managed to get together some £27,000 to start the Sunlight business. With it they leased a soap works in Warrington, which came complete with a works manager, Percy Winser, and his long-serving soap boiler Edward Wainwright. Fortunately these two men did know exactly what soap was made out of, and they were able to alter and adapt the newly purchased formula to iron out a few minor problems (its surface had a tendency to go rancid if it wasn't used for a few days) and create the definitive recipe for Sunlight Self-Washer:

Copra Oil	41.9%
Tallow	24.8%
Cotton Oil	23.8%
Resin	9.5%

When this mixture was boiled up along with lye, a strong alkaline solution, it separated into two substances: glycerine (which was drained off and sold as a valuable by-product) and raw soap, to which scents and preservatives could then be added. Copra – the dried kernels of the coconut palm – was imported from the tropics. Tallow, fat melted down from the less edible bits of cattle and sheep, came in large quantities from the cattle ranches of the US and Australian sheep farms, while the resin was extracted from pine trees all around the world. The citronella that gave the soap its strong lemony scent was imported from Southern Asia. You've probably never realized how well travelled the soap you slap on your face is – or that much of it is made of bits of animals (or sodium tallowate, as the packaging prefers to call it) either.

What was missing from Sunlight was silicate of soda, a chemical that was used by most manufacturers to fill out their soap and save on production costs. It was easy to source – the soap-makers Joseph Crosfield had a plant producing the stuff in Warrington, practically on the doorstep – but Lever wanted nothing to do with it. He wanted to sell his soap on its difference from anything else on the market, and using only natural materials (however unsavoury their source) allowed him to market Sunlight as 'pure' in contrast to its rivals. Ironically, in our post-Body Shop, organic days, Sunlight now seems very chemical, its scent too cloying for our refined tastes. It no longer sells on the British market, though it is still going strong in Belgium, the Netherlands and Ireland, where presumably they like their soaps cheap and cheerful. In 1885, however, it was revolutionary.

His biggest innovation, however, was in the way it was packaged. Gone were the long bars that William had spent years slicing for his father. Sunlight was cut at source, and each tablet was wrapped individually in parchment, an idea which he had imported from America after questioning his well-travelled brother-in-law about the world-wide grocery trade. But Lever went a step further. The parchment-wrapped bars came inside brightly coloured cardboard cartons, each proudly displaying the Sunlight logo with its two outsized serif Ss – Sunlight in white on blue, Soap on a red banner beneath. It created a whole new expensive stage in the production process, but it was worth it: the boxes stacked squarely on top of each other in shops and created an eye-catching and novel display all by themselves.

The first batches of Sunlight rolled off the Lever Brothers production line in January 1886. 'The Warrington offices were not palatial, but consisted of two storeys, which we designated the "top" and "bottom" offices,' recalled J. T. Furnivall, one of the original employees in the sales and invoicing department. 'The staff numbered about 30, and the office hours were: Monday to Friday, 9 am to 6 pm, and on Saturday 8 am to 1 pm, so that as you may imagine, it was somewhat of a task to remember to get to business each Saturday one hour earlier than on the other days.' His six-day week was eased by in-house entertainment, however – 'The cardboard making department was composed of girls from Bolton, and I have pleasant

34

recollections of those early days listening to the beautiful singing of the girls while they were engaged on their work.'

Lever himself was less pleased with the premises – 'the buildings pile storey upon storey, departments interlace and overlap, and some are badly lighted owing to the impossibility of getting daylight into them,' he complained – but he threw himself fully into the work, leading as ever from the front. Visitors to the office often could not believe that the fresh-faced young man who greeted them could be in charge of such an enterprise – one of Lever's favourite stories concerned a 'very stylish individual' who came in without an appointment and demanded that he inform Mr Lever that he had arrived. Lever said he already knew, and carried on with what he was doing. 'This kind of dialogue went on for a few minutes at intervals, the caller getting more pompous meanwhile. Those in the office began to titter, I being the only solemn one amongst them. Then suddenly the visitor asked, "Are *you* Mr Lever?" "All that is left of him," I replied. Well, after that, he could not get on with his work at all, and suddenly left.' One visitor even tried to tip him at the end of a tour of the factory, and threatened to report him to the manager for impertinence when he declined the cash.

He had no such problem earning the respect of his staff, however. 'In the early days sales increased so rapidly that office work was very strenuous,' recalled clerk T. F. Houghton, 'but always a pleasure, we having before us all the time the wonderful example of our chairman to lead and encourage us.' For Lever was on home turf – the business of selling was what he knew best, and much of the early success of Sunlight was due to his expertise and personal experience in the field. As well as sending agents out to shopkeepers to ensure that they stocked Sunlight, he cut out the middleman with a team of District Agents who went directly to the doorsteps of their customers. 'Ding-Dong every day, every hour, every minute – that's the way to success and happiness' was the mantra he repeated to his sales force, but he also furnished them with tips from his own days going door-to-door.

They should let children inspect the brightly coloured cartons of Sunlight, so they would 'bother their mothers to buy some'. They should ensure that they always closed gates behind them and took care not to tread their muddy outdoor shoes over doorsteps that had been newly washed, for 'small items as these, however small they may seem, generally have a great effect on housekeepers'. More than anything, however, they should get over the message that Sunlight Self-Washer could save a housewife hours. A whole day of the week – usually Mondays, because there were enough leftovers from the Sunday roast to feed the family without extra cooking – had to be set aside for the household wash. It was done in a vast trough, with bucket after bucket of water heated over the range. Soap had to be painstakingly flaked into the mixture and dissolved, along with soda or lye to burn away the stains on the more heavily soiled clothes. In the absence of bleach, housewives used home-made substitutes – urine, or, in more rural areas, a solution of pig manure, which is rich in ammonia. The whole mix had to be spun repeatedly with a wooden peg dolly like a three-legged stool on the end of a broomstick, before being pulled out and rinsed in more water that had been lugged in from the pump and heated up all over again. Sunlight offered them a magical alternative – 'while the wash is lying still, rolled up under water in the tub, and the housewife is making a beef-steak pudding, the unseen fairy fingers of the soap *are busy in the tub*, doing the work'. At least, that was how the sales patter put it.

But sending men out for one-on-one doorstep sessions was only one, hardly cost-efficient way of telling the public just how good this soap was. No sooner were the pans and presses in action at Warrington than the name Sunlight was appearing before the eyes of travellers all over the country. 'With great trembling I entered into a £50 contract with the London & North-Western Railway Company,' recalled Lever of his first advertising campaign. 'We ourselves chose the positions for our advertising plates on the railways, and the advantages of right hand or left hand side of a booking office were matters that received personal and weighty consideration.' Less thought seems to have gone into the slogan that was stamped on the enamel panels, but 'SUNLIGHT SELF-WASHER SOAP: SEE HOW THIS BECOMES THE HOUSE' was soon a familiar phrase among all those who frequented stations.

The art of advertising was still in its infancy. The first agencies had begun to open only in the 1830s, offering to place sober 'announcements' in the weekly and daily newspapers, and it was only in the last few years that such daring innovations as illustrations and typefaces that differed from the articles surrounding them had begun to be introduced. The first illustrated posters had appeared on Britain's streets only in the 1870s, to much bluster and consternation on the letters pages of *The Times*, and the general impression of advertising was that it was a vulgar activity of which no gentleman should have any need. All that was about to change. The streets and the minds of Britain were about to be flooded with irrelevant, irreverent and inescapable information. And William Lever, one of the shrewdest young businessmen in the country, was ready to ride that wave.

4

SOAP WARS

WHY DOES A WOMAN LOOK OLD SOONER THAN A MAN?

screamed the billboards on streets the length and breadth of Britain, in letters high enough to be read from thirty feet away. Cross the street to look closer, and you could read the message in full:

WHY DOES

a woman's health so often break down at an early age? Put a man at a washing tub: let him get heated with the hot suds until every pore is opened; then let him stand over the filthy steam that comes from scalding and boiling clothes, and his health certainly would break down before long and yet this terrible ordeal is exactly what

A WOMAN

has to go through on washing days; and besides, while over-heated at the hot work, she has to risk her life by going out

---

into the open air to hang up clothes. These facts, which
are known to every housekeeper, readily explain
why so many women

LOOK OLD

while yet young in years, and physicians and boards of
health cannot draw attention too strongly to the injurious
effects of the usual way of washing, with its necessary steam
and scalding or boiling to get the clothes pure and sweet.
Fortunately, this trouble can be avoided. Scalding, boiling
and steam done away with. Clothes made sweet and
beautifully white, and much

SOONER THAN

by the old way, by using the SUNLIGHT SOAP – a soap so
purifying and cleansing that the dirtiest clothing can be
washed in lukewarm water with very little rubbing, while
the work is so light that a girl of 12 or 13 can do a large
wash without being tired. Now that there is a remedy for the
great 'washing-day' evil, so economical in its use as to be
within the reach of all, there is not a woman or

A MAN

who is not directly interested in having introduced into their
homes that wonderful way of washing clothes which, when
properly tried, does away with the hard work, offensive
smell, and fearful steam on washing day, and makes the
white pieces whiter, coloured pieces brighter, and flannels
softer than they can be made by washing the old way, and
also leaves every article as clean and sweet and as pure
as if never worn.

Even now, it pushes all the right buttons. Female insecurity?
Girl power? Health scares? Time-saving? Purse-friendly?

Scientific pseudery? Whites whiter? All present and correct. It pulls every trick in the advertising textbook. Knock out a few words and it would win awards now.

Lever could not take the credit for this particular ad – he bought the text from an American soap manufacturer and simply adapted it to suit his own product – but it showed how swift he was to catch on to the possibilities of the new medium. 'By means of advertising the manufacturer is making less costly the distribution,' he explained to his staff. 'The consumer of an article goes into the shop with full knowledge of the article wanted, the shopman's time is not wasted in explaining it, the manufacturer's time is not wasted in the cost of salesmen explaining the merits of the article, reducing the number of calls and the cost of each sale. Advertising is as near bringing the manufacturing conditions of repetition to the selling side of the business as possible.'

And repetition was the key. A century before Britain's playgrounds rang with cries of 'Wazzup!' or orders to 'Tell Sid about it', no top-hat-doffing was complete without the greeting 'Good Morning, Have you used Pears' Soap?' The catchphrase, the invention of Pears' Thomas Barrett, was meaningless enough to be appended to almost any scenario, and it seeped from the series of posters on which it was originally printed far enough into the national conscious-ness for enraged letter-writers to complain to the newspapers that they could barely offer a civil greeting in the street without receiving a free advert in return. Barrett was possibly the first man in Britain to realize one of advertising's fundamental truths; as long as you engrave a brand name in people's minds, it doesn't matter if they don't know anything else about it. He hired Lillie Langtry, the Tara Palmer-Tomkinson of her day, as famous for her

scandalous connections to the royal family as for her subsequent career in showbusiness, to be the face of Pears, with
the personal endorsement, 'For years I have used your soap
and no other.' Men wandered up and down the streets of
London with the catchphrase emblazoned on sandwich
boards. Pears' name turned up in the most unexpected
places: on the back of stamps (Barrett bought exclusive
rights to the lickable bit of the Penny Lilac), watermarked
into writing paper ('Marvellous Effect! Hold this up to the
light!'), and even over-stamped on the coins in your pocket
– until an outraged parliament acted to outlaw the practice.
Undeterred, Barrett approached the government offering
to print up the 1891 census form for free, just as long as
every page could feature an advert for Pears. His generous
offer was politely declined.

When the novelty of simple posters wore off, Barrett
replaced them with elaborate optical illusions: crowds
gathered in the streets to stare for twenty minutes at a time
at his posters while the name Pears' Soap burned itself into
their straining retinas. He did not go as far as the rival firm
who attempted to hide the dome of St Paul's behind a vast
advertising hoarding erected on Ludgate Hill, or the
American company who daubed the white cliffs of Dover
with slogans praising their products, two of the excesses
that prompted the creation of the Society for the Checking
of Abuses in Public Advertising, aimed at stamping out the
'sordid joys of meretricious mart'. Barrett did, however, rig
up magic lanterns to project what *The Times* called
'gratuitous exhibitions of dissolving views' – every one an
advert – on to various London landmarks, including
Nelson's column. It's not quite Gail Porter's arse on the
Houses of Parliament, but it still caused a hell of a stir.

Barrett had a budget of some £120,000 a year on

advertising. While Lever was keen to get the Sunlight name out in front of the public as much as possible – during the 1880s it appeared in such diverse places as trams, books, bicycles and the bathing machines on Blackpool beach – he knew that he could not yet compete with the spectacles Pears could afford. Instead he chose another, equally novel route: he would simply point out just how useful and good a product he had. According to E. S. Turner in *The Shocking History of Advertising*, 'Lever was one of the first to see that whereas it had once been enough for an advertisement to be pithy, bright, original and humorous, the public now needed logical and considered arguments.' This was exactly what they got in *Sunlight Soap and How To Use It*, a promotional booklet which Lever himself wrote and distributed around potential customers in 1886. It gave simple instructions – 'brought down to the level of a working man's needs', as he put it – on exactly how Sunlight could be used for all manner of household chores, cleaning everything from clothes to carpets. Occasionally it advised adding some unusual other ingredients:

How To Clean Silk:

Take one third of a tablet of Sunlight Self-Washer Soap, a teaspoonful of brandy and a pint of gin, and well mix them together; when dissolved, strain through a cloth. With a sponge, spread it on each side of the silk, being careful not to crease. Then wash it in two or three waters, and iron on the wrong side. The silk will look as good as new.

But it wasn't just clothes that Sunlight could improve, as this tale of a hypothetical housewife shows:

She gives Sunlight Self-Washer Soap a fair trial, and is perfectly astonished at the easy way she can wash with this soap. Her washing is all over and put away before her husband comes home, and after tea they go out for a walk together, a thing they have never been able to do for thirty years. It seems like their old 'courting' days, and she never felt so happy before. She begins to think that life is worth living after all.

Removing marital strain alongside material stains was a favourite Lever promise. 'Don't let steam and suds be your husband's welcome on wash days' was a line used in early Sunlight ads, while much later the company would offer the following promise for another brand, complete with before-and-after illustrations:

> Dirty pan
> Supper late
> Angry man
> In Sad state
> 'What, no tea?'
> Swears Big D
> Wife, of course,
> Gets divorce
> Pistol shot,
> Gone to pot.
>
> Prudent wife
> Tea in time;
> Without strife
> Life's sublime
> Full of hope,
> Brooke's soap
> Keeps pans bright;

Meals all right
Married Bliss
Happiness.

As selling-points go, 'Buy our soap or your husband will divorce you and top himself' takes some beating. But if Lever's advertising was to be believed, there was little his soaps could not do. Sunlight was 'found to be better than so-called Carpet Soaps . . . has a special place as a washer of silver and electro-plate . . . painted walls and woodwork can be both cleaned and restored . . . the best hair-wash . . . for improving the complexion, Sunlight Soap stands un-rivalled'. Lifebuoy, a disinfectant soap which Lever launched in 1894, was sold under the all-encompassing slogan 'For Saving Life', amid confident claims that it could prevent cholera and cure foot-and-mouth disease.

All these claims were made in the *Sunlight Year Book*, a multi-purpose guide to life which was produced annually in the 1890s as 'a Treasury of Useful Information of value to all Members of the Household, including The Calendar and kindred matter, army and navy, trade, politics, the colonies, men and women of today, sport, literature, how to make the best of our homes, the fashions, popular games and amusements, the garden, domestic animals and pets, etc.' It also contained exhortations to buy Sunlight Soap at the top of every single page – 'See smiling faces all around, wherever SUNLIGHT SOAP is found', or 'Don't Worry! Use SUNLIGHT SOAP!' – which sat oddly with its long and densely written accounts of business in the House of Commons, lists of acquisitions by the national museums, railway statistics and tables of agricultural returns. It did, however, swiftly become the standard reference work for the schools to which it was given away free, and in those households which saved up enough Sunlight cartons, and lent the brand a respectability and ubiquitousness far beyond the bathroom and pantry.

The same worthy tone pervaded the first Sunlight promotion, in 1887. The company announced that they had £2,000 to give away to the 'Religious and Benevolent Institution' that the most customers voted for, asking them to send in the name of their preferred charity on the back of a Sunlight box. Only belatedly did Lever realize that the bulk of his customers did not share his philanthropic zeal, and an additional offer was tacked on for the selfish: the customer who guessed closest to the number of votes that the winning charity received would win £400 for themselves. When the RNLI came up trumps Lever scored a double dose of publicity: he presented them with a lifeboat named 'Sunlight Number One', and then commissioned engravings of its valiant crew in action in a choppy sea, which he gave to the *Illustrated London News*. Naturally, the nameplate was placed at the forefront of the picture, which appeared in the paper with the name Sunlight as prominent as it would have been in any advert, but at a fraction of the expense. Everyone was a winner. He repeated this trick when the first London to Brighton car-run was held in 1896, celebrating the end of the law that required men with red flags to walk in front of motor vehicles. Lever entered three vans emblazoned with Sunlight ads: to ensure he got the maximum press coverage, they set off in procession ten hours early, at midnight, in front of the invited cameras of the recently launched *Daily Mail*, who duly printed the story under the obliging headline 'Sunlight At Midnight'. He also sent an unsolicited twelve dozen bars of Sunlight to Commander Robert Scott to be used during his journey to the Antarctic, and supplied miniature cakes of Sunlight for the royal dolls' houses, milking the resultant thank-you letters for all the publicity they were worth.

The story that had really launched Sunlight into the headlines and made Lever himself a celebrity was not so carefully planned. In 1886 Barrett launched his famous *Bubbles* advert, the cutesy knickerbockered boy with the golden curls gazing up at the bubble he has just blown through a clay pipe. It was painted by Sir John Millais, the brilliant Pre-Raphaelite who forty years before had scandalized the world of art by depicting Jesus as a ginger in his *Christ in the House of His Parents*, but was now reduced to sentimental hack-work like this. *Bubbles* was an instant hit: so popular were the posters that Barrett issued the image, complete with the logo and bar of Pears that he had added to the original, as a collectible postcard, black-and-white engraving and even a jigsaw puzzle. It was a significant victory in the soap war that had sprung up between the two manufacturers as Sunlight's sales began to threaten Pears' dominance, and Lever badly needed a Sunlight Girl to rival the Bubbles Boy.

He found her at the Royal Academy Summer exhibition in 1889. For three years William and Elizabeth had made an annual pilgrimage down to London to view the show and pick up anything that would lend itself to selling soap – pictures like Louise Jopling's *Blue and White*, a painting of two young ladies caring for their crockery that managed the admirable feat of making washing-up sexy. That year one picture struck Lever as absolutely perfect: *The New Frock* by William Powell Frith, which he snapped up for the bargain price of 150 guineas. 'I liked Mr Frith's picture because it is of a little girl, and the mothers always like to look at a nice little girl,' he explained. Hmm. The little girl in question was holding up her gleaming white skirt to display her ruched petticoats, her face a rosy-cheeked mask of innocence: she was very definitely designed to appeal to the same 'cult of little girls' that made naked ten-year-olds the most popular subject for Christmas cards in the late 1880s. Still, it had worked for Pears (Millais himself was quite keen on small children, and regularly lent his own to Lewis Carroll to be photographed in the nude), it sold soap, and no one appears to have thought any of this was remotely dodgy at the time.

The first Frith knew of his picture's fate was when it appeared on hoardings across the country complete with the Sunlight logo and the caption 'So Clean'. It was the latter that really enraged him: he had intended the picture to be a sanctimonious comment on the little girl's pride, and had even given it the ponderous sub-title 'Vanity of vanities, all is vanity'. 'So Clean' didn't quite have the same effect. He also felt professionally insulted: he was a major-league artist with works in the royal collection (Queen Victoria herself had bought his landscape *Ramsgate Sands* for Buckingham Palace in 1854); now people would assume he was willingly prostituting himself for the advertising shilling. He fired off an angry letter to the *Pall Mall Gazette* disowning the advert and declaring his outrage at being used in such a vulgar manner.

SIR – I have what I consider a grievance, which I beg to be allowed to make public . . . as a warning to my brother artists. One of my contributions to the present exhibition of the RA is called *The New Frock*, a simple subject of a child raising its pinafore to show the new dress to admiring friends. The picture found a purchaser in a stranger, whose courteous treatment in the matter of payment &c. left nothing to be desired, and nothing that could be construed into constituting any difference from the ordinary patron of art.

Lively therefore was my surprise when I found a large representation of my picture with a new title of *So Clean* forming the part of an advertiser for a firm of soap manufacturers ... I warn all and sundry of my brethren that if their works should happen to display any peculiarity which could serve the turn of the advertiser, it would be well to retain a power of preventing such a fate as that which has befallen *The New Frock*.

It drew the following dismissive response from Lever:

SIR – In reply to the letter of Mr Frith ... yesterday, complaining that his picture exhibited in this year's Royal Academy, and purchased by myself, should be used by my firm as an advertisement for 'Sunlight Soap', would Mr Frith kindly say in which way I have unintentionally injured him by so doing? Pictures have been used for advertising ever since advertising was known, and the very fact that in the latter half of the nineteenth century advertisers are seeking the works of our best artists, making thereby their advertisements more attractive, is a change that many lovers of art will consider an advance on the old style of advertising. Surely the use of a picture in this way cannot detract from the reputation of the artist, but rather the reverse, because his picture will be admired by and give pleasure to millions who could otherwise never have seen it?

Bingo! Sunlight's name in the *Pall Mall Gazette*, one of the highest-circulation papers in Britain, two evenings running, and not a penny spent! Even better, the same day's edition carried a half-page advert for Pears, for which Barrett must have paid dear. But the affair was not finished yet. William Thomas Stead, the *Gazette*'s editor, knew a story when he saw one (he had practically invented the tabloid exposé four years before with his series on child prostitution). He cleared his front page on 17 July for an interview with Lever – relegating the headline 'JACK THE RIPPER AT IT AGAIN: ANOTHER WHITECHAPEL TRAGEDY' to page 4 in the process – and set about printing one of the least objective pieces of journalism ever printed. The paper announced itself 'wholly in favour of this high-class method of pictorial advertisement', which is hardly surprising since they made the bulk of their income from them, and occasionally Stead interjected phrases like 'Capital, Mr Lever, capital!' into his reporter's story just in case readers hadn't quite got the point. Lever himself was resolutely unapologetic, declaring that the painter was making a great fuss about nothing.

> Mr Frith reminds me of the young lady who is asked to play the piano. She simpers and says no, and after a struggle is led to the keyboard, and plays as she really wished to do from the first. My opinion is that Mr Frith is rather pleased to be in a position to point out the engraving to his friends and to say, 'Now look at that. Isn't it too bad? But I could do nothing you know. I really object to be made a bait for the soap-boilers to dangle with. Great Heavens! I wonder what they'll do next! Oh yes, I got my money all right, but it's going a little too far. And such a shock, too!'

He defended his failure to declare his intentions when he bought the picture – 'I looked upon the transaction as any other businessman might in making a bargain. If I had mentioned the word "advertising" the price would have gone up in a moment.' He pronounced himself quite willing to wedge a packet of Sunlight into any scene, and even substitute it for objects that were an integral part of the picture (for instance replacing the glasses of champagne in the picture of a wedding toast with bars of Sunlight), just so long as the pictures were 'reproduced as artistically as possible'. Asked why he didn't simply commission his own pictures, he replied that such an approach was 'quite useless. An artist if he knows he is painting a picture which is meant for advertising purposes lowers his tone unconsciously.'

This remark probably rang a bell with Millais, whom the *Gazette* subsequently solicited for his views on the use of *Bubbles* in an effort to 'wind up an interesting controversy by giving the practice of the profession in the matter'. 'It is an admirable reproduction, and a credit to Messrs Pears, and to my picture, which is a very good one,' the old man sheepishly admitted. He knew perfectly well that a number of artists were painting specifically for the advertising market, filling their pictures with non-specific soaps, bottles and packets and offering them to the highest bidder at trade fairs. The snobs like Frith were fighting a losing battle – Lever made good on all his promises in the interview, moving the furniture around in Charles Burton Barber's *Girl With Dogs* in order to accommodate a large bath in the foreground and rechristening it *The Family Wash*. Barber, Jopling and the dozens of other painters who found their work similarly rearranged and decorated with Rupert-the-Bear-style rhyming couplets ('Silv'ry age and ruddy youth/ Bear witness to this golden truth/ SUN-LIGHT IS BEST') learned to simply cash the cheques and keep quiet about their artistic integrity.

Besides, these 'admirable reproductions' were a big hit with the public. Lever had many of them printed up as postcards, which were inserted, unbound, into newspapers and magazines. They quickly found their way into frames and on to the walls of suburban houses and working-class tenements, so tiny references to Lever products – the Lifebuoy logo on a boy's sailor suit, the box of Sunlight in a girl's basket as she carried her shopping home for mother – embedded themselves subliminally amid the clutter of the Victorian drawing room.

Some pictures were even given away un-soaped. Prints of Sydney Curnow Vosper's *Salem*, a portrait of an aged crone in traditional Welsh dress making her way out of chapel, were offered to customers who saved up Sunlight wrappers, part of a massive gift scheme that replaced the initial philanthropy of the charity-vote that had benefited the RNLI. Small gifts like dominoes, 'waistcoat pocket diaries', magnifying glasses and paint-boxes were available for a handful of wrappers, while more could score you a wild array of riches – a poster from 1897 promises '£66,156-0-0! in PRIZES of CASH, BICYCLES, WATCHES, BOOKS, for SUNLIGHT AND LIFE-BUOY SOAP WRAPPERS'. It depicts a fashionable young couple fully kitted out with spats and gloves for a day's cycling: the craze for this new sport had continued unabated since the Rover Safety Bicycle with its new-fangled chain had been introduced in 1885, and Lever himself was an early fan – he could often be seen tottering around the lanes of Warrington on his own ramshackle machine. When motor cars became more common in the following decade, Lever offered a brand-spanking-new model worth £250 to anyone who could collect 25,000 Sunlight wrappers. The lucky recipient, a squeaky-clean grocer from Bradford by the name of Harrison, was photographed sitting proudly at the wheel of his rattletrap prize alongside a uniformed chauffeur who was supplied to teach him the basics of driving (his wife is in the back seat, a look of absolute terror on her face).

Lever could well afford such generosity. The Warrington works had started off producing 450 tons of soap a week;

within months Percy Winser was reporting that they did not have the capacity to meet the orders that were being sent down from the clerks' office. As happy to immerse himself in the practicalities of production as planning advertising campaigns, Lever bent his mind to the problem and came up with the idea of fixing three-foot-tall iron rings to the tops of the boiling-pans to increase their depth, and swell production by a third, but even this was not enough. By the end of the year a new boiling shed was put up to meet a demand of 3,000 tons a week. That total trebled again in the following year – the public could simply not get enough Sunlight. 'In some districts we were three months behind in deliveries; somehow or other, out-of-the-way places got neglected,' Lever recalled. 'The man who telegraphed for soap got some, the man who wrote got none, because there was none left after fulfilling the urgency orders.' He desperately needed to expand production – but he wasn't the only one who had noticed the cash flowing in. His canny landlord agreed to lease him more land on the site, but demanded more money for it than he had originally wanted for the whole soap-works. With much grumbling Lever had to agree, 'but I only covered it with wooden buildings, and only took it on a short lease'.

By the end of 1888 they were producing over 14,000 tons a week. Lever's explanation for his rapid success was characteristically simple: he had started locally, and 'when I got it established there and making money, I ventured forth to Liverpool and Manchester. Established there and making money I ventured as far north as Newcastle and as far south as Plymouth with the intervening country more or less opened up. Established there and making money I opened up in London, Scotland and elsewhere, and covered the

United Kingdom.' In doing so he had scandalized the Soapmakers' Association, made up of the old established firms who had divided up the country in a series of gentlemen's agreements years before and did not even consider encroaching on each other's patches. They were snobbish about the young upstart's success – 'the best-class neighbourhoods still stick to the bar soap trade in some form or another; Messrs Levers' trade is one kept as distinct as it can be from the rest of us' – but it troubled them enough to pass motions condemning his 'ungentlemanly' behaviour in advertising, and describing his gift schemes as 'degrading to the trade and demoralising to business'. Finally in 1889 they were forced to give up the ghost and invite Lever to join the Association, largely so that they could harangue him in person at their annual dinner, which amused him enormously.

In fact, the only people who appeared not to recognize Lever Brothers' extraordinary success were the banks, who refused to loan Lever the cash for a new factory on the grounds that Warrington already had a successful soap company, Joseph Crosfield & Sons, and they didn't trust that his would survive.

It was the start of a lifelong dislike for the banking profession on Lever's part – criticizing people for having a 'banker's mind' was one of his favourite insults till the end of his life. Frustrated, he stomped off back to his father and announced that he was going to cash in his share of the grocery business. And this time, seventy-seven-year-old James Lever surprised everyone and pledged his full support. In fact, he declared he would do the same, and proposed floating their first venture as a limited liability company. The prospect panicked the younger Lever brother – the pace of success had been too much for James, who fretted that further expansion was just asking for trouble, and wondered why they couldn't just sit tight and wait for all these customers to go away. His misgivings were swiftly bulldozed by his brother and father, and in 1887 the reins of the grocery business were handed over to W. H. S. Taylor, whose name quickly replaced that of Lever on the signs in Victoria Square, though the family retained a share in the company. With a fresh wad of cash in his pocket, Lever headed out in search of a new site for his business.

But he wasn't just looking for a new factory. Ever since the money had started to roll into Warrington, Lever had been bending his unique mind to the problem of how best to spend it. 'Whose was that money?' he recalled asking himself. 'We had the same works, the same manager, the same soapboiler and the same staff. The only difference was that all those men were paid more money than when they were working at a loss, and yet there was now a profit of £50,000 a year. Whose is that money? For I want to give it to the man that ought to have it.'

In finding the solution to that particular quandary, William Lever was about to create something totally new.

5

A TOWN CALLED SUNLIGHT

YOU KNOW WHEN YOU'VE ARRIVED AT PORT SUNLIGHT. There is an invisible dividing line which separates this Merseyside utopia from the surrounding suburbs, a border as rigidly defined as the thick black lines Lever sketched on his first rough map of the area back in 1888. New Ferry to the north of the village is the sort of area that makes you clutch your belongings and walk a little faster, a place of Kwik-Saves, fly-posting, fortified off-licences advertising Budget Booze and fried chicken takeaways. But the moment you turn right from the New Chester Road you are in another world. Port Sunlight is a pastoral vision of suburbia, all crazy-paved paths and hanging baskets. The place seems to have more bowling greens than any community could possibly need. What's even stranger is that even though they are unfenced, none of them have been vandalized. It's hard to believe you're still in Britain.

But this is no identikit housing estate either – no two buildings here look alike, and many seem to be competing for the most out-of-place architectural affectation. Some are half-timbered, with wooden colonnades stretching the length of their fronts. Others sprout Tudor-style chimneys from red-tiled roofs, or have turrets, towers or spires protruding from them. One house, now sadly demolished, was a perfect replica of Shakespeare's birthplace in Stratford-upon-Avon. Another so resembled a cuckoo clock that it went by the name of the Swiss Cottage. There are more differently shaped windows here than in a whole series of Playschool: portholes, bays, great picture windows, with panes that are frosted, leaded, bottle-ended or fashioned from stained glass in intricate designs. The place feels like a tour through 500 years of architecture, yet every building is somehow absolutely rooted in its time, with a solid dependency that speaks of the turn of the last century. For all the diversity of design, the angles of the gables and the lines of the roofs are in perfect harmony, ensuring that they work together rather than clashing.

Part of that is due to the vast amounts of space between them. The roads here are thirty-six feet wide, the pavements twelve feet from side to side. Even with cars parked down both sides of them, there's still room for buses to pass in the middle. You can hardly move for learner drivers joyfully practising their three-point turns. The sense of space is increased by the immaculate lawns which front every single house, their few shrubs and flowers neatly trimmed. There is not a leaf out of place, not a piece of litter in sight. After a while it just starts to become weird. You feel like you might be trapped in an episode of *The Prisoner*.

When William Lever first saw this place, it was nothing more than a group of marshy fields. In the distance lay the vast River Mersey, its tidal flow piddling away in a series of muddy creeks that stretched far inland. Only a few ramshackle cottages stood on the land: the nearest village was

Bebington, on the other side of the railway line which ran from Birkenhead to Chester and beyond. William Owen, the architect who extended his first soap works in Warrington and who accompanied him on many expeditions around the surrounding countryside in search of premises, saw nothing but problems in the landscape – floods, mud, uneven ground – but to Lever the view was full of possibility. The railway led to every town and city in Britain, nearby Bromborough Pool gave easy and deep access to the Mersey and thence to all the ports of the world, and best of all, it lay outside the area covered by Liverpool dock and harbour dues, which would save the business a fortune. 'I remember looking over the field gate, situated right in front of the present office door,' he said many years later, 'I saw the facilities and the railway, I said "here we are", and I never looked any further.'

On the afternoon of 3 March 1888, the Warrington steam barge puffed up Bromborough Pool from the docks at nearby New Ferry and disgorged a group of local dignitaries, Lever employees, friends, family and journalists, all in their best hats, on to a quay that had very recently passed from the ownership of the Bebington Cement Works into the hands of Lever Brothers. The quayside had been spruced up for the occasion and the barge itself covered by a large sheet of crimson cloth, but there was no disguising the fact that the 150 or so guests had arrived to see what was basically some muddy fields. Nevertheless, with due ceremony, a heavily pregnant Elizabeth Lever was presented with a silver ceremonial spade, which she proceeded to plunge into the soil to turn over the first sod of the town her husband had decided would be called Port Sunlight. He said a few appropriate words, the crowd let out a cheer, and they all filed back on to the barge, no doubt trailing a great deal of mud and cement dust on to the crimson covering in the process.

That evening the party reconvened across the river in the Bear's Paw Restaurant on Lord Street in Liverpool, and William Lever was able to outline his vision in rather more detail. 'Our idea is that profit sharing should be so managed that those who take the profits are those who are working at the works, and what we propose to do is apply it to the building of houses to be let at a reduced rental,' he told the crowd. 'It is my hope, and my brother's hope' – as usual he co-opted the nervous James – 'to build houses in which our work people will be able to live and be comfortable – semi-detached houses, with gardens back and front, in which they will be able to know more about the science of life than they can in a back slum, and in which they will learn that there is more enjoyment in life than in the mere going to and returning from work and looking forward to Saturday night to draw their wages.'

It was an admirable ambition. Ninety per cent of Britain's people did not own their own homes. In every city workers lived in jerry-built terraces, their homes sharing not only the side walls with their neighbours but often the back one as well. Thousands more families lived below ground in windowless cellars. Many households did not even have an outdoor privy, and children played in the streets among stinking dunghills. Typhus, diphtheria and smallpox were the real killers in the slums, far more of a risk than the vicious maniac who was slaughtering prostitutes in London's East End. Social reformer George Sims described the typical living conditions on Jack the Ripper's stalking-grounds: 'they must put up with dirt, and filth, and putrefaction; with dripping walls and broken windows; with all the nameless abomination of an unsanitary hovel, because if they complain the landlord can turn them out at once, and find dozens of people eager to take their places who will be less fastidious.' Those in rural areas fared little better – a survey by the Social Science Congress in 1873 judged that a third of the agricultural houses in Britain needed urgent rebuilding, though since the bulk of the dwellings were in the private hands of the farmers who dictated both working and living conditions for their employees, there was little they could actually do about it.

While Liverpool itself fared better than most – the then thriving docks allowed the city council to spend more on establishing a clean water supply and enforcing health regulations than most places managed – Lever knew from the poverty and desperation he had seen around him during his childhood in Bolton just how bad things could be. Philanthropists like Titus Salt had done much to improve their workers' housing – having failed to force his fellow factory owners in Bradford to cut the pollution that brought that city's life expectancy down to a miserable eighteen, he had upped sticks and moved his own textile business to the ready-built town of Saltaire, complete with lavatories, a water and gas supply to each house. But Lever had something greener in mind. Open spaces, trees and parks were as important to him as decent walls and toilets, for as he put it, 'a child that knows nothing of God's earth, of green fields, of sparkling brooks, of breezy hill and springy heather, and whose mind is stored with none of the beauties of nature, but knows only the drunkenness prevalent in the hideous slums it is forced to live in, and whose walks abroad have never extended beyond the corner public-house and the pawnshop, cannot be benefited by education. Such children grow up depraved and become a danger to the state.' Ten years before Ebenezer Howard put pen to paper to predict the fusion of town and city in *Garden Cities of Tomorrow*, and followed it up by building Letchworth and Welwyn in Hertfordshire, Lever was making his dream a reality.

His vision was probably appreciated rather less by the assembled guests than the sumptuous banquet he provided for them, accompanied by the finest wines the Bear's Paw could provide. No fewer than ten toasts were drunk, their order designed as much to appeal to the vanity of those present as to reflect Lever's own priorities:

- The Queen and Royal Family
- The Architect
- The Guests
- Success to Bebington
- The Press
- Success to the Firm
- The Travellers
- The Staff at Warrington
- The Staff at London
- The Advertising Staff

The architect in question was William Owen, who had in fact merely formalized the plans for the Port Sunlight factory as sketched by Lever himself. Working on sheets of white foolscap with fountain pens filled with red and black ink, the amateur had filled every inch of the intricate plans with technical notes and comments in his spidery hand-writing. Framed on the wall of the Port Sunlight Heritage Centre today, the plan is a tribute to Lever's obsessive interest in every last detail of his business. Just a few years after declaring himself 'as ignorant of soap-making as a baby in arms' he was confidently designing differently shaped boiling pans and a new heating method for the new factory, as well as a number of other technical innovations which he reckoned would increase production.

By the summer of 1889 the first Soapery was up and running along with its own glycerine plant and packing room; its 300-foot chimney towered over fields which were still piled with their last harvest before they too were swallowed up by the grand scheme. The first printing department opened nearby that November and became by default number 1 Wood Street. The first of the houses that would surround it did not follow until the next year, and the new plant was for much of the first year staffed by recruits from the local area, overseen by senior staff from Warrington, where production continued until the changeover in 1890. But the street plan had long since been drawn up by Lever – a grid of vast boulevards, designed more for aesthetic than practical reasons, for motor cars were still an exotic and rare sight. He left space between these vast avenues not just for the generous gardens that would belong to each house, but also for parks and recreation grounds. He named them for the people and places of his boyhood – Wood Street, Park Road, Bolton Road. At the edges of the site the roads led towards other areas he hoped to buy up in the future, for he always planned that Port Sunlight should expand beyond its initial boundaries. Even these were generous – of the fifty-two acres he had purchased, more than half were allocated for houses, the factory consigned to its own zone at the south of the village. Planning regulations stated that the maximum number of houses that could be built in an acre of land was forty-two, though less scrupulous developers often crammed in more. These days the government recommends twenty per acre. Lever decreed that Port Sunlight was to have no more than seven.

Naturally, his inclination to do things 'better than they were ever done before' did not stop with such accepted fundamentals as the layout of houses. The common practice of putting bathrooms upstairs with the bedrooms was a ridiculous one, he declared: far better to put them on the ground floor next to the front door so that those coming in from work could strip off and get washed without trailing their dirt and sweat all through the house. He sketched out two basic designs – the 'Kitchen Type', with one large room downstairs and two bedrooms above, and the larger 'Parlour Type', which had a separate front room and an extra bedroom upstairs. Beyond this, however, he was determined that the houses should be as different from each other as possible – thirty different architects were engaged during his lifetime, including Owen and Jonathan Simpson (and later both their sons), and a twenty-one-year-old by the name of Edwin Lutyens, whose seven houses on Corniche Road showed little of the stately grandeur he would later bring to New Delhi and the Cenotaph in Whitehall.

The architects were encouraged to add their own flourishes, details and eccentricities to the blocks they worked on, but the whimsy disguises innovations that keep Port Sunlight in the town planning textbooks of today. Professor Anthony Sutcliffe paid tribute to Lever in his book *British Town Planning*: 'Port Sunlight has an attention to architectural detail which is unique ... The Cadburys, the Rowntrees at York who founded New Earswick, the Reckitts at Hull, and the Colemans at Norwich were all non-conformists of one kind or another, but while they exchanged ideas, Lever always seems to have remained aloof, the individualist who did everything his own way . . . he forecast certain planning devices which were to be adopted more widely over the next two decades.' Chief among these was the concept that later became known as the 'super-block': grouped housing built around a central open area. Every house, as Lever had promised, had its own garden at front and back, but behind the houses was a large space devoted to communal allotments. There was more space than the inhabitants knew what to do with.

At the same time Lever was sorting out his own living arrangements. When work started on Port Sunlight in 1888 he rented the manor house in the nearby village of Thornton Hough from the impoverished Forwood family, who had built it fifty years before: they were only too happy to sell the place to him five years later, and he immediately set about 'improving' it with Jonathan Simpson's help. The process went on almost until he died, the original Victorian gothic house taking on a chameleon-like quality, its gables, bays and chimneys metamorphosing year by year according to Lever's changing preferences and favoured periods.

One of the first alterations he made was the installation of his first open-air bedroom, a fixture in every one of his subsequent homes. A narrow leaded platform between two converging roofs was strengthened to bear the weight of an iron bedstead and a stone washtub, a canopy placed above it to keep off the worst (but by no means all) of the rain. So much water did make it through to the bedroom that gutters had to be sunk into the floor to carry it away to the drainpipes and down into the dull paved back yard that the 'room' overlooked. 'Fancy, Bill,' remarked one of the workmen hired to install the outdoor room, 'a bloke getting £500 a week regular and sleeping on a roof.'

You can understand his confusion. Sleeping outdoors was – and remains – a crazy thing to do out of anything less than necessity. But Lever was not alone in his conviction that wind, rain and snow were the best bedfellows. Outdoor living was enthusiastically advocated by the poet Edward Carpenter in his 1889 book *Civilisation: Its Cause and Cure*, along with a host of other ideas – vegetarianism, pacifism, nudism – which made up an ideal 'simple life'. The architect Raymond Unwin, who designed much of Letchworth, was also a fan. It was just one of a whole bundle of fads and cranky beliefs that popped up in the 1880s and 1890s with differing levels of durability. Lever himself experimented with vegetarianism, and was a convert to a newfangled system of physical jerks. 'For the last year I have practised gymnastics almost daily and find the greatest possible benefit,' he confided in his diary for 1891, three years before the new sport became an Olympic standard. 'From this day I propose to book a daily record of dinners, cigars, wines and the exercises I have taken as a guide for the future.' He became obsessed with the new fad of dietetics, lecturing his employees at length on how they should aim to chew every piece of food at least thirty-two times, and dismissing cooked breakfasts as 'quite super-fluous for adults'. While he never went quite as far as advocating naturism or learning Esperanto, Lever followed new trends with enthusiasm, and he stuck with the ones he believed in. From 1891 onwards both he and the un-complaining Elizabeth spent every night that they could out of doors.

Part of the reason was simple masochism. Throughout Lever's career his abiding principle was no pain, no gain. 'Are you willing to sacrifice your ease, your comfort, and your enjoyment?' he demanded of an audience of students in 1915. 'Success in business . . . means absolute self-sacrifice, and nothing else. That is the prize you will have to pay if you want to aspire to the honourable positions occupied by the leaders in this and all other towns.' At Thornton he put his beliefs into action by insisting on baths that were never more than a few degrees above freezing, instructed the servants to wake him without fail at 6.30 every morning, and had his 'sanctum', or office, fitted out with a specially made high desk, because he insisted that he would work better if he had to stand up. In this, as in everything else, there was no arguing with him.

Three Levers moved into Thornton Manor, for only three weeks after she had cut the first sod of Port Sunlight, Elizabeth, at thirty-eight, gave birth to a healthy baby boy after a series of miscarriages. He too was named William, but he took his middle name, Hulme, from his mother, and it was the name by which his father always called him. His birth was announced by letter to the employees of Lever Brothers in a sweet little practical joke:

I write to advise you that I have been introduced to a gentleman who I hope will take over my interest and position in this business. It will be a trouble to me to retire from a business I have had to work very hard to build up, still I feel that this gentleman has qualifications that pre-eminently fit him for the post. In the short acquaintance I have had with him – only 11 days – I have not failed to notice his natural business instincts, not the least of which are that he hears what people have to say but keeps his own mouth shut and that he never meddles or interferes with what does not concern him. I have never known him to be 'talked over' from any object he had in view, he forms his own opinions and threats or persuasions are alike useless to turn him from his purpose. He shows great perseverance in attaining his object and is never quiet until he has realised his wishes. Of an unassuming nature he attaches more importance to the solid comforts of this life than to any mere outward show. He insists on the strictest attention to their duties in all those who are in a position of trust with him, but their duties performed he gives them the fullest liberty to follow their own affairs. He makes no promises and tells no lies and I may add enjoys the most robust health. With these qualifications I trust that WH Lever Jnr – my successor – will have the same hearty and generous support you have always given to

Yours truly

WH Lever

Elsewhere in the family, things were not so happy. In 1889, a year after the birth of his own eldest son, the younger James Lever was involved in a road accident. His behaviour, always nervous, became more erratic. He lost his enthusiasm for his work, insisting that his own contribution to the business was worthless. He was, in short, suffering from depression. The Port Sunlight project continued to terrify him, and William ensured that his brother's duties in the offices were limited to harmless paper-pushing and seconding proposals that had already been made, rather than facing his crippling fear of taking important decisions by himself. This was really little more than a formalization of the way their relationship had always worked. Lever Brothers was always the name above the door, but there was very definitely one man in charge. William's own son, who did indeed grow up to join the business, made an interesting choice of words when he came to describe the relationship between his father and uncle: 'William had always been the dominant partner, the originator, the directing mind, the controlling force, but his brother, until illness overtook him, gave him loyal, competent and unstinting support.' Controlling forces have a tendency to sweep the merely competent from their path without really noticing. How much responsibility the autocrat felt for the way his little brother ended up we shall never know.

6

CARE IN THE COMMUNITY

IN 1889 WILLIAM LEVER HAD TWO NEW FAMILIES TO WORRY about – his own newborn son, and the villagers of Port Sunlight, whom he intended to bond together as tightly as any clan. They would work together, live together, and even eat together – vast dining-halls were provided, dishing out over a thousand hearty meals at three pence a time for man and manager alike (though the managers got tablecloths and waitress service in a special room at the back). Every employee of Lever Brothers was free to apply for a house in the village, and the rules stated that they should be assigned 'irrespective of an applicant's position in the company, the general rule being that all types of houses are available to all types of employee, after size of family has been taken into consideration'. Rents were deducted directly from wage packets. The Kitchen houses cost between five and six shillings a week, the Parlour houses from seven to ten, well within the reach of most of the male employees, who were at that time earning between twenty and twenty-five shillings a week. When rates and maintenance were taken into account, Lever Brothers were actually running Port Sunlight at a loss. But Lever was unperturbed by the balance sheets. The equation that mattered to him was that a comfortable, secure workforce equalled a loyal and productive workforce, and he knew he would be more than repaid in the long term. 'There is no room for sentiment in business,' he declared in 1900. 'The truest and highest form of enlightened self interest requires that we pay the fullest regard to the interest and welfare of those around us, whose well-being we must bind up with our own and with whom we must share our prosperity.' By 1897, that prosperity totted up to assets of around one and a quarter million pounds, an almost unimaginable embarrassment of riches. There was plenty to go round. He rather enjoyed scratching his workers' backs, but he knew perfectly well that his own would be scratched in return.

So the villagers were provided with every amenity they could possibly want, and several they probably didn't. A primary school was built for their children. Shops and a post office sprang up. Tennis courts, bowling greens, a football and cricket pitch were installed, and the company provided equipment and refreshments during matches. Before long Port Sunlight boasted more clubs and societies than a university campus in freshers' week – a brass band, presented with a set of silver-plated instruments by the company, a thriving Horticultural Society which filled the village halls with blooms at their annual flower show, an Amateur Dramatic Society, a Philharmonic Society, Old English Choir, cycling, walking, croquet and quoits Clubs, and even a ping-pong team. The 'Mutual Improvement Society' – a very Lever organization – hosted talks by visiting lecturers on subjects as diverse as 'Science and Revelation', 'The Life and Times of Oliver Cromwell' and 'National Festivals of Physical Training Abroad'.

The less intellectually inclined men got a social club complete with bowling green, while the unmarried women who flocked to Port Sunlight from Liverpool to work in the packing department got their own Institute 'to provide the girls with a place where they can meet together for companionship, and under the supervision of a lady superintendent, attend classes in needlework, cookery and housewifery'. This would prepare them well for marriage, at which point they were required by the company to hang up their overalls for good and devote their days to looking after their homes. Actually meeting a potential husband, however, was something of a challenge. They were provided with a separate dining-hall at lunchtimes, and even a women-only hostel to which they could donate nearly half their wages in return for bed and board and ensure that their lives remained entirely unsullied by the sight of a male. The convent-like atmosphere proved unpopular, much to Lever's bewilderment. 'I believe the girls' objection was due more to the suspicion they had that they were being asked to live in what appeared to them an institution, and probably also to the ridicule of other girls, than to any other cause,' he declared when the hostel was left empty, overlooking the fact that the whole village was essentially an institution, albeit one with fancy windows. 'Their womanly pride preferred to be independent, and to find their own lodging accommodation with some working man's family.' No matter – he reopened the building as a free library and museum, and, situated close to the main works gates, it proved a popular lunchtime destination for employees who wanted to keep up with the newspapers or gaze upon such edifying sights as the very trumpet on which was sounded the Charge of the Light Brigade.

More popular was the Bridge Inn, which opened in October 1900. Originally its enormous bar was run on strictly temperance lines, but an official request was made to the Village Society (run from within Lever Brothers) that it should be allowed to sell beer. Lever seldom drank himself – 'I am fond of champagne, but it is not fond of me,' he declared after an early hangover – and he shared the popular view among the better-off that alcohol was a luxury when they chose to imbibe it, but a vice when it went down the throats of the working classes. He did, however, agree to bow to democracy and put the issue to a vote of all villagers. In this he faced stern opposition from his colleagues, the Church and even his wife, who regularly entertained the local branch of the Women's Temperance Society to 'pleasurable tea parties' in the gardens of Thornton Manor, but he held firm, swayed particularly by the fact that 'the women also supported the change, for they knew their menfolk wanted their glass of beer, and they much preferred that they should have it at the inn in their own village, where they were known, rather than further afield'. Eighty per cent of the villagers voted to end the booze ban, and in 1903 the Bridge Inn received its licence, though it was to remain dry on Sundays for a further seventy years.

Those disgusted by such indulgences could work out their frustrations in the large gymnasium in the centre of the village, which was kitted out with the latest equipment of which Lever himself was such a fan. In 1902 an open-air swimming-pool was installed alongside, its water warmed to a still-bracing 60 degrees Fahrenheit in the soapworks themselves. The following year saw the opening of something even more extraordinary: the Auditorium, a full-size proscenium-arch stage built of stone at one end of one of the drained creeks in the village, its banks providing open-air seating for an audience of 2,400 people. Far more than that turned up for its opening ceremony, but they proved not as wind-resistant or waterproof as Lever himself and in 1904 he grudgingly agreed to erect an iron and canvas covering for the spectators to shelter beneath as they enjoyed entertainments as varied as orchestral concerts and Sunday school services. The same year saw the opening of Christ Church, a pastiche-medieval church which Lever ran on the non-denominational lines in which he had been raised. A few days after the first service had been celebrated there he received an angry letter from the Bishop of Chester complaining that a peal of eight bells had been heard ringing out across the village: it was a well-established tradition that only parish churches were allowed to ring a full peal, and the upstart chapel should remove its seven extra clappers without delay. Lever replied that he would be happy to strip his belfry just as soon as the Bishop showed him the law of the land that declared he was only allowed a single bell. Unable to produce any document-ation, the diocese was forced with bad grace to accept the multi-tinkling cuckoo in its midst. Needless to say, Lever milked the ecclesiastical controversy for all it was worth in the pages of the press.

Port Sunlight was a strange little fiefdom that made its own rules, as self-contained and inward-looking as any medieval city-state. Its borders were rigidly defined: the factory dominated the south, while the New Chester toll road sliced dead-straight through the countryside on the east; the London and North Western Railway line marked the western limits just as clearly. There was some bleeding across the Bebington Road to the north-east (Hesketh Hall, opened in 1903 as a technical college, lay on the wrong side of the tracks), but the slums and estates that sprang up beyond the edges of Port Sunlight were as separate from the village as Soweto is from Johannesburg. People here behaved differently: they were healthier and better-off than those in the suburbs that surrounded them, and they were resented for it. 'I wonder whether the children who are spending their happiest years in a spot so habitable, so full of possibilities for healthy exercise and enjoyment, are even conscious of the existence of the thousands of unkempt, unloved little kiddies in the urban slum land, those drab and dreary centres further than the boundaries of the village,' mused an editorial in the Lever Brothers' in-house magazine in 1906. Sentimental, perhaps, but not exaggerated. Two years after the opening of the village's Cottage Hospital, funded and staffed by the company (and featuring two 'open-air wards' with beds which could be wheeled out through specially designed french windows on to a terrace for the patients to sleep in the Lever-approved manner), the death rate was way below the national average: in 1909 it stood at nine in the 1,000 while in Liverpool across the river it was over twenty per 1,000. The city's infant mortality rate was double that in Port Sunlight. Lever's experiment in the 'science of life' had proved a success.

Naturally, it had not been achieved without some serious social engineering. Not everyone was welcome in this benevolent kingdom. Port Sunlight might have had an unemployment rate of zero, but only because anyone who left Lever Brothers or was sacked (as two chemists were at an early stage for gossiping about the top-secret formula for Sunlight in public) was required to vacate their home in the village as well. And simply working for the company might not be enough to keep them in bed and board. 'The private habits of an employee have really nothing to do with Lever

Brothers providing the man is a good workman,' Lever declared, but, adept at holding two entirely contradictory opinions simultaneously, he added, 'at the same time a good workman may have a wife of objectionable habits, or he may have objectionable habits himself, which make it un-desirable to have him in the village'. 'Objectionable habits' could include slothfulness, drinking, gambling, dishonesty or simply a failure to play a full part in the extra-curricular activities that were laid on in the village. Self-improvement was all but compulsory, and wise workers ensured that they were regularly seen applauding the Port Sunlight Players in the auditorium, or browsing the displays of antiques and pictures from Lever's personal collection that he occasion-ally put on show in Hulme Hall.

This was his village, his creation, paid for by his cash, and here he could indulge his control-freakery to the full. 'If I were to follow the usual mode of profit sharing I would send my workmen and work girls to the cash office at the end of the year and say to them: "you are going to receive eight pounds each; you have earned this money, take it and make whatever use you like of it",' he primly explained in 1903. 'Instead of that I told them "Eight pounds is an amount which is soon spent, and it will not do you much good if you send it down your throats in the form of bottles of whisky, bags of sweets, or fat geese for Christmas. On the other hand, if you leave the money with me, I shall use it to provide for you everything which makes life pleasant, viz, nice houses, comfortable home and healthy recreation. I am disposed to allow profit-sharing under no other than that form."' Patronizing perhaps, but he was downplaying a very real generosity. There was no 'usual mode of profit sharing', most factory bosses being quite happy to pile up the cash for themselves without a thought for those who had made it for them. Many insisted their workers should provide their own tools, clothing and even coal for the stove if they wanted to work in temperatures above freezing. In the same year that Port Sunlight was founded, 1,400 women went on strike at the Bryant & May match factory in London over the management's system of deducting fines from their wages for such offences as talking or going to the toilet during their fourteen-hour shifts. It was only the publicity created by campaigners like Annie Besant, our old friend from the *Pall Mall Gazette* William Stead and George Bernard Shaw that forced the company to stop using yellow phosphorus in their factories, a carcinogenic substance that caused the workers' faces literally to rot away. Lever Brothers' staff knew just how lucky they were, and Lever's generosity was much appreciated in the village (although possibly not always quite as much as a bottle of whisky or a bag of sweets would have been).

They did, however, have to live by the whims and rules of the fussiest landlord in the world. In a 1909 study of the village, author W. L. George noted approvingly that the front gardens that were such an essential part of Lever's vision had been 'at one time given up to the tenants, but their aesthetic possibilities were not appreciated; they were used as fowl-runs, and even as dustbins, while the family washing was unblushingly exposed on the railings'. They were therefore taken back into the control of the Village Estate Department, and thereafter kept clear, neat and planted only with varieties of flowers of which Mr Lever approved. Villagers were also reprimanded for taking short-cuts across the allotments, and informed that the Chairman was disappointed with the quality of the vegetables they were growing there.

Even more preposterously, Lever sought to control the

love-lives of his employees. A dance was held every weekend in one of the village halls, which Lever often went to
himself, kindly ensuring that he asked any plain girls who
had been overlooked by everyone else to dance with him
(one employee recalled that 'he always had a dance with
Ethel Williams, the hunchback'). Whether or not he
attended, he insisted that girls submit the names of any
man they wanted to invite to something called the 'Social
Department, which issues invitations to them unless there
be reasons that militate against them'. Lacking daughters
himself, he was determined to be an over-protective father
to those of other people.

But then as far as William and Elizabeth were concerned,
the Sunlighters were their family. Having left it unusually
late to start a family of their own, they indulged their
natural affection for children through the village. They
entertained all the youngsters in Port Sunlight to
extravagant parties every year on their own birthdays, with
Punch and Judy, party games and dancing to the music of
the Port Sunlight Prize Band. Awards were given for the
fancy-dress outfit that the Levers deemed the 'most
marvellous and exceedingly picturesque' – in 1911, the top
prize was taken by eight-year-old Arthur Stuffins, who
turned up as Lever's Mini-Me in a miniature version of the
grey tailcoat and hard felt hat that was the boss's trademark
outfit. Every summer the entire village was invited to
Thornton Manor for a series of garden parties, the most
spectacular of which was the 'Sunday School Treat', with
merry-go-rounds, swings, donkey-rides, boats on the lake
and coconut shies, all of which, one attendee recalls, 'the
Old Man enjoyed as much as the children'. My favourite
picture of Lever dates from one of these parties, the stocky,
buttoned-up Victorian gentleman standing beaming in the

midst of a crowd of young girls, gleaming white in their Sunday best, each of them trying desperately to wangle a finger or arm to clutch and a place in the shade of his vast parasol. 'The great and most eager sport was for the company of "Uncle Lever" as a playmate,' one parent recalled of the picnics, 'with the right to hang on to him for a regular romp, half-a-dozen or more at a time, for a share of his big Japanese sunshade, and for a seat on the grass beside him when, in order to get rest, he resorted to the stratagem of telling them a tale.' Elizabeth, meanwhile, took care of the less boisterous children, who liked to 'gather round her and whisper confidences'. They insisted on being called 'Uncle' and 'Auntie' by all, which could cause confusion among the younger children, as Andrew Knox, then a lowly employee of Lever Brothers, recalled:

> He saw a small boy crying and picked him up. He tried to comfort the boy by asking 'Why don't you call me Uncle?' The small boy through his tears replied, 'Because you never asked me to!' On another occasion his eyes fell upon my small twin sisters. He told them, greatly to their chagrin, that they were really taps because they were little Knox.

The children were not forgotten on their own birthdays, either. As Lily Fay, whose parents moved to the village in 1902, recalled in Sue Sellers's book *Sunlighters*, 'from the age of 5 to the age of 14 all the children in the village were given a book on their birthdays. There were 6 children in our family, and the books were never duplicated. We had Little Women, Gulliver's Travels, Dickens. Often Mrs Lever would come in her carriage and deliver the books herself.' Each thoughtful gift was decorated with an embossed book plate complete with portraits of the Lever family, and individually signed. A regular census was taken of the village to ensure that no child was left out.

The adults did not do too badly out of the Levers, either. Every Christmas the entire staff of Lever Brothers were entertained at Thornton Manor in batches – the schedule for the winter of 1905–6 was as follows:

- December 22 – Part of the Staff
- December 29 – Members of Christ Church Choir, the Port Sunlight Prize Band and the Philharmonic Society
- January 2 – The remainder of the members of the Staff
- January 4 – Old Scholars
- January 6 – The Company's Agents, with their wives
- January 9 – The Social Workers at Port Sunlight – 'those who, whatever their station, take some part in the control of the various institutions and organisations of the village'.

Each group was treated to spectacular dances in the ballroom and a programme of 'songs, recitations and organ music' featuring everyone from Gilbert and Sullivan to Richard Wagner next door in the music room, all performed by the various village amateurs whose talents Lever had encouraged. Even 'those who prefer the fragrant weed' were not forgotten; smokers were allowed to 'indulge while admiring the many beauties and natural curiosities of the Conservatories'. 'Not a few of the village lads and lasses – and more mature inhabitants too – look forward to the Thornton Manor dances as the most brilliant and happy gatherings of the year,' enthused the company magazine, while the host professed his own delight: 'probably a prettier sight is not to be witnessed than that of healthy, vigorous youth indulging in the innocent pastime of dancing'. Naturally, some careful policing of the guest lists ensured that the dancing remained innocent at all times.

In the summer, Lever took his staff further afield. An excursion by steamer to Anglesey in 1890, to celebrate the opening of the works, was the first of many awaydays for employees. Subsequent summers saw trips to 'the kaleido-scope of pleasure' that is Blackpool, while in 1897 more than 2,000 of the company's staff were taken by train to London to join in the celebrations of Queen Victoria's Diamond Jubilee. Subsequent trips to Paris in 1900 and Brussels in 1905 were organized with military precision. For the latter both the works and village were closed down for a weekend; battalions of Sunlighters met at prearranged points around the village and were shepherded by their managers and representatives of 'Messrs Thomas Cook & Sons' on to special colour-coded trains at Bebington station. They travelled overnight on the ferry from Folkestone, and were met on the Continent by trains painted in corresponding colours, every passenger having been issued with a coloured badge in case they forgot which train they belonged to. Once in Brussels the 2,000 Sunlighters breakfasted in the town's restaurants, which had been specially hired out for the occasion, and were decanted into 'wagonettes and landaus to the number of nearly three hundred' and taken on a tour of the city, where, one tourist reported, 'the kindly greeting exchanged between residents and visitors was one of the most interesting features of the trip'. The opening of a new Lever Brothers' factory in the Brussels suburbs was followed by a formal lunch and a performance by the Philharmonic Society, whose instru-ments had no doubt been given their own colour-coded tickets to ensure that they made it across the Channel.

Port Sunlight was, by anyone's reckoning, an extra-ordinary venture. *The Times* wrote approvingly of its 'institutions which may well be envied by communities of higher social scale in older and larger settlements'. Thousands of visitors from across Europe filed round the factory and wandered down the village's leafy avenues every year, eager to experience this new experiment in living for themselves. But the praise that meant the most to Lever came from one of the highest authorities in the land. On 28 November 1891 the first of several multi-purpose halls, designed to be used as a dining-hall in the day, a meeting-place at night and a venue for religious concerts on Sundays, was officially opened by William Ewart Gladstone, the great Victorian statesman then between his third and fourth terms of office as prime minister. To Lever, a lifelong Liberal, the old man was a hero, and the heartfelt endorsement this architect of universal education and parliamentary reform delivered from the flower-strewn stage meant more to him than any statement of profit or loss.

Though labour was appointed for our bodies . . . yet we cannot look to that alone, that its depressing influences are too strong, and that we require something else, some redemption of a portion of our time, some opening to us of fair opportunities, in order to give exercise and fair play to the higher departments of our nature. If man is made of body, soul and spirit, that applies as much to the working man as to the very highest in the land; and the opening of this hall signifies and visibly asserts in the face of the community that you ought to be able to spare and liberate from your labour some portion of your time in the evening and devote it to useful, improving, and enobling pursuits.

A very powerful writer . . . said we were approaching a period when cash payment was to be the only nexus, the only link, between man and man. In this hall I have found living proof that cash payment is not the only nexus between man and man. There enters something else into the relations between yourselves and your employers, something that appeals more deeply and more profoundly to the inner and deeper sentiment of human nature . . .

The objects of this institution are twofold – one, I think, undoubtedly to improve the material condition of the workman, to give him, if you can, an increase in wages and a decrease of labour; but besides this to give him the sense of a common interest with his employers, and give him also the sense of a common *feeling* with his employers. Establish some kind of brotherhood between man and man; look to the qualities of the heart; look to the action of the conscience, as well as to appetite and to the desire to rise, for solving the difficulties which may from time to time occur, look to the action of that overruling Providence which shapes our ends, and recollect that high principle announced to us in the highest of all sources, and applicable above all things: 'Behold how good and how pleasant it is for brethren to dwell together in unity.' This day must inspire great thankfulness for the past, more hopefulness for the future.

Long after the politician and his wife had departed Port Sunlight, leaving behind them two trees planted in the grounds of the hall that would bear their name, Lever was running those words through his head. 'I could not sleep much that night,' he recalled. 'I had to walk up and down the park thinking of him. He made an extraordinary impression.'

7

AROUND THE WORLD IN EIGHTY WAYS

BRITAIN WAS NEVER GOING TO BE BIG ENOUGH TO CONTAIN Lever. The soap companies before him had been content to operate on a provincial scale – Pears, for all its fame, was barely sold outside London, while other brands enjoyed a local monopoly in their home towns or cities. From the start Lever had set out to spread Sunlight across the land. It was no accident that he had placed his first adverts with the London and North Western Railway Company, spreading brand awareness not through the local streets but straight down the central artery of England, closely followed by salesmen who would ensure that the bright primary colours of the new product shone from every grocer's window. He had set out systematically to lather up the whole kingdom, and the next natural step was to concentrate on washing the pink bits of the entire British Empire.

Soap-making necessitated thinking on a global scale anyway. Each and every bar of Sunlight contained palm oils from the South Pacific, citronella from India, cotton oil from the American South, sesame oil from Africa, and tallow from the sheep farms of Australia and New Zealand. The chaos theory that governs global economics meant that events thousands of miles away were felt on the production lines at Port Sunlight – when drought hit Australia, the animals were the first to die, and the vast influx of tallow on to the market pushed prices down and Lever Brothers' profits up, just as the growing popularity at the end of the century of the recently invented margarine spread the vegetable oil market far more thinly, rocketing up the price of the more palatable ingredients of soap.

At the same time, export was beset with problems. While Great Britain provided the bulk of the soap used in the countries over which the Union Jack fluttered (including many of the ones that provided the raw materials in the first place), selling to areas outside the Empire could be all but impossible. Every country imposed complicated tariffs on goods that were imported across their borders, in an effort to ensure that their citizens bought only home-made products. In many cases, the duties were so high it wasn't even worth bothering to try. In Britain, the argument for imposing 'Protectionist' tariffs in retaliation raged for decades, tearing apart the Conservative party in much the same way as Europe did in the 1990s, and causing no less a figure than Winston Churchill to storm across the floor of the House of Commons and join the Liberals, outraged at his party's attempts 'to make inside our planet a smaller planet called the British Empire, cut off by impassable space from everything else'.

Lever himself was, like Churchill, a passionate advocate of Free Trade, and he was quite prepared to argue its benefits with anyone who would listen. But there was little he could do to influence the governments of other countries. He had to settle for exploiting what loopholes he could find. Thus it was that for several years vast slabs of Sunlight, around six feet long and three feet wide, arrived regularly at the door of a private house in the suburbs of Vienna, where they were sliced, stamped and packed into cartons in the cellar. Had they come over the border pre-packaged, each bar would have been subject to a duty of several groschen by the Austro-Hungarian government.

Elsewhere it was easier. Lever Brothers had a ready-made market in the dominions that Britain controlled – a fifth of the world's land surface – and they were quick to move into the parts of Europe that welcomed their business. By 1889 they were operating agencies in Belgium, Germany, France, Switzerland and Holland, each under the leadership of a native. Lever realized that in this, if nothing else, he would have to concede some control. 'The most serious obstacle to international trade in manufactured articles is the great difficulty – I might also say the impossibility – while living in one country, of appreciating the tastes and requirements of another,' he declared sagely. That didn't necessarily mean he liked it when other people told him so. A colleague recalled an encounter between the Chairman and one of his men in the field: 'When he wanted to start up in Siam – now Thailand – he sent a salesman there. In due course the man returned and made a report that Siam was a "blue mottled market" and that yellow soap was not liked; all that had to be done was give him blue mottled to sell and he would soon produce orders. The Old Man sent for him . . . "I've read your report and I see that you can't sell Sunlight Soap in Siam. I'll have to find some-one who can, then."'

Some agents, however, succeeded in satisfying his requirements. In Switzerland F. H. Lavanchy-Clarke, a trained Egyptologist whose only business experience was in running institutions for the blind, judged the national character perfectly when he launched Sunlight with a 'Fête des Blanchisseuses' on the shore of Lake Geneva: the sight of 100 or more washerwomen in sparkling white uniforms assiduously purging their sheets of stains appealed to the fastidious Swiss, and orders came flooding in.

In Holland the soap was an instant hit, thanks largely to the energetic efforts of A. P. van Geelkerken, whom Lever recruited from a commercial agency in London to head his operations there under the name of Lever Zeep Maatschappij. Geelkerken had as much of an eye for an eye-catching promotion as his boss: he sent a wagonette painted in the Sunlight colours around the country manned by two men dressed in blue military-style uniforms with red piping, who distributed samples as they went. The venture was not an instant success: the salesmen's uniforms were too similar to those of the Salvation Army, who were pursuing an aggressive recruitment campaign in the area at the time, and they had their work cut out persuading potential customers of their non-God-bothering credentials. Those who did agree to stop and listen to their sales pitch were rewarded with a sample of Sunlight and a free leaflet by Phileas T. Barnum, the American freakshow magnate, entitled *How to Become Rich*, advice which Geelkerken quickly followed, even if the customers didn't.

So worried were the biggest Dutch soapmakers, Van den Bergh's, by this new competition that they planned an even more spectacular stunt. A live elephant was paraded through the streets of Rotterdam, complete with a veiled rider. The gimmick, which was designed to promote their 'Sultana' brand, rather backfired since hardly anyone noticed the significance of the supposed Turkish princess who was gingerly clinging to the beast's back. Still, they probably did well out of the few shopkeepers able to interpret their customers' subsequent requests for Elephant soap.

Importing was not a long-term aim: Lever Brothers was always intended to be a multinational operation. In a 1902 speech to the staff of Lever's associated companies in the low countries, he told them: 'I want you to continue your efforts a little longer until we can put a works down in your country and you are able to call upon your customers and say to them: "this soap is made in Belgium for Belgian people" or "this soap is made in Holland for Dutch people."' Let the Conservatives complain that he was unpatriotic, and the Socialists carp that he was stealing British jobs. Lever had created more business, and done more for worker–employer relations, than any man alive. And while his British business continued to thrive, there was no danger of redundancies on either side of the Channel.

America, however, was a different matter. Lever first crossed the Atlantic in 1888, ostensibly to help his journalist brother-in-law, W. F. Tillotson, set up a syndication service which would import short stories from American magazines and newspapers, just as Sherlock Holmes and other literary creations made the journey in the opposite direction. While he was over there, however, he did a little business of his own, setting up agencies in Canada (under the control of an old school-friend, Alfred Robinson, who had emigrated) and New York. The US office was managed by A. J. Wolfendale, who had joined the grocery business in Wigan at the tender age of sixteen and gone on to work as Lever's second-in-command on outdoor advertising when he launched Sunlight. Here, however, the soap was less of a hit. Americans, then as now, preferred quantity over quality, and were unswayed by demon-strations of Sunlight's efficiency and value. They stuck to 'filled' soaps, those bulked out with silicate of soda, which came in much larger bars. The fact that they had to be larger because they didn't last as long or wash as well did not seem to bother customers. While the antiseptic Lifebuoy sold well, boosted by an award-winning ad campaign featuring a white-bearded lifeboatman who looks suspiciously like Captain Bird's Eye's granddad, Sunlight just gathered dust on shelves. To add insult to injury, some retailers in Brooklyn rebranded their own soaps as 'Daylight' and 'American Sunlight'. Even they sold better than Lever's own brand.

Failure was a new experience for Lever, and not one he was equipped to deal with. His frustration was doubled by having to rely on Wolfendale's own account of affairs, rather than the evidence of his own eyes. He was used to absolute control of every aspect of his business in Britain – even the official history of Lever Brothers admits that 'practically the whole of the business was carried in his head and was directed by his verbal instruction'. And that made it successful. Now he had delegated, and it had all gone wrong. It stood to reason that his old colleague was simply not doing the job properly.

His next move was extreme, even for Lever. He hired a private detective in New York, and instructed him to keep tabs on Wolfendale morning, noon and night. He was to follow him from his home every morning, travel across on the Brooklyn ferry with him, and not let him out of his sight for the whole of the working day. He was even to stake out his house at weekends, for, as Lever knew from Port Sunlight, it was how he spent his leisure hours that really gave you the measure of a man. The detective charged with the job assumed he was looking for evidence that Wolfendale was defrauding the company; no, no, Lever assured him, nothing of the sort. He would trust Wolfendale with his life. He just thought he was lazy.

Fortunately for Wolfendale, three months of solid surveillance turned up no evidence of slackness at all. The target, the detective reported, was working all the hours God sent, and then some. The New York office was a hive of activity. The salesmen were dropping with exhaustion. And still it wasn't getting them anywhere.

Satisfied that the problem was not Wolfendale, Lever began to spend as much of his own time in the States as he could, convinced that somehow he could change the minds of the American people through the sheer force of his own personality. Between 1894 and 1898 he visited New York every year. Still Sunlight failed to break through. 'It is the biggest undertaking I ever had on hand, and I fancy it has depressed me,' he wrote sadly to his father in 1895. 'I should hate to face a failure here, and we have to run the risk. However, I hope it will be a success, as big as in England.'

Success would come, but not with Sunlight. In 1899 Lever Brothers purchased Benjamin Brooke & Co., manufacturers of Monkey Brand, the most popular soap in America, figuring perhaps that if you can't beat them, you might as well buy them. At last, the American operation went into profit. Sunlight limped on in the shadow of Monkey Brand and Lifebuoy until it was finally withdrawn some years later.

Along with the company they acquired a new US headquarters, in Boston, and a new board member, Sydney Gross, who was probably the most valuable asset the company would ever take on. Gross, a sharp-faced, bearded showman from Philadelphia, was well known for having made for Brooke's 'the largest sale of soap that has ever been known in the world in one transaction, £50,000 worth', and he was an advertising genius. 'I believe Mr Gross and Mr Barrett of Pears' have done more between them for the cause of artistic advertising than any other men in the world,' said Lever. 'No one had a keener insight into effective advertising. In fact, if I might use a simile, his brain seemed to be a sheaf of arrows from which he could always draw one to pierce right through to the bull's eye. Most advertisers are the slaves of habit and the followers of custom. Not so Mr Gross. Originality marked him at every step ... His methods were always founded upon reason, logic and facts – no taint of deception in laying his goods before the public – and hence his success.'

A hundred and twenty years before the ITV Digital monkey found a place in the hearts of the British public (unlike the service he advertised), Gross was releasing great apes into people's living rooms. The Monkey Brand monkey first appeared as a wild baboon startled by his own reflection in a gleaming frying-pan which had been scoured with the soap in question, but he evolved at a rate that would have sent Charles Darwin back to the drawing-board. By the time of his next excursion he had acquired the ragged clothes of a tramp and squatted in the gutter, his begging-bowl the same shining frying-pan which he claimed in a handwritten sign as 'all my own work'. He swiftly went up in the world, getting a job as a butler and scrubbing everything from pots and pans to willow-pattern plates, in a spotless white tie and waistcoat. At the same time his features were refined; he became more chimpanzee-like, more cuddly. He was an enormous hit: under Gross's leadership Monkey Brand expanded as swiftly in the US as Sunlight had in Britain. The simple simian was accompanied by an ingenious pitch which accentuated the negative: it 'WON'T WASH CLOTHES'. Small print, however, listed every other possible use Monkey Brand was perfect for:

Spotless Earthenware – *Smiling Housewives* – Clean Baths – *Happy Husbands* – White Marble – *Contented Servants* – Shining Pots and Pans – *In The Parlour* – Polished Stair-Rods – *In The Kitchen* – Bright Fire-Irons – *In The Factory* – Sparkling Glass-Ware
SIMPLE!! RAPID!! CLEAN!! CHEAP!!

Gross's touch was evident in the launch of a raft of fresh products that took Lever Brothers into the new century, shifting them on from the Victorian whimsy epitomized by the Frith portrait into a brave new world of labour-saving and linoleum. Until now the company's policy on new brands had been dictated merely by Lever's practical thriftiness: none of the leftovers from the process of making Sunlight were allowed to go to waste. Lifebuoy, the miracle carbolic soap that kept the doctor from the door, was simply the dark brown dregs known as nigres which were left behind in the boiling pans, mixed with the anti-septic phenol and coloured to make it look less cheap. Lever's Double-Refined Glycerine, a multi-purpose emollient and laxative which was a staple in the Victorian bathroom cabinet, was simply the liquid that was tapped off at the boiling stage. After Port Sunlight got its own mills to extract oils on-site in 1897, the dry husks of the various kernels, nuts and seeds that were left over were mashed up and sold to farmers as Sunlight Cattle Seed Cake. Even the scraps that were left over after the soap had been cut and shaped into tablets were gathered and sold as Sunlight Flakes, aimed at saving the busy housewife the few seconds it took to flake her own soap into the tub – and at bringing in a much wider profit margin for Lever Brothers.

It was with this last product that Gross first worked his magic. Despite the promise that they were 'milled wonderfully fine' (rather than just scraped up off the factory floor), Sunlight Flakes sold sluggishly. After a few months they were taken off the market, and in January 1900 they reappeared as Lux. The very name smacked of the future. The cherubic babe of the new century took a break from shooing out his aged scythe-bearing predecessor in every newspaper cartoon to appear on the Lux packaging, where he held a mirror up to reflect a beam of blinding light on to an exhausted woman toiling at a washtub. Customers who collected enough cartons received not reproductions of fusty old paintings, but 'high-class photographs' of celebrities to hang on their walls. The tradition, which began with Marie Corelli, Ellen Terry and the various princesses spawned by Queen Victoria and scattered around the royal houses of Europe, continued for almost eighty years and went on to feature such 'Lux Lovelies' as Bette Davis, Joan Crawford, Raquel Welch and Rosemary Clooney in their time.

Lux was just the beginning. As the soap market continued to grow, so too did the company's share of it. Smaller companies were helpless against the competition; they were swallowed up by Lever Brothers, their products refined, rebranded and revived and served up to the public in new and exciting ways. Y-Z Disinfectant Soap Powder was the next to be launched, its name both pun and selling point, for it was to be the only powder those with a 'wise head' would use. Vim scouring powder followed at 3d a can, complete with a proudly proclaimed technological innovation: 'a sifting top regulates its use'. Lever worried that the word Vim sounded too much like one of the potted meat products that had recently come on to the market, though he seems to have been blissfully unaware that it was also the name of a popular naturist magazine, 'devoted to promoting vigour of body and mind' and later incorporated into the veteran title *Health and Efficiency*.

At the same time Lever Brothers branched out into a huge range of cosmetic soaps – Velvet Skin, Plantol, Coral, Capitol, Villa and Sealskin, all available in different perfumes and sold as the perfect product for 'tender skins' and a 'delicate complexion'. Having cornered the multi-purpose economy end of the market with Sunlight, Lever had set his sights on a more exclusive sideline. Toilet soaps were smaller, but sold at a higher price. And Sydney Gross knew just how to sell beauty in a bar. 'A pamphlet on toilet soap needs picturesque handling,' he declared, rejecting the initial proposals for the sweet-smelling Plantol. 'Something about the tropic climates in which the materials are produced, the care that is exercised in refining the oils, the flowers that are picked by the women of the South on fields full of colour and beauty. That is rather the line that should have been taken, and not a treatise on perspiration, sweat and pores.' Plantol, when it did emerge, was christened a 'floral bouquet', but Gross ensured that his Gauguinesque vision was accompanied by enthusiastic endorsements from doctors and skin specialists, which must have lent as much reassurance to hypochondriac customers as the company's royal warrant, granted by Victoria in 1892, did to the snobbish.

*

All these tricks worked. By 1906 more than £4 million in capital was employed within Lever Brothers. More than a million of that was locked up in operations overseas. Every carton of Sunlight that rolled from the production lines at Port Sunlight, Brussels, Mannheim, Olten or Toronto carried a proud boast: 'HAS THE LARGEST SALE OF ANY SOAP IN THE WORLD.'

8

MORMONS, MISSIONARIES AND MERMAIDS

ENOUGH BUSINESS. WE NEED A HOLIDAY.

Rewind to September 1892. At Liverpool docks, William and Elizabeth Lever make their way to the first-class deck of the White Star liner *Germanic* to watch the ship cast off. As the vast engines shudder into action and they begin to move away from the shore, Lever lifts his four-year-old son Hulme up to wave at the crowds massed at the quayside. Together they watch the city recede into the distance before William hands the sleepy child over to Mrs Green, their housekeeper from Thornton, to be taken below to their cabin. He stays on deck a while longer, arm-in-arm with Elizabeth – 'my better three-quarters', he always calls her – watching Anglesey slip by to port and the mountains of Ireland appear in the distance.

The boat – part of the great fleet that would so tragically overreach itself twenty years later with the *Titanic* – was their home for a week, the cross-Atlantic voyage the first leg of a journey that would take them right around the world in the next five months. The route was dictated by business –

Lever wanted to check up on some of his overseas operations, and explore new areas and seek out ways of selling soap to their inhabitants. But first and foremost, this was a family holiday, a chance for the three of them to spend some time together. Even so, Lever could not entirely leave Port Sunlight behind: business followed him in a stream of wires, telegrams and letters which flooded in daily: sales figures, statistics, requests for orders and opinions, invitations to address meetings, reports on the progress of the construction work in the village, and here and there, a letter from one of his old friends wanting nothing more than to inquire about his wellbeing. He took his time to reply to every one, drawing fountain pen and paper from the battered black briefcase that was always by his side and jotting down brisk, definitive replies in his sloped, looping handwriting. While he was engaged on correspondence Hulme had strict instructions not to disturb his father, but William always made sure he had the time to take a few turns round the deck with his son each day. One morning he asked Hulme what he wanted to do with his future: that's easy, said the boy, I want to be a soap-maker like you. William beamed with pride. There's just one difference though, his son added: I'm going to make more soap than you, and better. His father considered this an excellent idea.

From the New York docks they made their way by train to Chicago, the windy city that sprawls along the western shore of Lake Michigan. The city was a vision of the future; since the great fire of 1871 its architects and engineers had been vying to create the most solid symbol of the new America, where anything was possible. Great square apartment blocks squatted on every street, their flat roofs punctuated by the bulks of water towers and chimney stacks, belching out black smoke day and night. Trains rattled through the city at street level, panicking horses at level crossings, or thundered overhead on raised boardwalks that plunged the alleys beneath them into Stygian gloom. Above it all towered the ten-storey Home Insurance Building, built seven years previously by Daniel Burnham and John Root as a whole new concept in architecture: the world's first skyscraper.

For Lever, it looked like hell on earth. 'One cannot help being impressed with the great speed at which the people are living,' he wrote in his diary. 'All is one perpetual drive, without cessation or rest. Business and pleasure, Sunday and week day, appear to be all the same. You notice at once the drawn, haggard, prematurely old faces of the work girls and youths going to the offices and stores each morning. They look more wearied and tired than they ought to when leaving their work at night. Compare them with the bright, healthy looks of English work girls and youths, and one sees at once that this rapid living tells most woefully on the young of both sexes ... I am very much mistaken if the "sweater" has not got a firm grip in Chicago, and it would not take much to convince me that, however much of a paradise it may be for the capitalist, it is the direct opposite for the workers.'

He was not wrong. The biggest employer in Chicago was the Union Stock Yards, a massive mechanized abattoir where 14 million pigs were carried to their deaths on over-head conveyors every year, their carcasses trundling past knife after knife until nothing remained but blood on the factory floor. The city worked in a similar way. Each of its million citizens was an insignificant cog in a machine thundering inexorably on; and the stock-market crash of the following year would fillet them with the same casual brutality. By 1894 President Grover Cleveland would be sending troops into the city with orders to open fire on rioting strikers.

For now, however, there was a mood of optimism in Chicago. The World's Fair – the Colombian Exposition, to give it its full title – was nearing completion, the fantastic buildings of the White City that would house all the wonders of the modern world taking shape in Jackson Park south of the city. The Levers watched tiny workmen swarm on the roof of the Manufactures and Liberal Arts Building, the largest man-made structure in the world. It, along with the hundreds of other buildings and pavilions that made up the fair, was due to be officially opened in just a few weeks on the 400th anniversary of Columbus setting foot in America. They couldn't help noticing that it didn't look as if it would be ready in time.

Some things were already in place, however. One extraordinary new invention – a vast wheel of steel, 250 feet in diameter, which would carry hundreds of passengers in hanging carriages as it slowly revolved – as yet existed only in the mind of a young engineer by the name of George Ferris. But many of the other attractions the city had dreamt up were complete. As the family wandered through Washington Park on the fringes of the fair's vast grounds, Lever was particularly taken by a series of sculptures fashioned from flowers and bedding plants. Three Red Indians paddled their way across one of the stately lawns in a canoe made of moss, their head-dresses made up of blooms of different colours. The faces of several US presidents were just about recognizable in a series of giant floral busts which predated the more permanent Mount Rushmore by forty years. Such satirical topiary delighted Lever. 'The aim should be to introduce as often as possible something fresh and novel, something that would draw the public to the park, into the fresh air, and away from the streets and slums,' he proclaimed, and his mind filled with possibilities for the creek back in Port Sunlight which he planned to drain and turn into a park for the residents.

All this Lever captured with his latest acquisition, a Kodak, a miraculous new kind of camera that could be easily carried around without the need for tripods, concertina lenses, hoods and all the heavy clutter of normal photography. When the pictures were developed he bundled them up neatly along with the observations he had jotted down in his diary and sent the package to the offices of the *Birkenhead News* back in Britain, suggesting that they might make an informative item for readers. The editor, who knew exactly which side his bread was buttered on, dutifully printed in full each of the reports that arrived from the local tycoon as he circumnavigated the globe.

Several days on a train brought the family from the booming metropolis to the eerie wilderness of Utah: if possible, Lever liked the stronghold of the Mormons even less than Chicago. It's said that the faults that most rile us are the ones we know we possess ourselves, and that is certainly true of his objections to Salt Lake City. 'The high priests arrogate to themselves the right to interfere in every affair of life,' spluttered the outraged King of Port Sunlight as he beheld the hard-working farmers offer up a tenth of their crops to the Church. 'Of course, education is not encouraged. It is only over the ignorant that such power could be held.' If Elizabeth saw any parallels with her husband's own experiments in social engineering on the banks of the Mersey, she wisely kept her mouth shut.

At least Lever was prepared to make up his own mind about Salt Lake City. In Britain at the time the polygamous

Mormons filled the same role that Jews and the Catholics had played in their turn: multi-purpose bogeymen whose way of life was not just sinful but actively sinister. Sherlock Holmes's debut in *A Study in Scarlet* just five years previously had reinforced their image as murderous aliens, uncloaked by the master detective as 'persecutors of the most terrible description. Not the Inquisition of Seville, nor the German Vehmgericht, nor the Secret Societies of Italy, were ever able to put a more formidable machinery in motion than that which cast a cloud over the state of Utah.' Lever, however, was happy to walk into that shadow with an open mind and have a good peer around before deciding he disapproved. After an earlier visit to Egypt he had pronounced himself 'much impressed with many of the ethical values of Mohammedanism', a view that was fairly unusual in the 1890s.

The Mormons were not the most misunderstood minority in Utah. The original inhabitants of these lands still remained, reduced to a rump and stranded out in the desert, a mildly embarrassing thorn in the side of the young country. 'The US government is trying to train them to some useful purpose, but I understand with very poor success,' Lever reported back to the readers of the *Birkenhead News*. 'The government is continually taking away his "reservation" hunting grounds, and therefore must keep him in idleness or let him starve.' He took Hulme and Elizabeth to visit the latest scheme, which was attempting to train Indians up to serve in the US Cavalry that had so recently crushed them. It was obviously not working. 'The "noble red man" will not work, and is too lazy to become a soldier,' he wrote.

Laziness. Of all the vices, the one Lever most despised. But it was also one of the most powerful tools in the colonial armoury. Just as industry was the summit of the Victorian achievement, so indolence was its dark, destructive, alien opposite. Lever was a man of his time. He proclaimed the virtues of Empire as strongly as any of his countrymen. 'We should take the sensible view that this land was theirs for development and the advancement of civilisation. I can never understand why a black man should be allowed to assume a different attitude, and neither develop his land nor allow other people to do so,' he wrote when his own activities took him to Africa in later years. Fortunately for the people who came under his rule, unlike many of his contemporaries he proved to be fonder of the carrot than the stick. 'If we really wish to give to native races the blessings of our civilisation and religion, so that they may become a happy and prosperous people, let us first teach them to make for themselves and their families the best use of their lands; let us make them into planters, cultivators and manufacturers of such articles as can be made out of the raw materials their lands produce; let us in short act as would wise guardians and trustees during the infancy and development of a ward,' he wrote in his diary during the 1892 trip. Sadly, the more he saw of his fellow Christians' efforts, the less he believed this was the case.

Their final American stop was on the west coast, in the youthful city of San Francisco, established only fifty years earlier. Here was an opportunity for pure relaxation, and the Levers took to the city's huge Chinatown with as much enthusiasm as any present-day holidaymaker. 'We visited the various opium dens and numerous other sights, finishing by taking a cup of tea at a Chinese restaurant,' William wrote in his diary, though he did not record whether he and Elizabeth inhaled. If they did, it is not so surprising as it might seem: opium was such a common substance that it was popular as a painkiller, used in gripe water for babies or even as a 'top' for pints of beer. Mrs Beeton recommended it as a household essential, and it was so widely available from pharmacists and street carts that the few opium dens which existed, complete with drapes, divans, pigtailed Chinamen and the other clichés fostered by the more excitable newspapers, were there more for tourists than anyone else. Lever was more bothered by the dishes of the day in their restaurant – 'we did not feel equal to making an attempt on the "bird's nest soup", "shark fins", "roast puppy" and other delicacies that can be found there,' he reported.

On they went. Another long sea journey brought them to Hawaii, then still called by the name Captain Cook had dreamed up a century previously, the Sandwich Islands. He was killed by the islanders in 1779, but the new germs and diseases his crew brought with them ensured a long, slow revenge: as Lever noted, 'in spite of the blessings of civilisation, it happens that while in Captain Cook's day the population of the island was 400,000, now it barely reaches 90,000, of whom only 35,000 are natives'. The state of the islands rather depressed him, especially the capital, Honolulu – 'we found there every sign of modern civilisation, even that latest product of the culture of the age, "ta-ra-ra-boom-de-ay"'. Hearing this music-hall hit was roughly the equivalent of spotting a local wearing a Manchester United strip today, and it filled Lever with a deep pessimism. 'After we had heard it yelled by a South Sea Islander's child, we were prepared for anything and surprised at nothing.'

All the tribal customs he had assiduously read up on before embarking on the journey seemed to have fallen by the wayside. 'If Captain Cook returned he certainly would not know the place, nor the habits and customs of the natives, for now-a-days instead of settling the question of the government by a "Battle Royal" followed by a banquet for the victors, cannibal-style, the islanders adopt the comparatively peaceful and unpicturesque ballot box.' Here, as everywhere else, he saw the last traces of ancient cultures being stamped out by over-zealous Christian brothers. 'The money spent on missionary efforts is worse than wasted,' he thundered in his diary. 'The same money spent in taking the little children out of the gutters in England, feeding, clothing and educating them decently until they are fifteen, then putting them in respectable service of the colonies, would do ten thousand times more good ... or had the same amount of money, time and labour been devoted to teaching such of the arts and sciences of civilization as would enable the natives to make the most of their country, and to raise themselves in the social scale.' Instead, he sadly concluded, 'missionary effort becomes merely a prayer for the souls of the dying, a sending of the chaplain previous to the execution'.

Part of the gloom that descended upon Lever in the tropical sunshine was down to simple homesickness. Much as he and Elizabeth were enjoying their trip, the starchy unsuitability of their English clothes in the constant heat made them think fondly back to the shady countryside around Thornton Hough. 'When once the novelty of these pretty scenes has passed away, we reflect that the majesty of the oak or the elm far and away surpasses that of the palm tree, that a field of wheat is more beautiful in its waving grace than a field of sugar cane, that a field of turnips, although it may not appeal so strongly to the imagination and fancy, is brighter and fresher to look at than a field of pineapples, and, not least of all, that our English meadows and hedges have a charm that the bare looking, yellow, dried-up lands of the tropics can in no way approach.' You can't help wondering how convinced his readers back in rainy Birkenhead were by this theory.

Hawaiian beachlife, however, pleased Lever enormously. 'The natives are passionately fond of sea bathing, and are great adepts at the sport known as "surf-riding",' he reported from Waikiki. 'To enjoy this they provide themselves with flat boards of a length and width varying according to taste. To onlookers the sport appears very simple and easy, but in reality it is not so.' There is a distinct tone of hurt pride and a bruised bottom in that final sentence.

The Levers lingered in Hawaii, embarking on several expeditions around the islands. They were taken out to Wai Momi, a bay on Oahu which the Americans were rumoured to be developing as a naval station, but found nothing there but high reeds and marshland. Lever scoffed at 'pretentious' predictions that the site would soon be home to a great city. 'It seems not unlikely that the whole thing will fall flat,' he wrote, displaying a rare failure in foresight, for the bay would soon be better known by its translated name, Pearl Harbor.

More successful was their excursion to the live volcano of Kilauea, though it involved a difficult journey past the leper colony on Molokai island and an uncomfortable seven hours in a carriage on an appalling road. 'We never got such a bumping in our lives. The road is so bad that in many places the driver preferred to leave it and take his chance across the country, rocks two feet high and hollows two feet deep occurring in the middle of the track. I thought if ever I met the man who made such a road, it would be some consolation to give him, in plain Lancashire, a bit of my mind.'

The hellish journey was worth it, however. William grasped Hulme closely as the family walked across a parched and steaming lava plain to the very edge of the volcano's mouth – 'the red molten lava was dashing like angry surf on a rock-bound coast, sending showers of molten spray some twenty to thirty feet high. Whilst the centre of the lake was alive with moving jets and fountains of molten lava, between these and the sides a thin crust kept forming as the surface of the lake cooled, to be broken up and cast into the air by fresh jets and fountains upheaving from below. This crust was seamed with glowing zigzag cracks, ever changing, giving in the darkness the appearance of forked lightning. It was a scene never to be forgotten. It was a veritable "lake that burneth and fire that is not quenched".'

Further adventures awaited in Samoa, where they interrupted their southbound journey in late November. They docked for only a few hours and did not even go ashore, but that did not stop the locals from trying to do business with them. 'The natives swam in the water, holding bunches of fruit over their heads with one hand, whilst with the other they kept themselves afloat, undeterred by the fact that sharks abounded in the bay. It is said that sharks will not touch a native, but whether the native is short of flavour or has too much flavour I cannot say. It is a fact that sharks were there, because three were seen close to the ship. Neither natives nor sharks took the slightest notice of each other.' Lever was pleased to gather more evidence of the pigheaded uselessness of missionaries here – a party of Jesuits had failed to realize they had crossed the international dateline, and spent years encouraging the locals to observe Saturday as a holy day. Their mistake uncovered, 'the missionaries offered the strongest resistance to any change being made, on account of the necessity they would be placed under of having to explain their mistake to the natives'. Lever's smugness was dented a few days later when he faced the same task as their own ship crossed the 180th meridian, and he had to explain to his four-year-old son why they had skipped straight from 1 to 3 December with nothing in between.

The biggest relief when they docked in Auckland was finding a pile of letters and telegrams waiting for them. Cut off from his correspondence, Lever became twitchy: he needed to know exactly what was going on at the office in his absence. Records of a later business trip show that in five months he sent 878 letters packed with instructions and inquiries to Lever Brothers' staff back at home; that was in addition to the 600 he wrote to relatives and friends in the same period. That year many of them received Christmas greetings on the notepaper of the Star Hotel, Wairakei, along with glowing reports of the country, which in Lever's opinion combined the best of Britain with the finest possibilities of the new world. 'It was hard to believe that we were not in Devonshire or the Isle Of Wight, but in the New Zealand mountains, so far removed from civilisation that even the hotel horses had to be sent over 50 miles to be shod, and that, as a matter of fact, we were nearer to the Maoris than to the white men. Everything has had to be brought here, roads made and trees planted, cottages built, and what was then a desert turned into a perfect garden. We all agreed that it was the most comfortable place we could possibly desire ... The more we see of New Zealand, its climate and its people, the more we feel constrained to say that if our home was not in England, we should wish it to be in New Zealand.'

Here at last he found locals and conquerors getting along

together to his satisfaction: 'I may remark that the Maoris are treated exceptionally well by the New Zealand government in all matters relating to their land, far better than any previous governments in any other quarter of the globe have dealt with the native races. Every acre of land that does not belong to the white man by purchase or treaty is viewed as belonging by right to the natives. You find the native races occupying the superior position of landlords towards the white man, granting leases and drawing rents. Surely this is "unearned increment" with a vengeance, for the land had practically no value till the white man came.'

He also approved of their taxation system, which penalized the rich more than the poor. 'This must appeal to all of us as merely just and right, and not an abuse of power such as we at home have suffered under, when, the power being in the hands of the wealthy landowners, the incidence of taxation was so arranged that the greater burdens should fall on the backs of the people, while the wealthy landlords should escape almost entirely free.' That's a fairly unusual view for a wealthy landlord to hold, but Lever's enthusiasm for the 'working man's government' in Wellington was unbridled. He devoted page after page of his diary to praising their efforts to set up labour bureaux, nature reserves and measures to regulate the hours of shop-workers. As for the threats by rich landowners to abandon the country, Lloyd-Webber style, in protest at fair taxation, Lever was scornful: 'The idea is too absurd . . . The fears of those who are alarmed for the future of the English race because of the probability that there will be in the future a greater share of political power in the hands of the Labour party than has been wielded by them in the past, are utterly without foundation. If these nervous people would only carefully study history, they would come to the conclusion that just as all the revolutions the world has ever seen have been brought about by the accumulation of wealth in the hands of the few, accompanied by the political serfdom of the people, so the best guarantee for the progress, development and prosperity of a nation is only to be found in the granting of full political power and liberty to the people.' They are words that could have come from the mouth of Keir Hardie, elected to Parliament for the Independent Labour Party that very year, rather than one of the richest businessmen in Britain.

Lever and Elizabeth chatted easily with the Maoris they met, including one man who claimed to be a reformed cannibal: 'If his tale be believed, the flavour was like pig, "only nicer". He seems to have been a bit of an epicure in his way, because he complained that "white man tastes salt", but he added "Maori never".' They admired the outdoor kitchens where the locals cooked by hanging bags of food in the mouths of the hot springs which sprang from the earth. 'How housewives at home must envy the sweet simplicity of this domestic arrangement! No smell of cooking in the house, no getting up at 5 o'clock to light the fires, the water always on the boil day and night . . . There is, of course, the trifling disadvantage that sometimes the children tumble into these holes, even whilst playing in their own little garden, and are seen no more. But this is only a detail which may or may not be a disadvantage.' Nevertheless, he kept a tight hold of Hulme's hand at all times.

Along with a party of other guests from the hotel, the Levers conquered their second volcano in as many months: Mount Tarawera. The journey here was even more hazardous than their first; they went by horseback, but 'none of the party could lay the slightest claim to being able to ride a horse. Some had never ridden in their lives. Others remembered having ridden ponies in their youth, and having still a lively recollection of the tricks the ponies resorted to in order to get rid of them, hardly felt equal to renewing their part in the performance.' Once successfully mounted, the group picked their way across a valley floor pitted with chasms forty feet deep, through the remains of the village of Wairoa, destroyed in an earthquake several years earlier. 'We saw just the top of the village mill and the water wheel, but the stream that drove it has disappeared, and only the top rail of the little bridge that spanned the running waters can be seen . . . the hotel is buried almost to the bedroom windows. At a point some eight miles nearer to the volcano, and on the shores of Lake Tarawera, two entire native villages with all their inhabitants are buried some eighty to a hundred feet beneath volcano sand and ashes, perhaps to be dug out some hundreds and thousands of years hence, like a second Pompeii.' Such an extra-ordinary landscape made the journey worthwhile, though Lever complained that 'to our town and city muscles it was a hard day's work of twenty two miles in saddle, sixteen miles in open boat, and six or seven miles of walking and climbing'. At least here Elizabeth was able to ride side-saddle in a ladylike fashion. Lever had been shocked in Honolulu to witness 'ladies of all ranks riding cross-stride like the men . . . it strikes one as very indelicate'.

Their one disappointment in New Zealand was Christmas: lavish as the celebrations were, and delighted as Hulme was with his presents, William and Elizabeth could not shake off the feeling that something wasn't right. 'Although we knew before leaving home that we should have Christmas day at midsummer, still we felt something like a shock,' he reported back to Birkenhead. 'The shops were decorated with evergreens in true Christmas fashion, the streets were crowded with eager purchasers of Christmas cards, and of toys to be given in the name of Santa Claus, but to view all this with the sun shining bright, the people in print dresses, muslins and summer suits, with nothing to suggest Father Christmas, covered with frost and snow, made it all look like a hollow sham, a mere masquerade of Christmas and a very poor one at that. We felt inclined to take some of the rising generation aside and ask them if they knew what Christmas really ought to be like.'

By the new year they were back on the ocean, joining hands with the crew and their fellow passengers in the ship's saloon to toast in 1893 with a rousing chorus of 'Auld Lang Syne'. 'It is wonderful how such an occasion will draw all the passengers together, cementing old friendships and making new ones. We thought of all our friends at home and tried to imagine exactly what they would be doing. Altogether, New Year's Day at sea has a solemnity and impressiveness which one never realises on land.'

They had one last stop on their journey: Australia, the fledgling set of states still a decade away from federation. The Levers visited only two of them, Victoria and New South Wales, but the wilful disparity between them was shocking. At the border between the two states the family was obliged to climb down from their train carriage and board another, because the railways in New South Wales ran on a different gauge to those of their neighbours. Neither could agree to adopt the other's system, so they just ran a transport system that was twice as complicated, twice as expensive, and half as useful. The cost of transferring freight between railways must have been crippling. 'The fact is that no one can realise the jealousy between the Australian colonies who has not visited them,' Lever observed. 'However, this jealousy is not so great today as it used to be, and there are signs that it will soon be a thing of the past.' Once again, he was being over-optimistic. While the Australian Commonwealth bound the states together in 1901 (except for the Northern Territory, which sulked on its own for almost another eighty years), the Australian railways were not regularized until 1970.

Little about Australia pleased Lever. He loved Sydney Harbour, and was much impressed by the efficiency of a butter factory he visited in Victoria, jotting down observations on their fat-refining process to be considered back in Port Sunlight. But on the whole he felt the country, which had only stopped being a dumping ground for British convicts twenty-five years previously, had retained much of the worst of England without embracing the new possibilities that its neighbour New Zealand had so enthusiastically taken on. 'I was not long enough in Australia to arrive at such an advanced state of knowledge, and therefore can indulge to the full in that greatest of all pleasures to the globe trotter, which, as all the world knows, is to point out some of the shortcomings of the country and the way to put everything to rights,' claimed Lever with appealing self-deprecation, and, boy, did he make good on that promise. Page after page of polemic was published in the *Birkenhead News*, covering targets as diverse as Australia's immigration policy, land management, taxation system, and, above all, keenness on taxing imports. 'America, Canada, Australia, and the continent of Europe have all got the protectionist drag and clog on their wheels of progress,' he stormed in a lengthy rant that perhaps went over the head of the average workman in Wallasey or Rock Ferry. The 'one man one vote' legislation that was going through parliament in Canberra during his visit came in for scrutiny, Lever recalling his hero Gladstone's travails in getting his own Reform Act through in Britain a decade before. 'Upper Houses of Parliament the world over . . . all appear to be impressed with one idea – that they exist solely to maintain the power and influence of property on a basis altogether out of proportion to what property is fairly entitled to, that they must stand through all eternity, a faithful band, pledged to keep back the rising tide of democracy, or perish like heroes in the attempt,' he sneered.

Lever was able to exercise his political muscles further on the long cruise home, when he discovered that one of his fellow travellers was George Curzon, the Conservative politician who had just completed a tour of the Far East after leaving the government at the previous year's election. The long arguments the two men engaged in on the decks and in the saloons of the P & O liner *Australia* must have been lively events – Curzon was a passionate protectionist, had served in the recently jettisoned government of the Marquess of Salisbury, the last British prime minister to serve from the House of Lords, and believed that 'all civilization was the work of aristocracies'. The journey lasted ten weeks, and the two men never ran out of topics to disagree on, though they disembarked with a profound respect for each other. 'He will undoubtedly become a bright and shining light in the Conservative party,' Lever wrote in his diary. He was also impressed by another travelling companion, John Cook, 'a particularly shrewd man, keen and strong', and predicted a bright future for the tourist agency he was running, Thomas Cook and Sons.

William, Elizabeth and Hulme arrived back in Liverpool on 9 March, tanned, relaxed and delighted to be back. Lever brought with him a head full of ideas which would resurface and be refined over the next two decades as his business and social schemes expanded around the world; his wife returned with a taste for travel that would eventually see her elected as a fellow of the Royal Geographical Society.

They also brought back another object, one that had caused Lever a great deal of worry ever since he had purchased it in Sydney. He had been told by a taxidermist that it was an example of a species that was plentiful in Australia, but the more he looked at the unlikely creature, the more he suspected he had been conned. 'Our friends at home would be quite justified in believing we had the specimen made to order, like Barnum's mermaid, and as we have never seen the animal in its native lair, why of course we can only refer to the shopman. It is a very weak and ridiculous position for travellers to have to take up.' Even the name, the more he repeated it, sounded unlikely, and after displaying his acquisition to just a handful of people he quietly stashed the duck-billed platypus away in one of the lesser-used rooms at Thornton Manor.

9

OFFICE POLITICS

THE CURTAIN RISES. A PICTURESQUE SCENE IS REVEALED OF
an English village, its houses half-timbered, the streets
lined with leafy trees. A large sign reads 'PORT
SUNSHINE'.

Enter a chorus of maidens in bright white aprons and
bonnets, skipping across the stage.

> When you want a cake of soap, to finish off your toilet,
> We're the folks who boil it, with your needs to cope.
> Ev'rywhere we take the cake, we always take the prizes
> Hence the term arises, 'Where there's life, there's soap!'

They are joined by a troop of cloth-capped workmen, their
thumbs hooked into their waistcoats in the traditional
manner as they gambol from the wings.

> We do the toilin' work!
> Boilin' work!
> Oilin' work!

> We do the soilin' work,
> All the 'ole day through!

Back come the lovely ladies:

> Soap for pauper, peer or Pope!
> Honey Soap and Sunny Soap and Simply Soap!

And the audience chuckle, settling in their seats, sure that they're going to get their money's worth.

The Sunshine Girl opened at the Gaiety theatre in London's West End in February 1912. It was the work of Paul Rubens, whose speciality was sub-G & S romps about princesses, Persians and perilous predicaments, but who had decided to turn his hand to satire for a change. So the audience were treated to jokes about the suffragette movement:

> In the future man as man is absolutely dead and gone,
> Woman's going to wear the breeks when man has sewn the
>   buttons on!

and the peoples of the Empire:

> When I got there
> It gave me a scare
> Half of the folks were black!
> Just like the sort
> You see at Earl's Court
> Low neck'd all round the back
> One often sees
> A lack of rupees
> But it's clothes they seem to lack!

It was met with a rapturous reception. 'The great merit of *The Sunshine Girl* is that it sends us away feeling we should like to see more,' raved the *Times* critic. 'We have never known a gayer evening in the gay and absurd world behind the footlights of the Gaiety.' The general assumption was that Lever had arranged the whole thing to get his soaps a bit more publicity, but the papers were wrong (he would have made sure the composer got the name right, for one thing). In fact the first anyone at Lever Brothers knew of *The Sunshine Girl* was when it was advertised in the press, though they were quick to offer assistance to the producers, including some props from the real Port Sunlight. The villagers themselves got the chance to see their fictional counterparts the following year when canny producers transferred *The Sunshine Girl* for a run at the Royal Court Theatre in Liverpool, and bookings poured in from across the Mersey.

In fact the show borrowed little from the real village. Port Sunshine is in the suburbs of London – allowing the in-clusion of a song spoofing the current trend for rail trips to Brighton, 'London-by-the-sea' – and its boss is a handsome young stockbroker and aristocrat, Lord Bicester, referred to by his employees by the unlikely name of 'Bingo', who disguises himself as a workman in order to woo the 'pretty fairy' Delia, the Sunshine Girl of the title. And while the Sunshiners spend most of their time skipping about requesting kisses from one another, the factory on Port Sunlight was run in a rather more orderly fashion.

The working day started at eight thirty – not a minute later. Lever himself was woken at half-past six, and had generally already worked his way through a pile of reports on the company's activities, annotating them in red pencil, by the time he sat down for breakfast with his wife an hour later. 'During the whole of our married life of forty years, however early business called me, I never breakfasted alone,' he recalled after her death. 'She was always up and saw that the breakfast was properly prepared.' This was certainly more out of love than necessity – the Levers had their own cook, and at least three other servants who were probably rather better at making breakfast than Elizabeth was, and anyway Lever hardly ate anything in the morning (though he was careful that every morsel that did pass his lips was chewed the requisite thirty-two times). He allowed himself ten minutes with the newspapers (largely to ensure that the advertising that appeared tallied with the measurements he had paid for), before making his way to his office in the extraordinary headquarters that were built for Lever Brothers in 1896. The General Offices still stand in Port Sunlight, where they sit incongruously in the sylvan domesticity of Wood Street. Stuccoed, balustraded and topped with an enormous clock bearing the royal warrant in stone, they look like a mini-Versailles or Winter Palace that has somehow got lost in an English suburb. The fact that the building is only one storey high does not prevent it from utterly dominating the landscape.

Lever's office was slap-bang in the middle of this building, behind the clock and beneath the lion and the unicorn. It was walled with glass, and gave him a view over both the east and west wings, where hundreds of clerks toiled away at row after row of identical desks. He could see all of them, and they could all see him. And that was exactly how he wanted it. An internal telephone system allowed him to buzz straight through to the manager of any man he suspected of wrong-doing or laziness. Latecomers made the long walk to their desks to find the phone tinkling away, and the slightest yawn between 8.30 and 5.30 would be rewarded by a receiver pealing out like an alarm-clock. Imagine the opening scenes of the movies *Brazil* and *Clockwise* mixed together, and you have an idea of the atmosphere that reigned there.

When it came to finding the ideal employee, Lever believed that body language said it all. 'My first attention is given to the applicant's eye and expression of face. If his eye meets mine with clearness, candour and frankness; if his features indicate activity without excitement, and self-control coupled with ambition; if in walking he does not shuffle his feet; if he is perfectly natural and free from nervousness in the placing of his hands during the conversation, I am so far favourably impressed with him.' He infinitely preferred promoting long-serving staff within the company, rather than bringing in applicants from outside, and, though he later sent his own son to Cambridge, he scorned the idea of university education. Publicly he declared that 'Oxford and Cambridge dull the edge of a man for business', but his son knew the real reason for his prejudice: 'he firmly cherished the belief, in which no argument could shake him, that the University Professor does all his work in the small hours and arises at an atrociously late hour in the morning'.

In the works behind the Offices, starting time was staggered. The girls arrived ten minutes before the male workers, and left a full half-hour before them, lest they should be tempted into indecency while clocking on and off. As one observer approvingly put it in 1909, 'it would not be conducive to discipline for the men and girls to leave the works in a confused stream, particularly during the reaction following upon the release from work'. The distaff side were permitted entry to the Office, however, in the form of Lever's team of lady stenographers. This capable bunch, led by the redoubtable spinster Miss Alice Harding, were the first visitors to his eyrie each morning, where they spent an hour or so taking dictation. Lever insisted on at least two, and if possible three, stenographers being present, so that none of his precious words would be lost and he wouldn't have to waste any vital time repeating himself. He would work his way through the comments he had scribbled on his papers that morning, refining them into letters that 'gave the fullest vent to his feelings and conveyed his censure in unmistakable terms' to underlings who had failed to do things as well as he would have done. More often than not, however, he read such blasts over and tore them up, replacing them with a milder version. 'The man who makes no mistakes does not usually make anything,' he was fond of saying, but staff who had been on the receiving end of his wrath were generally extremely careful to avoid a repeat performance.

In later years the sheer volume of Lever's daily corres-pondence led to the introduction of two innovations: all internal memos were to be presented on special paper divided down the centre, with the report on one side and an area the same size left blank ready for the Chairman's re-action, corrections, thoughts and general observations. Even then his red pencil often ran over the dividing line. For external mail, things were done differently. Andrew Knox, who spent his career with Lever Brothers, describes the system in his memoirs: 'He had a number of small stick-on labels in different colours and carrying various instructions – each member of his staff having a different colour label. Altogether there were twenty-seven different instructions on the full set of labels, but many appeared on more than one label. As he went through his corres-pondence he set aside those to which he wished to dictate a reply and on the others he licked and stuck on the appro-priate label, ticking the instructions he wished carried out.'

From ten o'clock onwards, Lever met with his senior

managers and directors in person. Although many of them had been with the company for almost as long as he had, and given sterling service, that didn't mean they were any less terrified of the boss than the clerks were. Knox recalls that one board member fixed up a mirror outside the door of his own office so that he could spot Lever striding down the corridor and arrange himself into a suitably dutiful stance before he arrived. A rumour persisted for years that the Chairman held signed, but undated, resignation letters from all his directors in the safe in his office. It probably wasn't true, but no one was in any doubt that they held their appointments at Mr Lever's pleasure.

The morning appointments ran to a strict timetable. No one was allowed more than a few minutes, and many staff found themselves only half-way through the presentations they had carefully prepared before Lever scribbled a *WHL* against their name on his agenda and gestured towards the door. 'What's the next?' he would bark at Miss Harding, and she always knew. Managers soon learned to be ready as the door swung to behind their predecessor – the Chairman rang a bell on his desk to summon the next supplicant, and anyone who left him waiting for more than a few seconds received a gruff lecture on just how much of his time they had wasted, and exactly how much their tardiness had cost the company (no one was ever brave enough to point out that the time spent telling them off wasted even more). Few had the chance to take in their surroundings, admire the large mahogany desk behind which Lever sat, the high sloping worktop at which he stood to work, the vast map of Great Britain with its different coloured sales divisions, or the large portraits of his wife and parents that hung on the wall in front of him as inspiration in all that he did. Some never even got to sit down before they were dismissed. The man who eventually succeeded Lever as Chairman was fond of recalling his own first encounter with the boss. 'I was told to take my report round myself in case he wanted to ask any questions. I thought that here was a chance of telling the great man not only of the financial position but also what I thought of the personnel and of the future of the business. I was shown into his room . . . I said "I have brought the report on the so-and-so business." The only reply was, "Thank you, put it down there, good morning." I was in and out in fifteen seconds.'

Lever was not a man for discussion – 'Aye, nay, we won't argue: you're wrong' was a phrase he often used with employees – and he never changed his mind. He gave short shrift to anyone who questioned his judgement, or asked him to sleep on a decision before making his mind up. 'If I decided everything twice I would double my work. Take it away.' Even senior figures within Lever Brothers were regularly put in their place. When the company secretary dared to suggest some tactics for fielding difficult questions at the firm's AGM, he received a scathing dressing-down from Lever. 'I have always viewed you as thoroughly alive as to what is correct and proper for a secretary to take upon himself,' wrote the Chairman. 'I am always glad to have your free expression of opinion on all matters that I may discuss with you. But until I do discuss a matter with you, I think you will agree with me that it is not within your province to lay your views before me. I hope that this will be the last time on which you will venture an expression of opinion as to what course I should take at a Meeting unless in response to a request from myself that you should do so.'

How did he get away with it? Why did his board, and his shareholders, allow him to run Lever Brothers as an absolute kingdom? Part of the answer lies in the way that he prepared the company for flotation. The private company that William and James registered in 1890 went public four years later, its capital swollen from £300,000 to £1½ million. While demand for preference shares (which guaranteed a dividend from the company's profit) was more than four times their availability, Lever retained every one of the ordinary shares (which carried 'such dividend as the directors may decide to distribute') for himself. That meant that he retained sole control of the company, and when doubts were raised about any major expenditure he proposed, he was fond of responding: 'Well, gentlemen, I don't think the ordinary shareholders will raise any objection.' And indeed, he never did.

The board, meanwhile, was comfortably on side. Lever's first fellow directors were his brother, his father and Percy Winser, the soap-boiler whose job he had rescued in Warrington. Later the board had to grow to take in the representatives of other companies that had been absorbed into the Lever empire, but a strong family presence was maintained – two of Lever's nephews, and later his own son, were made directors, though not without a lengthy apprenticeship. He was proud of boasting that every single one of his directors had worked his way up from the works, the office, or the sales department of the company. It meant they were loyal, and, more to the point, it meant they had got used to doing what they were told.

Board meetings were few, and, as the company's official historian puts it, 'such consultation as he found necessary took place at informal dinner parties held at Thornton Manor, where wives accompanied their husbands, and Mrs Lever would entertain her lady guests in the drawing room, generally far beyond the conventional limit of time, while the men sat talking over their cigars'. It was another example of the blending of domestic and business life that came naturally to Lever – when asked to grade his priorities in life, he placed 'home first, and business second first' – but which must have sat less easily with his less workaholic colleagues. Nevertheless, they quickly got used to the idea that their mornings, afternoons and evenings belonged to Lever, and that their affairs could be organized in any way that saved his own precious time.

Whereas now a company director might 'call in' on his mobile from a business trip, and have any necessary documentation faxed over to him, Lever simply took the office with him. Literally. He travelled like Elizabeth I, dragging a peripatetic court around the country. Miss Harding and her team of stenographers got used to hauling their typewriters on to first-class train carriages and bashing out Lever's letters as he trundled from city to city, dictating as he went. As cars replaced trains as his favoured mode of transport, arrangements became even more elaborate. 'I have known him to transact a morning's business during the course of a motor run,' recalled Hulme of his father. 'Two cars would be engaged, and he and his colleagues would ride in one while those he wished to interview would follow in the other; from time to time a halt would be made, the person with whom he had been talking would leave the car and another would take his place, and this would be repeated every few miles until all the matters under consideration had been dealt with.' It was an ideal system for Lever, though less convenient for the managers who got left by the roadside, hundreds of miles from their desks, as their boss sped off in a cloud of dust to his next appointment. Woe betide the man who tried to claim a solo taxi ride back to the office on his expenses – Lever insisted on cramming as many of his directors as possible into cabs, even if they had to sit practically on each other's laps. 'Do you think you are all millionaires?' he would roar.

His own habits, when not related directly to the efficiency of the business, were exemplarily frugal. His interviews done, he usually lunched at his desk – poached eggs, cold meat or tomato soup, followed by biscuits and cheese (his favourite was Cheshire) and an apple. An underling recalled him ordering his usual meal in a hotel during a trip overseas, and being presented with an entire basket of fruit.

'How much is it for an apple, Knox?'

'Five shillings, sir.'

'What will it be if I take more than one?'

'Still five shillings, sir.'

'Right, then I'll eat one now and put two in my pocket, and you can put two in your pocket, and we'll be all right.'

He also preferred to use the normal staff toilets to the executive washroom attached to his office, largely because he suspected they might not be cleaned properly. The story of Lever's visit to the company's branch in Norway became legendary – the beaming manager had met him and proffered a sales sheet and the exciting news that the last month's sales were an all-time record, only to receive the blunt reply, 'I've no doubt about that, but what about the staff lavatories I complained about when I was here a year ago?'

The afternoons brought more paperwork for Lever, but not before he had practised another of his daily routines – a forty-minute sleep, which he took in a chair in his office. He had the ability to sleep on command, wherever he was, whatever his surroundings. Trained to sleep through rain, wind and cold in his open-air bedroom, it was no problem for him to attain unconsciousness in the noisiest of surroundings. After exactly forty minutes his eyes clicked open and the slightly maniacal gleam returned to them as, entirely refreshed, he threw himself into three hours of forward planning, much of which was spent drawing up a 'datum' – a detailed projection of profits – for every branch of his businesses in the UK and overseas. These were distributed on a monthly and quarterly basis to his managers across the globe, where they were treated in much the same way as the tribes of Israel treated the Ten Commandments – failure to match the datum was too terrifying a prospect even to be considered. Lever was the ultimate remote controller, each stroke of the pen in his glass-walled office on the Wirral setting off action and reaction far across the globe. As one flowery contemporary profile put it, 'he is a mighty autocrat in his own world, and it must require a strong character not to become arrogant and possibly aggressive when all around bend their knees, and thousands of puppets dance all over the world as he pulls the string'.

Fortunately for the thousands of workers whose livings depended upon him, he was a benign puppet-master. He remembered all too well the effects of bad labour practice he had seen around him in his own childhood. 'In the late '50s, amongst male operatives, you could only see two patterns of legs – the knock-kneed and the bow-legged. That was the result of immature youths being forced to work long and laborious hours in the vitiated atmosphere of mills and foundries.' He was determined that his own operatives would never suffer in the same way. The works at Port Sunlight were exemplary, a world away from the cramped and toxic conditions of the Bradford that Salt had abandoned, or the lethal match factories of London's East End. The works were designed to be as unlike the dark warren in Warrington as possible – the buildings were single-storey, sprawling over a massive twenty-four acres, and huge windows allowed daylight to penetrate right into the hearts of their vast interiors. Men who worked on abrasive scourers like Vim were issued with respirators at the company's expense and a strict rota system ensured that no one worked in dusty conditions for more than a week at a time. Lever Brothers was one of the first companies in Britain to employ a full-time safety inspector, as well as a company doctor who gave medical examinations to all new recruits and was on call at all times. Later a voluntary ambulance corps and fire brigade were set up on site, its members receiving an extra shilling a week in their pay packets for their troubles. The fire brigade was aided by the provision of alarms and sprinklers in every department, decades before such measures were made a legal requirement. When the Factory Acts were introduced in 1901, Lever Brothers' works exceeded the clean-air target by fifteen times.

Children worked at Port Sunlight from the age of thirteen upwards. That might seem shocking now, but in the late nineteenth century it was practically middle-aged. The under-nines had been banned from employment only in 1874; school was compulsory only up to the age of ten, and in much of the English countryside, where the law was less firmly enforced, children barely old enough to walk took turns in the fields scaring birds or caring for livestock. From the moment he set up his business, Lever insisted that all his junior staff devoted a portion of their time to education: they were given evening classes in languages, English literature, accountancy, basic science and engineering, all paid for by the company. At the same time that Thomas Hardy had Jude being turned away by the intellectual snobs from Christchurch, a generation of teenagers were emerging from the Port Sunlight Technical Institute able to speak French and quote Shakespeare to their hearts' content as they packed box after box of soap on the production lines.

Lever wanted to extend his educational experiment to adult employees too: he persistently tried to rearrange the shift system in his factories, shortening the working day from eight hours to just six. Naturally there was a catch: the two 'spare' hours were to be spent in 'absolutely compulsory' education in academic and technical subjects, as well as the slightly sinister-sounding 'training for citizenship'. His staff objected. The women in particular were concerned on two fronts: those who commuted to the village from Liverpool would have to make their way to the morning shift (6 a.m. to 1 p.m.) during the hours of darkness 'with all the great danger of molestation in a cosmopolitan seaport town', while working the evening shift (1 p.m. to 8 p.m.) would leave their gentleman friends home alone and open to temptation. Opposition from the trade unions scuppered the double-shift idea, though Lever never stopped being convinced he was right. 'The time is coming when it will be the rule and not the exception,' he warned an Australian audience in 1913. 'In the reduction of hours of labour you have one of the secrets of the well-being of a country. If you have a country devoting the whole of her time to work, so that her people go to bed weary, and rise with still weary bones to attack the next day's duties, you will never produce a physically desirable class of men and women.'

Lever's relationship with the trade union movement was good. Their aims were not dissimilar. 'You can overwork and kill any machine and that is sound policy,' he believed, 'but to be lacking in consideration in any way for the life, health and happiness of the employee is the most short-sighted policy a firm can adopt.' It was often the case that Lever was already offering his employees more than their own representatives dared demand. The country's first major strike in 1889, by the National Union of Gasworkers and General Labourers, was for a reduction in the working day from twelve to eight hours, a luxury the Sunlighters already enjoyed. The same year 10,000 dockers walked out demanding sixpence a day, while men at Lever Brothers took home more than two shillings. Lever's pay policy was generous: 'A salary should be as large as, or more than, the man could get under any other circumstances that I could possibly imagine.' Not only that, but pensions were introduced for both male and female employees in 1905, years before the government was persuaded of the need to make national provision for the elderly. While many of his fellow businessmen – those who believed rather that salaries should be as small as they could get away with – were thrown into outraged panic by the increasingly militant demands of their employees, Lever could not have been happier. 'Many people have expressed alarm at what they call Labour unrest,' he told pupils at his old school in 1915. 'In my opinion, there is no healthier sign than that, as, after all, discontent is infinitely better than self-satisfaction and complacency. There is an awakening amongst the people for what they know they ought to have, and a determination to have it. That means development.'

Lever often said he would have been a proud union member himself if he had found himself on the factory floor – indeed, he saw collective bargaining as a natural extension of the rules of trade, rather than some new-fangled bit of Bolshevism. 'I cannot see how we could with advantage attempt to deprive a body of men of the right to use this means, common to all of us, in connection with the only article that they have to sell, namely their labour,' he declared in 1919. He was happy to negotiate with union representatives, if he felt their demands were really in the best interests of their members, though he drew the line at allowing a man from the shop floor to sit on the board of directors, a gesture he dismissed as 'futile and sentimental'.

The only really significant strike that occurred at Lever Brothers in his lifetime centred on a dispute between two unions in 1920 over which should have the monopoly on membership in the works – an argument in which Lever refused to intervene. He was delighted to hear that Lever Brothers had been praised as 'ideal employers' at a meeting of Keir Hardie's Independent Labour Party in 1908, announcing the news with much fanfare in the company's in-house magazine.

Lever, however, could never have been called a socialist. He might have passionately approved of the 'awakening amongst the people', but he had no time for the ideological alarm clock that lay behind it. 'The Socialist claims equality with all above him, whilst denying equality to all beneath him,' he ranted on one occasion. 'Neither King, nor priest, nor politician, nor people, nor capitalist, nor employer, nor employee who has ceased to serve can survive, and no socialist "cure-all" can produce equality in value or fruits of service until our Creator sends us into this world all equal in health, strength, energy and ability.' As was often the case with Lever, however, he was cursing the theory with one hand whilst quietly putting it into practice with the other. For in 1909, when his business had spread far beyond the confines of his profit-sharing-by-property experiment at Port Sunlight, he launched a new, even more ambitious scheme: Co-Partnership. The scourge of socialism had decided to hand ownership of the company over to its workers.

The co-partnership scheme was meant as a practical lesson in economics for Lever's workers; a demonstration that industrial prosperity was in their interests as much as that of their bosses. Rather than relying on trickledown, Lever shoved in a pump and created a fountain. More than half of the profits that were due to him as the sole ordinary shareholder would be redistributed among the staff. Each and every co-partner would receive a dividend every year that the company showed a profit, and it would come, effectively, from his own pocket.

Naturally, there was small print. Co-partnership was not automatic. At the launch of the scheme in the Port Sunlight Auditorium in February 1909, certificates were issued to just over 1,000 of the longest-serving men and women on the staff ('I know it is a little outside the usual plan to take ladies into partnership, but when ladies do their work as faithfully as the Port Sunlight girls do, I don't see why they should be left out,' said Lever). Another 17,000 staff would be accepted on to the scheme during his lifetime. But not everyone was welcome.

Every co-partner had to promise not to 'waste time, labour, materials or money in the discharge of his duties, but loyally and faithfully further the interests of Lever Brothers, and its associated companies to the best of his skill and ability'. But they were also warned that their certificates could at any time be cancelled on the grounds of 'neglect of duty, dishonesty, intemperance, immorality, wilful misconduct, flagrant inefficiency, or disloyalty to employers'. Substitute 'Party' for 'employers' and it reads like a sentence from Mao's *Little Red Book*. Lever was determined to reward only those staff whose lifestyles he approved of – the self-deniers, the non-drinkers, those who never gambled, kept their gardens tidy and had their own well-worn pews in church. 'A man of high character should receive a more generous allotment than a man of equal ability, but not of the same high character,' declared Lever when he designed the scheme. He selected the sort of people who were already assured of their reward in heaven, and gave them a little down payment to spend on the way.

And little it often was. Charles Wilson, the company's official historian, describes the handouts as 'a drop in the bucket'. He cites the figures from 1912, when 2,000 co-partners had been created, their certificates bearing a nominal value of £350,000. The 10 per cent dividend that was paid out that year provided an average of £20 per head – but many lower-ranking members of staff had much fewer certificates, and therefore received much less. In less successful years, the company made no payment to co-partners at all – a good lesson in economics perhaps, but not one that was appreciated. The Lever Brothers staff quickly came to regard their annual payments as an automatic right rather than a privilege dictated by the state of the soap trade, and resented their bosses more, not less, when they were unable to pass any profits on. 'We have all of us felt disappointed that men and women could be Co-partners, and still be quite apathetic and uninterested in efficiency and output,' moaned Lever to a colleague after one particularly bad year.

But at least the intention was there. William Lever's staff knew just how well provided for they were compared to many of their contemporaries, and they showed their appreciation. Perhaps they weren't quite as enthusiastic as their fictional counterparts on stage at the Royal Court Theatre in 1913, but I suspect that more than one of them joined in with the triumphal chorus that closed act one of *The Sunshine Girl*:

> We shall all come in for a going concern
> We shall divide all the profits we earn!
> Oh we shall be able to play old Harry
> Monarchs of all we survey!

10

HATE MAIL

READ THE *DAILY MAIL* FOR MORE THAN A WEEK, AND YOU may conclude that it is very unwell indeed. The paper appears to be in the advanced stages of paranoia. Every headline, every news item, seems to drip with the poisonous conviction that someone, somewhere, is out to get you, diddle you of what should rightfully be yours, and probably give you cancer in the process. It seems to unerringly identify the basest prejudices of its readership, whip them up and serve them back to them with a side order of bile. But it's getting better. A hundred years ago its nickname on Fleet Street was the *Daily Liar*.

The *Mail* was launched in 1896 by Alfred Harmsworth – an Irish immigrant with a talent for self-promotion and a habit of impregnating people other than his wife – and his penny-pinching brother Harold. It was, like the eleven other national morning papers then available, a broadsheet, but its Old English masthead was almost identical to how it appears today. It cost a halfpenny, but it was very carefully designed to look more expensive – its readers wanted to look like the sort of people who could afford to read the *Daily Telegraph* at a penny, or *The Times* at thruppence. But they were cost-conscious enough to have a healthy fear of being diddled, and it was this fear that Alfred – raised to the peerage in 1905 as Lord Northcliffe – played on in a campaign that nearly destroyed everything that William Lever had achieved.

The price of Sunlight Soap had gone up only once in the first twenty years it was on the market, in 1898, when Lever signed up to an agreement with the Soapmakers' Association aimed at avoiding unfair competition by fixing prices between producers. He didn't need to. Sales of Sunlight were buoyant and the company was showing a healthy profit (this was partly the reason his competitors were so strapped for cash), but he was a member, and price-fixing was a long-standing tradition in the soap trade. He left the Association in 1905 'for no special reason at all, except that after long experience we have failed to find any benefit in continuing members', but the memory of the blip in his sales which the unnecessary price rise had caused was enough to make him think twice about a further jump when a hike in the price of raw materials hit the business in 1906. A one-pound tablet of Sunlight cost 3d; to go higher than that took it into the same price range as the luxury toilet soaps like Carnaval and Plantol which the Lever Brothers had recently launched. A price rise now would do the company a double disservice, making their luxury soaps look cheap, and their budget ones expensive. It was the last thing they needed.

Instead, the board decided on a different tactic: they would keep the price the same, but reduce the size of the tablets from 16 to 15oz. It is a tactic that has worked well for a number of retailers since, and Lever ensured that the change was well signposted on Sunlight's packaging, so that no one could feel too hard done by.

That took care of the immediate problem, but the raw material dilemma was not going to be as easy to solve. The increasing popularity of margarine, first produced in Britain in 1889, was likely to continue to push up the price of every kind of vegetable oil, and Lever had already decided he needed to get involved at the other end of the equation, buying up mills and plantations across the world in order to safeguard his own supply. But that took time. As his surveyors toured the globe in search of suitable palm trees, his mind turned back to the way the Association operated. When his company had first started shaking up the industry, he had objected to the idea of cartels, because the fledgling Lever Brothers had nothing to gain from them. Now, however, they were a major player in the industry, particularly since their purchase of the long-established firm of Hodgson & Simpson that summer. If they were in control of such an association, it could be the answer to all their financial difficulties. A working arrange-ment – call it a 'combine' – between soap companies would allow them to co-operate on the purchase of raw materials, thus keeping the cost down, as well as save money on adver-tising. They could even share research facilities and parts of the manufacturing process. Everyone would be a winner.

On 27 July Lever called a meeting with representatives of all the major soap firms in the north of England. They met in an anonymous hotel room in Liverpool – he wanted this business kept as secret as possible, though he did not for a second believe he was proposing anything to be ashamed of. 'I believe by amalgamating we shall be in a better position to serve the public well and give better value than ever, and also to better serve the interests of the distributors, both wholesale and retail,' he earnestly explained to the gathered chairmen. 'This will be the policy of the amalgamation, and it is on this policy that the business will be founded, rather than grasping for excessive profit, which might endure for a year or two but could not be permanent.'

An agreement was hammered out. Eleven companies, including Lever Brothers, exchanged a number of their shares. Complicated arrangements were negotiated for dealing in raw materials. It was agreed that the necessary dismissals – almost entirely among the travelling salesmen that each company employed – would be phased in gradually, to avoid 'large volumes of men parading the country giving out disgruntled talk'.

In the meantime, however, he set about making some of the other savings the combine allowed. He and Sydney Gross calculated that the non-competition pact they had made with their major competitors would save them some £200,000 on advertising. In September they decided to cancel several expensive contracts they had taken out over the summer – including one for £6,000 with the *Daily Mail*.

It took them a while to make the connection. The *Mail*'s first mention of the combine, the day after its existence was publicly announced, was brief and neutral. It had been created, the paper said, 'to lessen the costly competitive advertising and other expenses which had arisen owing to keen competition'. That was on 13 October. At some point during the next five days, Lord Northcliffe must have talked to his advertising manager.

SOAP TRUST ARITHMETIC
How 15 ounces makes a pound

screamed a headline on 18 October, presenting the drop in weight as a new discovery. It was the beginning of the sort of targeted and obsessive campaign at which the *Mail* excelled. Northcliffe was simultaneously attacking the 'shameless hoydens' who paraded at the seaside with 'bare heads, bare necks, bare arms and bare impudence', and attempting to have the 'wastrels' who ran London City Council removed from office, but nothing exercised him like the Soap Trust crusade. A hastily arranged interview, in which Lever explained the change and told the paper that 'Lever Brothers will not depart from the practice of their business principle of absolute purity of goods and the largest possible lump of pure soap for the money', was not enough to save him. The paper carried an attack on what it named 'the Sunlight Trust' every single day. Later in the month came a report by Edgar Wallace, detailing the

SOAP TRUST VICTIMS

complete with heart-rending details of a poor washer-woman who was a shilling and sixpence worse off every week because of the combine. 'The rise in the price of soap means all the difference between bread and butter for my children, and dry bread,' she sobbed to the sympathetic reporter. In case readers had missed the point the first time, the news desk followed this up with the shocking news

YOUR WASHING WILL COST YOU MORE

because the Trust was

SQUEEZING THE PUBLIC

before rounding up a number of stories of destitution from disgruntled ex-employees from Port Sunlight, which were liberally improved upon back in Fleet Street and printed under the headline

DISMISSAL OF EMPLOYEES BEGINS

Perhaps most damagingly, however, the paper actively encouraged its readers to boycott the soaps of the combine's members. A list was printed each day of 'approved' brands, alongside ones that should be avoided. Sunlight was always at the head of the latter. The rest of Northcliffe's publishing stable got in on the act. In his *Daily Mirror* Lever himself was depicted in a cartoon as a monstrous, bloated capitalist in a top hat, squatting behind the counter of a grocer's shop decorated with posters of 'Port Moonshine'. When a little old lady customer queried the weight of her purchase, he spat back barely literate speech bubbles: 'We don't care about you we want more of your money' and 'You may think yourself lucky I let you live, I'm boss of the situation, and I'll put as few ounces in the pound as I like.' Northcliffe and his fellow editors finally had an opportunity to voice their long-held prejudices about this weird, progressive social experiment on the banks of the Mersey, and they were not going to let Lever get away with it. Reporters were dispatched round the grocer's shops of the country with sets of scales, and even managed to get questions asked in the House of Commons about the matter. The company's share price fell by a third. Sales for November were down by 60 per cent year on year.

On 23 November the combine's members met again, at the instigation of Watson and Crosfield, the ancient firm against whom Lever had first found himself competing in Warrington twenty years previously. It was proposed that the whole plan be abandoned. The vote was carried almost unanimously. Lever abstained, unable to bring himself to vote against an idea he was still convinced could have worked.

In a letter to Joseph Watson after the meeting, he expressed his heartfelt regret, and a burning sense of injustice. 'It is one of the ironies of the situation that yourselves and ourselves, that of the United Kingdom have spent most with the newspaper Press, come in for most of the attack. Those firms like Messrs Gossage, who have never spent a penny in advertising, have never received any. In fact, I doubt whether the Editor, sitting on his stool in his office, has ever heard of Gossage's name.'

But the *Mail* was not finished with him yet. Gross took out newspaper adverts to announce the demise of the combine, and encourage customers back to Sunlight. But, unsurprisingly, he didn't put them in the *Mail*. The sniping redoubled. This was twisted into an attempt by Lever Brothers to bribe the press into approving their dastardliness – a crime they would have got away with had not the selfless *Mail* held out against their inducements. Northcliffe continued to take every opportunity to shoehorn a mention of 'the fifteen-ounce pound' into his pages, and to cast aspersions on the quality of the company's products and their ingredients, accusing them of using low-quality blubber bought on the cheap from the whaling industry in place of sturdy beef and mutton tallow. Finally, by December, Lever had had enough. His solicitor requested an opinion from the eminent barrister F. E. Smith, who, knowing exactly how lawyers ought to behave, sent out for a dozen oysters and a bottle of champagne and worked through the night in his chambers. In the morning his response was brief, and to the point. 'There is no answer to this action for libel, and the damages must be enormous.'

The writ was filed on 4 December 1906, and a trial date set for the following summer. Much of the following year was spent in the company of lawyers, with varying degrees of success. In March Lever Brothers successfully brought an injunction against the Titan Soap Company, who had shamelessly launched their own bars of fake Sunlight and sold them through a chain of shops in Manchester owned by their chairman. A case against a co-operative store in Rotherham to attempt to force them to stock Sunlight as well as their own-brand soaps failed, and was denounced by the Master of the Rolls as 'a somewhat audacious claim to a monopoly without warranty in law'. And in July the House of Lords was called upon to adjudicate a complicated case involving a bus service that the Mersey Railway Company had launched to link Port Sunlight to the station in Rock Ferry, on the very line that ran in front of the houses in Greendale Road at the west end of the village. The London and North Western Railway had, in their infinite wisdom, refused to build a station servicing the village itself, and then objected to anyone else providing an alternative. The Lords agreed with them, and the penny bus service ceased running after less than two months, increasing Port Sunlight's sense of isolation from the surrounding area.

When he pitched up at the Liverpool Assizes on 15 July, however, Lever was feeling positive. He knew that the *Daily Mail* were feeling the heat. Just a week before the hearing, he had received a personal letter from Lord Northcliffe offering an apology and a 'refrain from all further comment' in his papers, a sure sign that he was worried about his defence. Lever gave him short shrift. 'I like the cheek of the *Daily Mail* – it is simply colossal,' he wrote to Sydney Gross. 'They have had their detectives round Port Sunlight, and no doubt myself also if I only knew, for the last eight or nine months and have been interviewing every discharged, disgruntled, dissatisfied malcontent that there is or ever was in Lever Brothers' employ any time during the last 22 years. They have raked in all the scrap heaps and refuse heaps they could find. If they had discovered anything that would enable them to still further bully and browbeat us they would have had no suggestion of settlement . . . it is quite obvious that either they themselves are feebleminded, or they think we are feebleminded, and especially myself.'

Sir Edward Carson, the courtroom legend whom Lever Brothers had lined up to represent them, went straight for the jugular with his opening statement.

This libel, gentlemen, is of an exceptional and serious character, deliberately carried on for several weeks, and was made with the object of smashing up Lever Brothers . . . The defendants, having made up their mind to smash the combine, instead of attacking it in a fair way, have stooped to methods of libel which have rendered Mr Lever and his company liable to be branded as men with whom no honest man could have any dealings in this country.

The first and most serious charge is that the plaintiffs sold their soap in such a fraudulent manner as to deceive the public as to the weight of the soap. The next charge is that the plaintiffs, in consequence of the combine, have dismissed large quantities of employees. Another charge is that they have cornered all the raw material in the market. Messrs Lever Brothers are also accused of having, along with others, attempted to bribe and buy the press, and it is suggested that the attempt had to be abandoned because high-class and patriotic papers like the Daily Mail refused to be bribed. A number of the libels also contained hostile criticism of the plaintiff's soap, and alleged that unsavoury fish oil has been used in their manufacture . . . it was also suggested that the conduct of the plaintiffs in the matter of the combine tends to the oppression of the poor.

Lever, his public speaking skills honed by two decades at the lectern of the Port Sunlight Sunday School and, lately, on the benches of the House of Commons as part of the Liberal government that the *Daily Mail* despised (see Chapter 14), performed brilliantly in the witness-box. He elegantly refuted every single one of the paper's claims, pointing out that the weight change had not only been publicly announced by the company, it had taken place weeks before the idea of a combine had even been suggested. The *Mail*'s lawyer, Rufus Isaacs, failed to land a single blow. The following morning, he requested a meeting with Carson and offered £10,000 to settle the case then and there, a proposal which Lever took great pleasure in refusing.

The trial dragged on for just one further day. Carson challenged the *Mail* to produce the washerwoman interviewed by Edgar Wallace whose children Lever had so cruelly deprived of bread and butter: Isaacs was forced to admit that she could not be found. Carson dissected the figures Wallace had provided on her behalf: to lose one-and-sixpence, she would have to be using ninety-six bars of Sunlight every week. Not very likely, was it?

The following morning Isaacs returned with a new proposition. Lord Northcliffe suddenly found that he was able to offer £50,000 in damages – might that be acceptable? It would. 'I did not want two or three days' wrangle with all the books of Lever Brothers displayed in open court, showing the districts in England where trade had suffered,' Lever explained to his colleagues. Besides, the amount on offer was astronomical, a libel record – more than a million pounds in today's terms. The only comparable settlement in recent times is the million pounds that Elton John took from the *Sun* in 1987, after a lengthy campaign of vilification which involved them fabricating completely untrue stories of kinky sex with teenage rent boys and surgery on dogs whose barking annoyed him.

The *Mail* was obliged to cover Lever Brothers' costs, and the company collected a further £41,000 from a number of papers, including the *Daily Mirror*, which had repeated the libels. But it still wasn't enough to cover the damage the whole business had done to the company. Lever had invested £70,000 in setting up the combine by the time it was abandoned: he estimated that the loss of earnings from the *Mail*'s boycott cost him over half a million even after the damages were taken into account. Building work at Port Sunlight had to cease, and no new developments took place in the village for a further two years. 'The last four years our fleet has had to be steered through fogs, round sunken rocks and over sand banks represented by the Daily Mail attack,' Lever wrote sadly to a colleague in 1910. But he nevertheless gave away his libel winnings to Liverpool University, in order to found schools of Tropical Medicine, Russian Studies and Lever's particular passion, Civic Design. 'I have felt for many years that some help is necessary to be given both in educating the public on the matter, and also in providing the requisite knowledge available for Towns and Cities in the near future to be able to deal on broad lines with their suburban areas,' he told reporters. So impressed was Lever with Liverpool's Professor of Architecture, Charles Reilly, that he invited him to redesign the centre of Port Sunlight the same year, filling in a number of ravines and creating a grid system in the village centre centred around a new formal park, which was rectangular but inexplicably called the Diamond.

So some good did come from the whole messy combine business in the end. The secret negotiations between rivals were not entirely wasted, for several companies which had expressed an interest in sharing resources ended up coming entirely under Lever Brothers' control, including the best-selling brands of Knight's Castile and Rinso washing powder. And, ironically, those companies which had remained outside the combine and found themselves on the *Daily Mail's* approved list found demand for their products suddenly shot so high that they had to buy in emergency supplies of raw materials – and Lever Brothers were in the perfect position to dictate prices for the stock they had sitting on the quayside at Bromborough Pool.

Lord Northcliffe later found his perfect job, as Director of Propaganda in Enemy Countries during the First World War. Not long afterwards he went spectacularly insane and became convinced that he had been given poisonous ice cream by Belgians, ringing up his editors at odd hours of the night and instructing them to investigate why he was being followed around by young men in suspiciously tall hats. Naturally, this proved no obstacle to him continuing to dictate the *Mail's* editorial agenda.

William Lever never forgot his brush with the might of the *Mail*, having, like so many celebrities since, experienced just how unpleasant it was to get on the wrong side of the media. 'I consider the old highwayman of a hundred years ago was a gentleman compared to the modern newspaper proprietor,' he told colleagues. 'My spirit rebels against letting my business drift into where blackmailing methods and corruption prevail as in the English press.'

11

THE OTHER LEVER BROTHER

VISITORS TO LEVER BROTHERS' GENERAL OFFICES ON PORT Sunlight were generally kept for a while in the sumptuous surroundings of the vestibule before being ushered upstairs to the gallery that housed the directors' offices and William Lever's glass-walled lookout post. There they could cool their heels on the mosaic floor, peer through the interior windows at the hundreds of clerks working away at their regimented desks in the identical east and west wings of the building, or study the two busts of the company's founders that topped the newel posts at the foot of the splendid staircase. The clerks are still there, though they now sit among the computer terminals and partitions of the modern office, incongruous beneath the vaulting and cornice work of the vast interiors. And the busts remain, even if the name on the glossy, statistic-filled display boards that decorate the walls is no longer Lever Brothers.

On one side is the stout, jowly William, his large eyes bulging from his head, his hair swept up from his forehead, his thin lips tightly clamped but turning up in his customary welcoming smile. On the other is James, more handsome than his brother, hiding his baby face behind a curling moustache and sideburns. A man of fashion, his hair is slicked and ridged with pomade, his collar higher and more fashionable (at least in 1896 when the building went up) than William's stiff, purposeful garb. But there is no trace of a smile on James's face. His sunken, delicate eyes gaze off into the middle distance with none of the fiery intensity of his brother's. His expression is inscrutable. He looks neither happy nor sad.

This was as close as James Lever ever got to the office.

He is the vanishing man, dropping out of our narrative before the General Offices were even completed, and barely spoken of again in any of the newsletters or publications of the company. The official history of Lever Brothers records his departure in a line: 'Illness attacked him in 1895, and from that time onwards his part in the business was purely nominal, though he did not finally resign until 1897.' William Hulme Lever, writing his father's biography in 1927, devotes even less space to his uncle, noting only in passing that he was forced to retire in 1897 'through ill health', sudden news of which had forced William and Elizabeth to rush home early from another round-the-world journey the year before. The Port Sunlight Heritage Centre, a multi-media shrine to the memory of William Lever, makes it very clear that this was a one-man show. 'He didn't really do anything,' explained the attendant when I inquired why there was no information available about the other Lever Brother.

It was not just his office where James's presence was missed. The set of marble busts that William commissioned from Edward Onslow Ford between 1895 and 1906, which now adorn the entrance hall of the Lady Lever Art Gallery, feature the mutton-chopped James the elder, statesmanlike in old age, the plain Elizabeth and the familiar piercing gaze of William, but James Darcy is absent. At the coming-of-age ceremony which was held in 1909 to celebrate the twenty-first birthday of his eldest son, confusingly also called James, the entire family gathered bar one. Uncle William had to stand in as chief toastmaster. 'My brother, you remember, was among us in the early days of Port Sunlight, and, in the time he was with us, endeared himself to the hearts of every one of you,' he told the assembled throng. 'We all regret that the state of his health does not permit him to be with us today, but he will hear of what you have done, and it will give him the greatest possible pleasure to know that his son has had such a hearty and cordial welcome from every one of you.'

So where was James? What happened to him? The obituaries that appeared in *Progress*, the company's magazine, after his death in March 1910 are hedged with vagueness and euphemism. 'The younger of the Lever Brothers had for many years unhappily been laid aside by ill-health from active duties at Port Sunlight . . . As early as 1889 he met with an accident while driving which permanently affected his health, ultimately obliging him to give up business and live a life of comparative repose and retirement. Happily he enjoyed, as well as his strength permitted, the pleasures of a country life, and the reminiscences stored in a marvellous memory . . . His final illness was short, and his end was peace.'

We know, however, that his behaviour before leaving the company had been erratic and anxious. Even the obituary acknowledges a certain oddness about his attitude to the various schemes the business was involved in. 'These were his elder brother's conceptions, and Mr James Lever would often indulge his warm fraternal pride and affection by insisting upon this fact, even to the extent of disclaiming his own legitimate share in the development of Port Sunlight. But the records, including Mr [William] Lever's frequent personal testimony, stand to show that all the enthusiasm and robust energy of Mr James Lever's early manhood were brought to bear on the hard work of establishing the business, and that he was especially sympathetic and whole-hearted in seconding every proposition for the welfare of the workers.' Someone protests too much, methinks.

James Lever's death certificate records his death at Thornton House, the home he shared with his wife Ann just down the road from his brother in Thornton Hough. In looping copperplate handwriting the registrar records the opinion of Dr W. Henry Dobie: James had been suffering from acute gastritis – an inflamed stomach lining – for four days, before a gastric haemorrhage finished him off. In modern terms this probably means a gastric or duodenal ulcer – and what it definitely means is a very unpleasant way to die, vomiting and shitting blood and in great pain. His end may have been many things, but one thing it wasn't was peace.

But the death certificate also records something else: James Lever was diabetic. According to Dobie he had been suffering from diabetes mellitus for fifteen years before his death – ever since he stopped working for Lever Brothers in 1895. It is unlikely that the condition led directly to the gastric problem that killed him (although a newly introduced wonder drug by the name of aspirin which he may have been prescribed for some of the painful side-effects of the disease is now known to damage the stomach lining), but it was obviously significant enough a problem for the doctor to think it should be mentioned.

Diabetes is a twentieth- and twenty-first-century epidemic.

It was first recognized in the second century BC, but it only became widespread in the 1930s, and the number of cases accelerated in the 1960s as we settled down to a sedentary lifestyle of fast food and TV dinners. These days it can be easily treated with special diets or regular injections of insulin, the hormone which controls the amount of glucose in our blood, and which sufferers lack. But insulin was only identified in 1922. When James Lever was suffering from the disease, there was very little, other than the usual prescription of fresh air and cold baths, that anyone could offer him. What dietary recommendations there were varied massively between doctors, ranging from thrice-boiled vegetables three times a day to almost absolute starvation.

At first he probably didn't realize he was ill. In the early stages of diabetes many sufferers are unaware that they are passing water too frequently. If they do notice, they are likely to attribute it to the amount they have been drinking – they've been so thirsty lately. Often it is only with the onset of hypoglycaemia that people realize something is wrong. They become confused, and drowsy. They can't concentrate, and don't seem to know what they are doing half the time. They feel completely incapable of making decisions, weighing things up, or doing complicated calculations. As their blood sugar drops further they can become aggressive, and begin to tremble and sweat. If things get worse, they can even slip into unconsciousness and begin to convulse. The relatives of sufferers from chronic hypoglycaemia often report that their loved ones suffer a complete personality change, becoming difficult, uncommunicative and failing to take care of themselves and their appearance.

All this would explain James's behaviour prior to his retirement. But unfortunately in the late 1890s, any or all of these symptoms would also have been enough to get you locked away as a madman. The asylums that sprang up in every county following the Lunatics Act of 1845 were filled not just with the mentally ill, but with the epileptic, the paralytic, the syphilitic and the senile. We know that James Lever had been diagnosed with diabetes by the time he died in 1910, but we do not know at what point in his fifteen-year illness doctors actually identified what was wrong with him.

What we do know is this: the 1901 census does not record him as a resident at Thornton House, where Ann presided over an all-female household with her daughters, a twenty-year-old cousin and six servants while her two sons were away at boarding school. Instead James Darcy Lever is found some 200 miles away, as a boarder in the home of John C. Barker, in Clarendon Road, Watford. Barker records his profession as a 'Medical Practitioner' on his 'Own Account working at home'. He lives with his wife and two children, and five servants, including a 'domestic valet' who, it seems likely, was in the employ of the wealthy patient upstairs.

It is possible that Dr Barker was an early pioneer in the treatment of diabetes mellitus, though if he was, he never published any works on the subject. But it seems more likely that he was a part of the 'trade in lunacy', one of the hundreds of doctors who cared privately for wealthy patients who, for one reason or another, failed to fit the standards of behaviour deemed suitable by late Victorian society. There was a long tradition in Britain of the mad being 'boarded' with sympathetic and discreet medical men, but as Professor Roy Porter puts it in *Madness: A Brief History*, published in 2002, 'the early history of private asylums is obscure, for they prized secrecy: families would wish to avoid publicity'.

This certainly seems to have been the case with James

Lever. We do not know how long he spent with Dr Barker – the census records only who was present on the night of 31 March 1901 – though we do know that he returned to Thornton Hough and his family before he died nine years later. The symptoms of chronic hypoglycaemia would explain what we know of his behaviour, but so would those of depression. Perhaps he suffered from both physical and mental problems, each exacerbating the other. The onset of diabetes has long been associated with unhappiness and emotional stress. In Lever's time the Victorian psychiatrist Henry Maudsley attributed the disease to 'violent passions', an attitude which lingered on after the discovery of its real causes – in the 1930s doctors were still identifying a certain type of 'weak, irritable, hypochondriacal and changeable' personality as going hand in hand with diabetes. Today practitioners are more sympathetic. 'It can be a puzzle to distinguish symptoms due to diabetes from those due to depression or anxiety, which require different treatment,' writes Dr Joan Gomez in *Living With Diabetes*, a guide published in 1995. She adds that 'it is a statistical fact that diabetics are likely to have had more upsetting experiences and conflicts than other people during the three years before the disorder comes out. Bereavements, losing your job, moving house, especially to a new locality, someone you love being ill, financial stringency, divorce, failing an exam – all these count.' James Lever, who had opposed the move to Port Sunlight and all that it entailed in 1888, and who lost his mother in 1893 and his father in 1897, had suffered many such anxieties. Enough to increase the risk of diabetes – but also enough to send anyone off the rails for a while.

James Darcy Lever is buried in the churchyard at Thornton Hough beside his wife Ann, who outlived him by fifteen years, and two of their four children. On 28 December 1911 there was a special memorial service for him at Christ Church, Port Sunlight, where his brother unveiled a new stained-glass window dedicated to his memory. 'He was a kind and loving husband, a good father, a generous friend, and a true and loyal brother,' a clearly emotional William told the congregation. 'If each pane of glass in this window, and in each window of this church, had to commemorate a generous act and deed of him whose memory we hallow and revere, then all the windows in this church, and the church itself, would be a monument all too small to commemorate his memory.

'He was a child in frankness, candour, and sincerity, and a man in all that makes for manly qualities of mind and heart. He was a loving brother, and will always remain so.'

He concluded with a few lines from the book of Ecclesiastes.

Remember now thy Creator in the days of thy youth, while the evil days come not, nor the years draw nigh, when thou shalt say, I have no pleasure in them. While the sun, or the light, or the moon, or the stars, be not darkened, nor the clouds return after the rain . . .

Also when they shall be afraid of that which is high, and fears shall be in the way, and the almond tree shall flourish, and the grasshopper shall be a burden, and desire shall fail: because man goeth to his long home, and the mourners go about the streets . . .

Then shall the dust return to the earth as it was: and the spirit shall return unto God who gave it . . . For God shall bring every work into judgement, with every secret thing, whether it be good, or whether it be evil.

12

FOR EVER ENGLAND

THORNTON HOUGH IS AN OLD, OLD VILLAGE. IT APPEARS IN the Doomsday Book as Toritone, but by the early fourteenth century the local landowners had poshed-up their name to de Thornton in time for the marriage of their only daughter to local hunk Richard de Hogh. The various peasants in the locality who depended on the two families for their land obligingly renamed their village as a kind of cheap wedding present, and the name stuck. The villagers got a new church, school and row of cottages in 1870 courtesy of the Huddersfield textile magnate Joseph Hirst, but for the most part the village quietly sank into dilapidation over the course of the centuries.

So it is strange to visit Thornton Hough now, and find yourself in the heart of an Elizabethan village. The timbers of the small-frame cottages are bolted together with wooden stakes like Shakespeare's Globe, their walls brightly whitewashed and intricate renaissance designs cut into their plasterwork and beams. Low doorways open on to shared porches: tiny plots front and back are filled with hollyhocks, foxgloves and marrows, the quintessential English Country Gardens. On one corner a giant cartwheel marks the smithy, its forge billowing smoke. Even the cricket pavilion is half-timbered.

It's all fake, of course. Look closely at the elaborately carved lintels on the cottages and they read 1893, not 1593. Not content with his extraordinary transformation of his own house, William Lever bought up the surrounding village, knocked it down and started again. He was fulfilling a desperate need. The tied cottages that housed the local farm workers had long been neglected and had fallen into insanitary disrepair, their inhabitants too desperately poor to do anything about their rotting beams and stinking middens, and their landlords unwilling to bother.

But there was an important difference between Port Sunlight and Thornton Hough: the villagers here were not Lever's responsibility. They worked not in the soaperies of Port Sunlight, but in the fields around the village, breaking their backs to bring in the harvests for the local farmers, and receiving a pittance in return. By now Lever's natural generosity had gone far beyond the bounds of cause and effect, of wealth-sharing employer and wealth-producing employee. Despite his repeated protestations of pure self-interest – 'we will work on business lines, and we will have nothing to do with philanthropy', he liked to tell those he helped – he was determined to right inequality wherever he saw it, whether there was anything in it for him or not. He was particularly moved by the experiences of Betty Jones, an elderly widow who had spent her life in Thornton Hough caring for twelve children on an income of just sixteen shillings a week, and who now found herself destitute, reliant on the charity of her neighbours to keep her fed and housed in her tumbledown cottage. State

Eight-year-old William (*left, sitting on the right*) poses with his brother, James Darcy, and their oldest sister, Elizabeth Emma, in 1859. The family grew up in Wood Street, Bolton, which is largely unchanged today (*below*). From thirteen the boys attended the Church Institute a few streets away (*above*).

PORT SUNLIGHT

Where SUNLIGHT and LIFEBUOY SOAPS are Made.

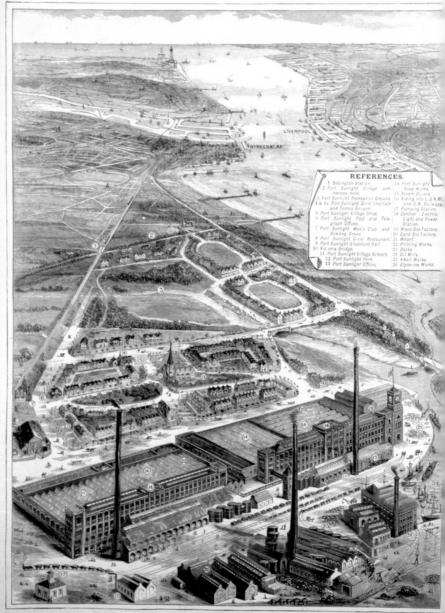

A BIRD'S-EYE VIEW OF WORKS AND VILLAGE.

The village created by Lever out of the marshes beside the Mersey came complete with every facility and institution its inhabitants could have desired – and a number they probably didn't. This bird's-eye view dates from 1898: the village continued to grow throughout Lever's lifetime.

Port Sunlight

Prosperity and Sharing

Part I.
The Works

Part II.
The Village

LEVER BROTHERS LIMITED,
1903.

ABOVE: 'Houses in which our work people will be able to live and be comfortable – semi-detached houses, with gardens back and front, in which they will be able to know more about the science of life than they can in a back slum.' Factory girls (*top*) turn out to welcome George V on a royal visit in 1914. Their elation was short-lived. 700 men from the village signed up to fight in August 1914; 481 were killed during the battle of the Somme. A devastated Lever bore the colours of the Port Sunlight Pals at their memorial service (*right*).

A scandal erupted in 1920 when Lever commissioned Augustus John to paint him and so disliked the result that he hacked out the portrait's face (the repair job, undertaken long after his death, can clearly be seen here). Hostile press comment – such as this Max Beerbohm cartoon (*opposite page, centre*) – reached the levels of the 1906 feud (*opposite page, bottom*) with Lord Northcliffe, owner of the *Daily Mail* and *Daily Mirror*, which ended in libel victory for Lever.

SUNLIGHT SOAP.

THE FAMILY WASH

ABOVE: Lever was happy to take any liberties with paintings he purchased to make them suitable for advertising his products: here Charles Burton Barber's *Girl with Dogs* is transformed into 'The Family Wash' by the simple addition of a badly drawn bath and the distinctive packaging of Sunlight Soap. He did, however, neglect to inform the artists of his intentions when purchasing their work, which caused many ruffled feathers in the art world.

THE GREEDY SOAP TRUST.

IF YOU DON'T LIKE IT — LUMP IT!

SOAP TRUST

PORT MOONSHINE

WE DON'T CARE ABOUT YOU WE WANT MORE OF YOUR MONEY

SOAP

SOAP. 15 OZS TO THE LB. — AND IF WE HAVE ANY OF YOUR CHEEK WE'LL MAKE IT 14 OZS

AT PORT MOONSHINE

OPPOSITE PAGE: The regular parties thrown by Lever for his employees were lavish and spectacular (*below*) – here men from his factories dine among priceless Pre-Raphaelites and Wedgwood pieces in the Music Room at Thornton Manor. By contrast the Levers' own living conditions were Spartan (*top, right*) – upstairs was the open-air bedroom and bathroom where he and his wife Elizabeth (*left*) slept all year round. The extent to which the rain came in can clearly be seen by the state of the floor. Even when Elizabeth, his 'better three-quarters', died of pneumonia in 1913, he could not be dissuaded from the practice.

The grounds of 'the Bungalow' – Lever's pre-fabricated wooden home a thousand feet above sea level at Rivington Pike (*below*) – were opened to the public on special occasions. Visitors could admire the flamingos, zebras and lions which were kept in the grounds, or visit the fake castle he had built in the nearby park. Almost as spectacular was 'the Pergola' (*above*) in the grounds of his London home, built with the stone excavated during the building of Hampstead underground station.

When Baron Leverhulme bought the Scottish islands of Lewis and Harris as a retirement project in 1917, he found their inhabitants living in poverty in croft cottages (*below*) which were unchanged from the dark ages. He invested millions to try to create 'the Venice of the North' (*above*), an industrialized Utopia 'full of thriving prosperous cities' like this one, from a visionary sketch he commissioned from Raffles Davidson in 1920. Unfortunately, neither the man nor his dreams were welcome on Lewis.

allowances for people like Betty had been all but done away with by the Poor Law Amendment Act of 1834: 'out-relief' was replaced by 'in-maintenance', the dreaded workhouse, explicitly intended as a deterrent from poverty rather than a solution to its problems.

Betty, like all her neighbours, got her own Tudorbethan doll's house to live in. Thornton Hough also received a new school, the smithy and a village club like the one in Port Sunlight, all courtesy of Lever. He even added a second (non-conformist) church next door to the Church of England which had been built by his predecessor, turning the tiny village into perhaps the most theologically over-provided community in Britain. St George's was probably erected more to satisfy Lever's architectural needs than his spiritual ones. 'I hold very strongly that in addition to what we may call the orthodox believers, and those who attend a regular place of worship, there are a great number of men and women, and I am one of them, who do not and cannot be bound by creeds as we understand creeds,' he explained in 1916. 'I have never joined a church in my life, yet I have always had great happiness in attending Divine Service. I cannot imagine a life to be well passed that does not have some ideals in connection with God as the Supreme Being . . . but there is so much of what I call "hard and fast rules" in so many creeds, that I prefer to just be going my own way.' He was, however, a regular member of the congregation at St George's, along with his less ecumenically inclined father, who moved to Thornton Hough after the death of Eliza Lever in 1893. William built a new house for his father and unmarried sisters Emily and Alice at the foot of his own drive, calling it Hesketh Grange in tribute to his mother's maiden name. Another sister, Jane, moved in nearby with her husband John Smith Ferguson, a manager at Lever Brothers. When James was in residence with Ann at Thornton House across the road, the top end of the village was one big happy family.

The Lever family Christmas at Thornton Manor was certainly an event to remember. William would gather the whole family together – Hulme recalled how 'sisters, nephews and nieces, their families, close personal friends, old friends of early days and their families' would start to arrive on the afternoon of Christmas Eve, in good time for William's traditional reading from Dickens's *A Christmas Carol*, complete with all the voices and a set of ghosts that never failed to make the little ones squeal. Fifty or more people would sit down to a turkey and plum pudding dinner the next day, and stay all the way through to Boxing Day afternoon to take their parts (however unwillingly) in the annual performance by the 'Manor Mummers', an impromptu play thrown together and performed on the ballroom stage as thanks to their hosts, under the direction of Hulme himself. While the servants were required to produce meals in industrial quantities each year, they were warmly invited to involve themselves in the various entertainments. An honoured guest each year was William's sister Mary Tillotson, who was, against all odds and customs of the time, making a terrific success of running her late husband's newspaper empire back in Bolton.

Thornton Manor was a truly extraordinary house. When Lever bought it in 1891 it was an impressive but bog-standard Victorian villa; the sort of house that announces The Money Is Here without flashing its wallet around. It wasn't good enough for Lever. Architectural features multiplied during its first renovation in 1896: the windows sprouted mullions and bays from attic to outhouse, pediments and pilasters grew from the roof, but the house at least retained its basic shape. That was not true of the next transformation in 1902: a vast semi-circular music room was added, complete with a projecting organ gallery in marble and an inglenook fireplace the size of most people's front rooms. Between 1912 and 1914 a whole new wing was added to give the frontage a more 'disciplined' air, and a timber-framed gatehouse added at the foot of the drive. Stables were erected according to his own plans, but turned out to be too close to the kitchen, so they were turned into an open-air dining room, and the simple fernery that had housed his collection in Bolton was extended into a parade of magnificent glasshouses.

The gardens were also redesigned to fit Lever's particular view of how the great outdoors could best suit his needs. 'One central feature is easily carried in mind and easily walked around, but a number of them, and a number of breaks and levels, I find to be irritating and annoying,' he instructed the landscape architect Thomas Mawson. 'I have tried sitting down in retreats and garden shelters, but I cannot rest in them two minutes,' and indeed in later life Hulme was unable to recall a single 'intimate and companionable talk between father and son' that had been conducted without their pacing up and down a garden path or passageway. Mawson provided the necessary formal gardens at Thornton, and also created a twenty-acre artificial lake, complete with canal, bathing pool, lagoon and its own island. Despite Lever's initial misgivings about approaching him – 'I have wanted to consult you for the last two years,' he wrote in 1905, 'but all of my friends warned me that it would be useless, as you never worked for anyone holding less social rank than a Duke, whereas I am only a poor and indigent soapmaker' – the two men became firm friends. In Mawson's opinion Lever was 'a veritable

Napoleon in his grasp of all factors dominating any problem to be tackled', while Elizabeth 'shed the radiance of a truly gracious spirit over the household'. For her own part, when asked what she thought of her husband's improvements, a wistful Elizabeth usually replied that one day she would rather like to experience what it was like to live in a house which didn't have a team of workmen in it.

The Manor, like every one of Lever's other homes, ended up as a crazy but charming mish-mash of competing styles that borrowed from every period and added some baroque touches that were entirely Lever's own. While most of his architect friends were left cold by the mixture of influences, Lever rejoiced in his carefully selected clash of cultures. 'I prefer Georgian dining-rooms as the rooms in which to give large dinners,' he averred. 'For small dining-rooms I prefer Tudor. For drawing-rooms I prefer what is called the Adam style; for entrance halls the Georgian. For a large room, such as a music room, I prefer the Inigo Jones type of Renaissance.' What he ended up with was something like *The Crystal Maze*: a bizarre set-up of interconnected zones that bore no relationship to each other and precious little to their originals. But within each room he was at least consistent: he scoured auction houses for genuine furniture and artworks contemporary with his fake interiors, snapping up chairs, tables, cabinets and escritoires alongside vast lots of wood panelling, plaster mouldings, doorways and chimneypieces. Each room was carefully hung with artworks from the correct period: works by Reynolds, Turner, Gainsborough, Constable and Canaletto were scattered around his interiors as if hung by some bygone patron before their paint was even dry. So keen a collector was Lever that even when he acquired (and extended) large homes in Rivington and London every room felt overcrowded and museum-like, 'rooms to be looked at, not lived in', in the regretful words of his son. Amid all this time-travelling splendour one item stood out: a shabby two-seater sofa from the mid-Victorian period, threadbare, horsehair bristles bursting pubescently from its covers. This, the Levers took great pleasure in telling their guests, was the first piece of furniture they had ever owned: it had travelled with them from their first home in Park Street, Bolton, back in 1874 and it would remain with them as long as they lived, a reminder of those happy, impecunious days that followed their wedding, its fabric fading over the years even as their love grew stronger.

Much of Lever's art collection was sold off in a series of auctions following his death, in 1926, which bundled together 1,256 weird and wonderful lots culled from his various households:

lot no. 326 A William IV charter, parchment with wax seal
lot no. 327 Three pairs of roller-skates

The best of it, however, remains in the Lady Lever Art Gallery, the purpose-built Portland stone wedding-cake erected slap-bang in the centre of Port Sunlight in 1922 and adopted as a national museum in 1986. Here you will find everything from sixteenth-century tapestries depicting the trials of the Israelites to Arthurian myths as sketched by Burne-Jones, capering porcelain demons from the Ming dynasty to armchairs alleged to have graced the bottom of Napoleon. The finest collection of Wedgwood jasperware anywhere in the world sits alongside several of the Pre-Raphaelites' most peculiar masterpieces: Frederick Walker's carelessly pederast *Bathers*, Millais's vision of sentimentality in armour *Sir Isumbras at the Ford*, and William Holman

Hunt's *The Scapegoat*, the painting of which required its unfortunate four-legged model to actually expire of starvation in the Dead Sea while the artist worked on the finer points of the weird Technicolor background.

'I really am blind on music and poetry. The whole of my artistic tastes are in colour, representing pictures, porcelain and furniture,' said Lever, and indeed he bought anything and everything, purchasing others' collections wholesale rather than hunting down individual pieces for his own. James Orrock, a dentist and lover of English watercolours and Chinese porcelain, painstakingly built up three separate personal collections before selling each in its entirety to Lever; the Wedgwood collection built up over a lifetime by the first Lord Tweedmouth was similarly snapped up along with a group of Greek and Roman antiquities that Thomas Hope had travelled the world to acquire. It is typical Lever: though he continued to buy from the RA's summer exhibition each year, to devote his time to tracking down individual pieces on the open market would have seemed to him like pure self-indulgence. Instead he simply identified his target – an art collection – and proceeded down the most direct route to acquiring it – buying someone else's. The fact that he bought his artworks in bulk did not mean that he loved them any the less. And besides, they weren't just for him. Even before the gallery was built, he shared out the pieces from Orrock's collections that were not to his taste among the various works buildings and canteens in Port Sunlight, ensuring that everyone got a view, and even some of his favourite items were lent to the village and displayed in the cramped conditions of Hulme Hall. Not that any of this was philanthropy, of course. Enlightened self-interest, all the way. 'The whole history of the world has proved that, so far from the love and cultivation of beauty and art threatening disaster to trade and industry, they have on the contrary proved a most powerful stimulus to their rapid growth and expansion,' he told an audience of artists in 1915. 'Art and commerce are the obverse and reverse of the same medal, both commemorating the nation's progress and development.'

The last of the Levers departed Thornton Hough in July 2000, with the death of the third Viscount Leverhulme. The Manor was sold nine months later along with its extra-ordinary contents, which raised a record-breaking total of more than 9 million pounds. The dining table alone (French, nineteenth-century, once belonged to Napoleon III) went for £323,000. When I visited in early 2003, the builders were in, the property surrounded by hoardings hung with contractors' boards and signs warning KEEP OUT – 24 HOUR PATROLS, complete with silhouetted alsatians with slavering jaws. None of them seemed to be about at the time, so I nipped up the back drive and peered up at the open-air bedroom, the bed long removed, but the swallows whose yearly arrival and departure Lever delight-edly noted in his diary still in residence under the eaves. The glass roof of the open-air dining room was cracked and open to the elements; the windows opened on to dusty voids, cables trailing from holes in the plaster, workbenches and toolboxes their only furniture. The glasshouses were dilapidated; long thickets of grass pushed up through the gravel on the driveway.

A sharp *tap tap* on a window revealed I was not alone. In one of the ground-floor windows stood a man in the standard property-developer garb of hard-hat and fleece over blue twill shirt and bright tie: they must hand this stuff out free with the company Rover. He tried to open the window, failed, and moved on to the kitchen door. That wouldn't yield either, and he was reduced to alternately wagging his finger at me through the thick glass and trying every key on an oversized ring on each lock in turn. After a while it became apparent to both of us that he was stuck on his side of the wall (for all I know he had been in there for months), so he just glared at me as I waved and wandered off back down the drive. On the way I met two builders in overalls who greeted my trespassing with the insouciance cultivated by years of casual contracts, and were happy to chat about what was going to happen to Thornton Manor in the twenty-first century: 'It's going to be a hotel, and luxury apartments, like.' The local paper preferred to call it an 'upmarket health spa', and said the new owners had promised to hold classical concerts and summer camps for children in the grounds, so I suppose there's a chance Lever would have approved. But I hope his ghost will stride up and down the corridors banging on doors if he feels the guests are staying in bed too long in the mornings.

13

MOVING MOUNTAINS

THERE WERE PLENTY OF REASONS FOR WILLIAM TO BUY Rivington Pike. It was a family tradition – in the seventeenth century, much of the estate had belonged to his eminent ancestor Robert Lever, benefactor of many a Boltonian institution. It was a way of reinforcing his links to Bolton, the town he had left more than a decade before but which he continued to love. But most of all it was a chance to go back to his courting days: he could own the area where he and Elizabeth had picnicked as teenagers, and they could build themselves a home on the very spot where they had first declared their love.

The fact that the site in question was 1,000 feet above sea level and, in the words of the *Manchester Guardian*, 'often wreathed with cloud-rack and drifting sea fog' bothered him not one jot.

The Rivington Hall estate was put on the market in 1899 by its near-bankrupt owner John Crompton. He had little use for the 2,100 acres of rough moor and woodland that came with the ancient manor, but he was fond of the

Georgian manor house, so it was made a condition of sale that he be allowed to continue to live there.

Lever already had a manor house of his own, so he found these conditions acceptable: he was less keen, however, on the asking price of £70,000 for the rest of the estate. He offered £40,000, and cannily instructed his solicitor not to reveal his name, knowing that Crompton would push higher if he knew the purchaser had several million in the bank. But Crompton only received one other bid, from the Liverpool Corporation, which owned several reservoirs nearby. They refused to go above £35,000, and in the end Crompton agreed to sell to Lever for £60,000: for this bargain price Lever also got a number of farmstead holdings, two Ango-Saxon tithe barns and the site of a beacon which had been lit to warn locals of the approach of the Spanish Armada in 1588. Much of which he almost immediately gave away.

Rivington Pike had long been a party site for the people of Bolton. The Pike Fair that was held every Whitsun turned the hillside 'like an ant-hill, covered with a moving mass', and during Lever's childhood it had been notorious for scenes of drunken revelry, much to the disgust of his father. Much of this had been stamped out by the end of the century – or at least relocated to Blackpool courtesy of a cheap train service – and by 1893 a writer commented that 'now the Pike's visitors are more of the class who come to drink in the health-giving breeze which gently fans its summit and from its ancient watchtower scan the Ribble and its wandering course'. Lever well remembered the stifling grimness of Bolton before its one and only park opened in 1866, and the continued difficulty in accessing Lancashire's moors still frustrated him. 'Your citizens could fill their lungs with fresh bracing air, making their cheeks ruddy with the glow of health,' he scolded the councillors of Oldham at one public engagement. 'Working in the confined air of workshops and factory, their blood requires the oxygen and ozone from your moors to revitalise it.' Now, in his own home town, he had the chance to do something about it.

He made his proposal in a letter to the council in September 1901, most of it in a single epic sentence:

> I shall be obliged if you will communicate to the Mayor of Bolton on my behalf an offer to give to the Town of Bolton a portion of the lands in the parish of Rivington belonging to myself, which are enclosed within the undermentioned boundaries and more clearly shown on accompanying plan, to be used as a Public Park for the use and enjoyment of the Public for ever, but subject to the understanding that during my lifetime I may, provided same be done at my own sole expense, erect on such land any building or buildings for the use of the Public, or make any roads or footpaths thereon for the proper opening up of the land for the use of the Public and generally deal with the land as may appear to me to be desirable for the purpose for which the Park is intended, viz. its free and uninterrupted enjoyment by the Public.

Only Lever would so politely ask permission to carry on giving his own money away. The people of Bolton could barely believe their luck. In his formal acceptance of the 400-acre park that December, the mayor called it 'a magnificent Christmas gift'. But in another town hall, another group of men had a very different idea.

The Liverpool Corporation did not take kindly to defeat. They had wanted Rivington Pike for themselves to guarantee the purity of the water in their eight reservoirs in the valley below, whose 4 billion gallons supplied much of the city to their west. On several occasions the cesspits of the Black a'Moors' Head pub in Rivington had overflowed into one reservoir, putting 800,000 scousers at risk of typhoid and other diseases. In 1899 Liverpool had spent £25,000 on the nearby Anderton Hall estate to stop the development of a mental asylum on the land, fearing that insane could only mean insanitary. Now Lever was proposing to invite tens of thousands of day-trippers to wander all over the land above their water supply, and who knew what they would do with their faeces.

That October the Corporation petitioned Parliament for the powers to compulsorily purchase not just Lever's newly acquired estate, but 6,000 acres above and around their waterworks, 'to enter on and take, and hold for the purpose of protecting their reservoirs, works and waters in the county of Lancaster'. Almost immediately Bolton presented a counter-petition, and Lever himself swore to fight the case to the death.

The fate of the Rivington estate was decided in a Commons Select Committee which met in May 1902. Lever's legal team pointed out that the creation of the park would involve the rehousing of 108 residents and the demolition of all the dilapidated cottages whose sanitary arrangements the Corporation had so objected to: they would also erect iron railings around the reservoirs to ensure that no one could bathe or throw rubbish in the water. They even donned metaphorical white coats for a lengthy discussion of exactly how many bacteria per cubic centimetre presented a public health risk in their efforts to prove that Liverpool was 'fighting a phantom'.

It was not enough. On 15 May the Committee ruled that Liverpool should be allowed to take over almost all Lever's land, leaving him only enough for the hilltop house he had already built and enough land around it 'to preserve the amenities of the place'. The park, however, they liked. Liverpool Corporation were ordered to provide the agreed 400 acres for the use of the people of Bolton, and to 'expend money on the waterworks account for the keeping up, maintaining and management of the park, and to make bye-laws'. And just to add insult to injury, they had to call it Lever Park.

It is hard to say who gave in with worse grace. Liverpool's lawyer threatened to abandon their proposed revisions and fight the case in the House of Lords, while Lever played extraordinarily dirty over the compensation he was due. He had purchased the whole estate two years previously for £60,000; now, for the three-quarters of it that the government had ordered him to hand over, he demanded £107,000. When Liverpool queried his figures, he was, according to his son, 'not a little surprised' and 'saw no alternative but to fight the case as strenuously as he could'. It's something of an understatement. He upped his price to £450,000.

It was only through the efforts of a lengthy Arbitration Tribunal organized by the Board of Trade that the parties reached agreement: Lever got £140,000, more than doubling his original investment (even then the saga was not over: a writ had to be served to force Liverpool to pay up, which they contested by accusing the chair of the tribunal of being 'mentally incapacitated' at the time). Liverpool got a guaranteed clean water supply, though this was thanks largely to the demolition of the Black a'Moors' Head in 1903. And Bolton got a park, on which Liverpool imposed as many strict by-laws and as little maintenance as they could get away with.

It didn't matter that much. In William Lever the town

had found a perfect party-host. In 1901 the *Manchester Guardian* had waxed lyrical over his plans for the park, where 'nature will have its own wild way, deer and rabbits will crop the grass and wild birds will enjoy perfect sanctuary'. In the event the wildlife proved rather more spectacular. Paddocks near Rivington Hall were stocked with emus, zebras, yaks, wallabies, buffaloes and deer, while a specially constructed den built of rough stonework was home to a lion cub imported from Africa. The lake in front of Rivington Hall was split in two, one half housing white English swans, the other black ones from Australia. The house itself, after the death of John Crompton, was turned into an art gallery.

The two great tithe barns, which had stood at the foot of Rivington Pike for the best part of a millennium, were restored by Jonathan Simpson using materials and construction methods as close to the originals as possible. They were opened as tea-rooms, serving a range of refreshments to visitors, and the larger one was the venue for the official opening ceremony in May 1904, when several hundred invited guests and the representatives of twenty-one newspapers feasted on such delicacies as ox tongue, brisket beef, liqueur jelly and prawns in aspic. When it came to entertaining Boltonians, no expense was spared.

The same was not true of Lever's own home at Rivington, Roynton Cottage, or, as it was generally referred to, the Bungalow. He spent rather less on this house than he did on the replica of Liverpool castle which he began in 1912, and always intended to look ruined (though its lines are still rather too clean to have really withstood a Roundhead bombardment, as the real one did before its demolition). Roynton Cottage was purchased from the Portable Building Company of Manchester and delivered to

Horwich station by train: it was built entirely of wood, its pine verandas more suited to an Indian summer than to the frequent fogs at the top of Rivington Pike. So unwelcoming was the bleak, windswept site that the company moved the building when they used it in promotional materials: it was pictured nestling cosily at the foot of the mountain amid some entirely imaginary neighbours on postcards that the firm sent out to publicize their valuable commission.

Inside, however, the Bungalow was palatial: it had thirteen bedrooms (including those of the servants), five of them en-suite, and its own billiard room with magnificent views down the hillside. But the house was not Lever's first priority: the forty-eight acres of land that the select committee had granted him gave him the opportunity to create an extraordinary garden, and he intended to indulge his imagination to the full.

He had two allies in this, his oldest friend Jonathan Simpson and Thomas Mawson, the landscape architect who had created the formal walkways of Thornton Manor. Here, however, he wanted something completely different. The gardens, he told Mawson, should be 'in perfect keeping with their natural environment'; however, that didn't mean the natural environment should prevent them from doing anything that they wanted. No plants flourished on the barren hillside, so Mawson was charged with finding him ones that would survive. He wanted lawns, but the gradient of the land meant that that was impossible – so the hillside would have to be flattened. Oh, and one other thing. He handed the designer a copy of the blue-and-white willow-pattern plate that had been fashionable in Britain for more than a century. He'd quite like something like that at the southern end of the garden: could he sort it out?

Japanese gardens were the height of fashion in the first

decade of the century. Josiah Conder, whose book *Landscape Gardening in Japan* was published in 1893, was the Alan Titchmarsh of his day, setting off a craze for everything oriental. At the same time that Lever was working on his slice of Japan at Rivington, the finishing touches were being put to similar gardens at Friar Park near Henley-on-Thames and Hinchingbrooke in Cambridgeshire. Wisterias, peonies, irises and lilies began to spring up in gardens across Britain, courtesy of a thriving horticultural trade with the Far East. In 1906 the Yokohama Nursery Company claimed to be exporting more than 5 million Japanese bulbs a year to Britain and the US; four years later, after the Japan-British exhibition at White City in London (to which Lever took a party of Sunlighters), that figure had gone up to 15 million. More important than the plants were the accessories: the red lacquered bridges, brightly coloured pavilions, thatched tea-houses and stone lanterns to which stores like Liberty devoted whole departments. Naturally, few of these were authentic – lacquered bridges are a Chinese tradition, and no garden in Japan has ever featured a painted pavilion. Nevertheless, Lever bought the lot, and, just to add to the cross-cultural confusion, installed a flock of flamingos (native to South America and Africa) on his brand-new, concrete-bottomed lake. Surprisingly, the mish-mash worked: the sandstone cliffs that were exposed by Lever's excavations have that unusual horizontal layering familiar from a million Japanese woodcuts, and at night when the lamps were lit in the grottoes and behind the rice-paper shutters of the three pagodas that overlooked the lake, the effect was bewitching. 'It is difficult to believe that the scene is not in Japan itself,' wrote one visitor, 'whereas if one turns about, one surveys a panorama of Lancashire coal-mines, factories and cotton-mills.'

The Japanese garden is only a fraction of the forty-five-acre site: there were great formal lawns in front of the Bungalow which were used for croquet and dancing in the evenings, vast heated greenhouses for Lever's beloved ferns, a boating lake complete with a statue of Neptune and a series of stone buildings scattered throughout the lower terraces which doubled up as viewing platforms during good weather and sturdy shelters during bad. At the garden's northernmost end is the pigeon-tower, a three-storey folly which housed a collection of doves and other birds, and where Elizabeth would sit and sew and gaze out over the gardens like Rapunzel awaiting her prince. A guest once asked her what she thought of her husband's latest acquisition, and she replied, 'It's very nice, but it is like having two houses and no home.' But she was fond of this room, with its mock-medieval fireplace embossed with her initials alongside those of her husband, and the motto he chose for himself when he was made a Baronet in 1911 – *Mutare Vel Timere Sperno*, 'I spurn to change or fear'.

Personally, she preferred the inscription on the sundial that her husband had placed at the corner of the great lawn, on the very spot where they had sat and confessed their love for each other forty years before: 'Live today, not regretting yesterday or fearing tomorrow.' Looking around at this unlikely paradise, the hanging gardens of Rivington, hewn out of the unforgiving hillside by an army of workmen and planted with the best treasures the Orient had to offer, it truly seemed that for the Levers anything was possible.

14

ACCIDENTALLY ELECTED

IF YOU WANT TO KNOW HOW DIFFERENT THE POLITICS OF the 1880s were from those of today, consider this one thing: the *Daily Telegraph* didn't support the Conservatives. The most true blue of broadsheets was founded in 1855 as a radical voice pushing for reform of the House of Lords and against capital punishment; it nailed its colours firmly to the mast of the Liberal party under the leadership of Gladstone, 'the people's William'.

It was Gladstone who had dominated the youthful Liberal party, formed from the ashes of the patrician Whigs half-way through the century. He had fostered its reforming zeal and focused it in a series of emancipating measures: education for all; the extension of voting rights; newspapers that everyone could afford. 'All the world over, I will back the masses against the classes,' he declared in 1886, and he was not afraid to face his hidebound opponents head on. 'You cannot fight against the future,' he told the Tories as he extinguished the last of the rotten boroughs that had ensured the domination of the landed gentry over British democracy for centuries. 'Time is on our side.'

Gladstone, however, made one serious mistake: not his conversion to home rule for Ireland, then still a full part of the United Kingdom, but the way in which he allowed news of it to dribble out. The 1880s saw a mainland terror campaign by the Fenians that was in every way as effective as that of the IRA a century later: bombs exploded in Manchester, Glasgow and London, and threats were issued against the capital's spanking new underground train system. Senior staff from the Viceroy's office in Dublin were murdered. Gladstone publicly insisted on a policy of 'firm government' in Ireland, giving the administration summary powers to crack down on the violence. But he continued to negotiate behind the scenes. The agreement he bashed out with Charles Parnell, the leader of the Irish Land League, involved the release of political prisoners, with the public outrage that always provokes. And it was against a background of worsening violence that in December 1885 Gladstone's son Herbert announced to the newspapers that his father had become convinced that Ireland should rule itself.

It was a political disaster for the Liberals. The party split down the middle, the pro-Unionist faction peeling off under the leadership of Joseph Chamberlain, whose son Neville failed so spectacularly to deal with Hitler half a century later. They would eventually be absorbed into the Conservative party, but their independent stance at the 1886 election ensured that their former party lost more than 100 seats, and returned the Tories to power with a hefty majority. The *Telegraph* jumped over the fence, and the Liberals were left in disarray. Their seventy-seven-year old leader looked increasingly out of touch. If they wanted to see power again, party officials knew they needed to bring in new blood.

They found it in William Lever, a lifelong supporter of the party. 'His liberalism was always more than a party label, it was a deeply ingrained habit of thought', according to his son: it was evident in every measure he introduced for the benefit of his workers at Port Sunlight. Until 1892, however, he had taken no active political role. That February, less than three months after Gladstone's speech at Port Sunlight had so inspired him, Lever was elected as chair of the executive committee of the Bebington and New Ferry district Liberal party. This was simply a stepping-stone along the way: the party were determined to make him their candidate in the coming general election. He was perfect for the role – his famous concern for the condition of his employees ought to divert working-class votes from the worrying new Labour movement; his self-made status made him an attractive alternative to the Conservative incumbent, the Viscount Bury, heir to the ancient seat of Albemarle. He was perfect for the job. Benjamin Disraeli, Gladstone's great Tory rival, could have had Lever in mind when he outlined the ideal legislator: 'an English gentleman, born to business, managing his own estate, mixing with all classes of his fellow-men, now in the hunting-field, now in the railway-direction, unaffected, unostentatious, proud of his ancestors'.

There was just one problem. He didn't want to do it. Lever was happy to fund the Liberal campaign, he would speak in their support at every opportunity, he would throw open the Gladstone Hall in the village for them to hold their meetings. But he had no desire to be an MP. He hadn't the time. He had a business to run.

He was assured that he had nothing to worry about. The Tories had a majority of over 1,200: with the state the national party was in, he hadn't a hope of getting anywhere near Westminster. Home Rule, to which Gladstone remained passionately committed, was less popular than ever. Parnell, his new best friend, had been exposed as an adulterer, which in the 1890s was regarded as a far worse crime than consorting with murderers: no, he would be fine. If he could just make a show at the hustings, shake a few hands, kiss any babies that happened to come his way, then he could be safely back behind his desk on the morning after the election. This is how Lever recalled his conversation with the constituency chairman:

'Will you give me an honest answer to a frank question?'

'I will.'

'Good. Now, if I stand for Birkenhead, what chance have I of getting in?'

'Not a dog's chance, but it will pull the party together.'

'All right. You can nominate me.'

They were right. Gladstone somehow managed to scrape his way back into power, buoyed by the support of the Irish nationalists. But Viscount Bury was indeed returned as the honourable member for Birkenhead, and William Lever lived to work another day. He had, however, by force of personality alone, reduced the Tory majority in the small constituency by half. Only 604 votes stood between the business he loved and an unlooked-for career in Westminster. He had had a lucky escape.

Just two years later, in 1894, the seat became vacant again, when Bury succeeded to his father's title and a seat in the House of Lords, and didn't have to bother with the inconvenience and indignity of actually getting himself elected any more. This time, Lever was even busier. He had floated the company just a few months before, and made employment history by introducing an eight-hour day as standard. He did everything he could to wriggle out of having to stand, including offering to meet the expenses of any alternative candidate, but the committee insisted that no one else could be found (no doubt while crossing their fingers behind their backs and adding the silent proviso 'that has as good a chance of winning'). In the end their appeals to Lever's ego held out, and his name appeared on the ballot sheets for the by-election. He did, however, flatly refuse to campaign door-to-door, declaring it 'highly improper ... nothing but moral suasion and argument should be employed'. Instead he toured the constituency addressing public meeting after meeting, Elizabeth at his side, and chipped away even more of the opposition's majority. Elliot Lees was returned for the Conservatives with a majority of just 106.

Meanwhile things went from bad to worse for the Liberals on the national stage. Gladstone's second attempt to force a home rule bill through Parliament ended in ignominious defeat at the hands of the House of Lords. The old man resigned from the leadership of his party, and in 1895 the country prepared to go to the polls once again. And once again, a deputation was sent from the local party to Port Sunlight to beg Lever to stand.

He was getting a taste for it now. Whereas he had been visibly, painfully nervous at his first public speeches, he now spoke with confidence and worked an audience well. His son recalled the long, narrow pieces of card on which his father jotted down notes, the points he wanted to make listed in black ink, the jokes etched out in red. 'Whenever he heard a good story he made a note of it. He was always on the look-out for anecdotes in books, magazines and newspapers. He carried about with him a waistcoat pocket diary, in which the salient points of the stories in his repertoire were jotted down under different headings –

Scotsmen, Lawyers, Doctors and so on – so that he could readily turn up a story appropriate to the occasion.' He was good at off-the-cuff ripostes, too. When Elliot Lees referred to the Liberals in Birkenhead as 'the scum of the town' during a public debate, Lever quickly pointed out that he knew as a soapmaker that it was the scum that floated to the top, while the lees were left behind on the bottom. The Tories took the threat from Lever so seriously that their leader Arthur Balfour made a personal visit to Birkenhead to canvass on Mr Lees's behalf. Lever kept their majority down – it was a mere 204 votes – but his local popularity was not enough to overcome the national mood, which had taken against the Liberals. The Conservatives were emphatically elected, and would remain in power for a decade, which gave them plenty of time to do what they have always been best at, tearing themselves apart.

And so to 1905. Lever Brothers was a worldwide concern, with factories across Europe and North America rolling out more than twenty brands of soap. Port Sunlight was almost completed, with nearly 2,900 residents. Hulme was preparing to leave Eton for Oxford, having received the sort of gentleman's training his father could only have dreamed of as he cut soap in the warehouse in Bolton. And Lever's political usefulness had been exploited by the party on a local, rather than a national, level: he had sat as the chair of the Bebington District Council and served a term on Cheshire County Council. Still he professed no desire to move on to the House of Commons. When Prime Minister Arthur Balfour announced a general election for the following January, Lever was pleased to hear that the local party had found themselves another candidate. He fired off a generous donation to party funds, wrote offering free use of all halls and meeting rooms in Port Sunlight, ensured that similar letters had been sent to every other party that was contesting the seat, and settled back to concentrate on running his business.

It was mid-December before the Liberal candidate for the neighbouring constituency of Wirral announced he was pulling out. This time the party really didn't have any alternative. Lever accepted the nomination once again with a heavy heart, set the printing presses in Wood Street to producing banners that read 'LEVER THIS TIME' and went out on the road once again. He had a massive work-force behind him – and this time, they were angry.

'One or two statements made and repeated by the opposite party roused the Port Sunlight workers to a pitch of excitement hardly to be conceived,' reported *Progress*, the Lever Brothers in-house newsletter. 'It was freely stated that no man was allowed to continue his employment at Port Sunlight after attaining the age of 45 years, and that the full trade union rate of wages was not paid.' They were particularly stupid claims to make, since they were so demonstrably untrue – in fact Joseph Darby, a long-serving member of staff, was able to refute them from the audience at one election meeting, pointing out that he was over forty-five, and that he was not only paid generously to work for Lever Brothers, but he was also paid not to, thanks to the company's revolutionary policy of paid holiday which had been introduced the year before. Along with some politically minded colleagues, he organized a group of Lever Brothers staff between the ages of forty-five and seventy, who processed through 'some of the principal centres in Wirral, especially those in which the slanderous statements had been made', accompanied by the village brass band. According to *Progress*, 'the sight of so many old men taking the trouble to drive in open conveyances on a cold winter's day for the sake of their appreciation of and love for their employer, did much to convert many strong Tories'. The pensioner-pity trick doesn't always work – just look at Michael Foot in 1983 – but this time, it paid off.

Support for Lever was evident throughout the village. At the packing department in Wood Street 'entire rooms were very tastefully decorated with festoons, chains and mottoes in the party colours', despite the fact that the staff there were all female, and unable to vote. Restriction of suffrage to those who owned property, or paid above a certain amount in rent, meant that only 60 per cent of the male population had a voice in the running of the country, but in the event only eight of the 535 Sunlighters who were registered to vote failed to turn up at the polling station, and while a few no doubt took their chance to rebel anony-mously against the boss who controlled so many aspects of their lives, the number of X's beside the name of 'Lever, W. Liberal' on ballot papers far exceeded those recorded for anyone else.

Elections a century ago were not the nail-biting race for the TV cameras that they are now. There was no single polling day. London and the other major cities went to the polls part-way through January, while results from the hundreds of rural constituencies dribbled in over a period of nearly three weeks. The final result was not declared until 7 February, but by then it had long since become obvious that a landslide had taken place. Just as in 1997, the electorate had grown sick of a tired and bickering Conservative government. The party had all but destroyed itself over the issue of free trade and the repeal of corn duties in 1903. Joseph Chamberlain had walked out of the cabinet – it was becoming a habit – Winston Churchill had crossed the floor, and Prime Minister Arthur Balfour had managed to manoeuvre himself into a position where he had no choice but to resign from number 10, something even John Major never managed. Balfour lost his seat in the subsequent landslide, which saw the Liberals returned with a stonking majority: their 184 seats shot up to 399, more than half the House. One of those was the Wirral. On 26 January Lever had been elected by 1,071 votes.

It might have been the news he was dreading, but Lever couldn't help being carried along with the euphoria. Five thousand Lever Brothers employees packed the Auditorium to hear his victory speech: more were waiting outside to offer their congratulations. 'As Mr Lever left for his motor, he was literally besieged by workpeople and girls, with whom he warmly shook hands until his arm must have ached,' reported the *Birkenhead News*. 'Several of the girls were so elated that they seized Mr Lever and kissed him, and then, "just for fair play" as they said, they also kissed Mrs Lever, a proceeding which caused both Mr and Mrs Lever to shake with laughter.'

The celebrations were not entirely disinterested. Most of the staff reckoned that if they looked chuffed enough, it would be enough to get them an afternoon off work. Lever's last words as he left the platform were a half-hearted attempt to persuade them to return to their posts, but in the end he left the decision up to them, and the production lines remained silent for the rest of the day. The same was not true of the streets outside: someone managed to organize a wagonette to carry the brass band around the village, with a crowd of people following and singing along. At Christ Church, the Reverend Samuel Gamble-Walker instructed his bellringers to peal out until their arms ached.

Much of Lever's elation had faded three weeks later, when he reported to the Palace of Westminster to be sworn in as an MP. It is impossible to cross the threshold of the Houses of Parliament without feeling awed: its atmosphere is otherworldly, its ecclesiastical architecture designed to hush you into respectful silence, its staff superior in white tie and tails. Everywhere you look, imposing statues and murals abound to remind you that here you are in the very presence of history – this is where Guy Fawkes and King Charles I were put on trial; this is where the realm has been shaped for the past eight centuries. To enter knowing that you have been charged with continuing that tradition, that you are expected to play a solemn part in Britain's democracy, that the political will of thousands lies in your hands – anyone could be forgiven for feeling a twinge of terror.

Perhaps as Lever stood before the speaker's throne to take his oath of allegiance to King Edward, he might have reflected on the history that was being made on that particular day. Alongside him twenty-nine representatives of the Labour party entered the Commons for the first time: Ramsay MacDonald stepped up to promise to be faithful and bear true allegiance to His Majesty just minutes after Lever. One day this party would swell and eclipse his own: within two decades MacDonald would enter Downing Street as Prime Minister, but for now the leadership of the country rested in the hands of the seventy-year-old Henry Campbell-Bannerman. His energies had largely been spent on the long struggle to unite his party: his time in Downing Street was undistinguished, his government carried along largely by the vigour of his Chancellor, Herbert Asquith, and the young radical David Lloyd George, President of the Board of Trade.

They came to power fired with reforming zeal, swearing to help the 10 million Britons who had fallen through the net and were living destitute in the richest nation on earth; as Campbell-Bannerman put it, to make Britain 'less of a pleasure-ground for the rich and more of a treasure-house for the nation'. This was a government of which Lever was proud to be a part, and his opportunity to make his mark was to come sooner than expected.

'We have a duty of doing something for those members of the community who are not in a position to do it for themselves,' William Lever declared to the House of Commons on 20 February 1906. His was one of the first maiden speeches of the term, just twenty-four hours after the King had declared Parliament open. His request to catch the speaker's eye had been favourably received, and he had only had to sit through a few hours' debate on 'Kaffir and Chinese Coolie labour' in the Transvaal before his name rang out across the chamber. Not for him the usual gushing thanks to his predecessor and empty words of praise for his new constituents: instead, clutching his notes in a shaking hand, he issued a heartfelt demand for action. 'It is quite beyond the reach of the workers themselves to provide sufficient for their old age,' he told the House, relying on his fame as an enlightened employer to give weight to his words. 'It is equally certain that the question cannot be dealt with by individual employers.' Instead, he proposed, the state must introduce pensions without delay, whatever the cost. 'With regards to the means of providing the money, I suggest that in addition to a graduated income tax, of which I cordially approve, there are probably some economies that can be made in existing expenditure.'

The subject of old age pensions was not a new one. It was one of the treasonous proposals of Thomas Paine in his revolutionary *The Rights of Man* in 1791. Joseph Chamberlain had been campaigning for their introduction since

Germany had adopted a national insurance scheme in the 1880s. Lever pointed out that 'there was no topic on which the country had so often and so emphatically expressed an opinion', but he did suggest something new. Pensions had previously been dismissed out of hand because of the expense of suddenly funding a whole generation (Lever placed the expense between 18 and 20 million a year, which was optimistic); instead, he proposed a gradual introduction which would begin by alleviating the suffering of only the very oldest in society. The droll hand of a Hansard reporter records the reaction on the opposite benches:

> If they had not the money available to provide pensions at the age of 65, which in his opinion was the proper age, let them commence the pensions at 70; and if not at 70 then at 75 ['Oh!']. But let them resolve that these were only to be stepping-stones to the full and complete scheme.

Here things might have rested had Lever not got lucky in one of the Commons' odder customs, the ballot for Private Members' Bills. A handful of MPs each year succeed in this lottery, their lucky numbers selected by the speaker and a few precious hours cleared on the parliamentary calendar for the House to discuss their particular bugbear. So on 10 May 1907 Lever stood in the chamber again, this time to formally propose that his graduated pension scheme should be introduced over a period of three years, five years being knocked off the commencement date every twelve months until every man and woman over the age of sixty-five – 'excluding paupers and criminals' who were actually resident in either workhouse or prison – could report to the post office every week to collect their allowance of five shillings a week.

He told his honourable friends about Betty Jones back in Thornton Hough (though he left her anonymous to save her shame), with her twelve children all kept well on sixteen shillings a week, now reduced to living on the charitable handouts of her neighbours. Should she have deprived her kids in order to save for her old age? 'From a national point of view she has fulfilled her duty to the State in a higher manner by bringing up a family respectably than if she had saved any amount of money for thrift.' He reminded them that 'there is an obligation on the part of the State to do for individual citizens what individual citizens could not do for themselves'. And he appealed especially to the 398 MPs on his own benches to use their massive majority for good. 'I am certain the result of this scheme would be to produce better citizens; I believe this five shillings a week would encourage thrift by giving a stimulus where at present there is blank despair.'

Bless Lever. He had a saint's desire to do good in the world, and a martyr's ability to deny it. 'This is not benevolence,' he assured the House, for 'if it were, I do not think the working man would have anything to do with it.' He possessed not a shred of cynicism, and was simply unable to conceive of anyone not sharing his own pride and honesty – he laughed off Conservative suggestions that his scheme would be scammed by the well-off, maintaining in all honesty that 'only the poor man would want to stand at the end of the queue', and thanking his opponents for the opportunity to point out that the government stood to save a fortune on his hypothetical good citizens who would graciously decline their windfall. He demonstrated his lack of self-interest by proposing a higher tax rate on the rich to pay for the scheme – 'The logic is that wealth requires the most protection, by armies, navies and so on, and therefore must pay the most' – and sighed at Harold Cox's suggestion that a pensioner 'might have spent his life not in helping his country but in injuring his country by his own vicious conduct: he might have been an idle, drunken blackguard, yet when he reached the age of 65, he was entitled to draw five shillings a week out of the pockets of hard-working, sober, and thrifty men'. Cox, MP for Preston, was a Liberal in name but not mentality: he was eventually slung out by his constituency association, sick of his vitriolic opposition to every social reform the party stood for. The Hansard reporters produced another tiny masterpiece in their account of an exchange between him and Lever:

> **Mr Cox (Preston)**: Challenged any Member to rise and say that he told his constituents that he was prepared to support a Bill for Old Age Pensions that was going to cost the country £26 million a year.
> **Mr W. H. Lever**: I think I did.
> **Mr Crooks (Woolwich)**: And so did I.
> **Mr Cox**: Said that at all events the Government were very careful about committing themselves.

But Mr Cox was wrong. Lever's bill was carried by 232 votes to 19: a delighted Lever concluded that 'what he desired was that the House should express its opinion so that when the Chancellor of the Exchequer came next year to fulfil the pledge he had given, he might know exactly the views of the House upon this great subject'. Asquith was as good as his word: the 1908 budget provided £1.2 million per annum to be shared out in five-shilling instalments between every man or woman over the age of seventy in the land. They had first 'to satisfy the pension authorities that their yearly means as calculated under this Act do not exceed thirty one pounds ten shillings', but the question 'Are you an idle, drunken blackguard?' would not be asked.

It was the delayed start of the Liberals' new dawn. After a series of heart attacks Campbell-Bannerman had been carted out of Downing Street in February; he died two months later. Asquith took over as Prime Minister, and installed Lloyd George as Chancellor. Together they raised death and land value duties, and introduced a super-tax which took from those with incomes of more than £3,000 a year, sharing out their wealth among the poor in the form of labour exchanges and pensions, and instigating the national insurance scheme with all its attendant benefits. It was Lever's Port Sunlight dream writ large: enlightened self-interest on a national scale. But he nearly wasn't around to play a part in it.

The years between 1906 and 1910 were difficult ones for Lever Brothers: the instability of the raw materials market forced the company to look for alternative sources overseas, while the controversy over the soap trust and the *Daily Mail* attacks nearly ruined them at home. Just as Lever had predicted, it quickly proved impossible for him to perform both jobs. He shared his time between Thornton Manor and his new London home on Hampstead Heath, and did much of his work from the company's offices in the capital, at Caldwell's Yard near Blackfriars. But there was no room in his punishing schedule for the extra responsibilities of a career in Westminster – duties he had not sought, and could not bear to shirk. Instead, just a few months after the election, he had decided that he would have to give up his seat.

Naturally, this being the British Parliament, you cannot just resign. MPs who have had enough of life in the House must either die, go bankrupt (and be automatically expelled), or get themselves elevated to the peerage. The only other way out is to accept a paid office of the crown which, unless you are qualified to become a High Court Judge, means the Chiltern Hundreds.

Unlike the Chancellor of the Duchy of Lancaster, a fairly high-ranking cabinet minister (whose duties can range from minister without portfolio to cabinet enforcer, but can be guaranteed to have nothing to do with Lancaster), the Crown Steward and Bailiff of the three Chiltern Hundreds of Stoke, Desborough and Burnham is an utterly meaningless title. The Hundreds are a real place, in Buckinghamshire – the House of Commons will provide you with a map of them if you ask nicely – but they need no more stewarding than anywhere else. The title exists merely as a way for MPs to jettison their jobs, and it has been used in recent years by figures as diverse as Ian Paisley, Matthew Parris, Robert Kilroy-Silk and Neil Kinnock. There's even a Stewardship of the Manor of Northstead if more than one of them want to jump ship at once. Apparently it all made perfect sense in the seventeenth century.

The Liberals' massive majority meant they could easily afford to lose Lever. But he was useful. 'Mr Lever is extremely popular in the House, and has been a most excellent member,' wrote George Whiteley, the chief whip, to a worried Prime Minister. He also had a public profile outside Parliament, unlike many of the new intake, whose inexperience had caused some commentators to question whether they were capable of forming a competent admin-istration. Best of all, Port Sunlight and the rest of Lever Brothers' business were a shining demonstration that the social reforms they were trying to push through Parliament, against entrenched opposition from the Conservatives and the House of Lords, could work in practice. His departure was bound to be spun by the opposition into a loss of faith in the Liberal vision. It would be particularly galling to lose him because of the efforts of the *Daily Mail*, which was busy violently opposing every social reform the government attempted to push through and deriding the dying Campbell-Bannerman as 'the Incubus'.

It was the size of their majority that allowed a compromise to be worked out. In an extraordinary arrangement, the whips agreed to waive Lever's attendance claims for a year, and let him get on with his day job. 'I discovered in conversation with him that where the political shoe really pinches is in regard to next year – 1907 – when Mr Lever's business duties will be of such an onerous character as to prohibit him attending regularly,' Whiteley reported to Number Ten. 'At the same time, I find that after the lapse of next year, the business demands on his time will be reduced.' So it was simply agreed that for the next twelve months, the honourable member for Wirral need not report to the House unless he wanted to. In return for continuing to represent the party – no one seemed all that bothered about his constituents – he would be allowed to stand down at the next election, on condition that he agreed to contest a different seat that was guaranteed unwinnable, to demonstrate his continued support for the party. In the event he still managed to significantly reduce the Conservative majority in Ormskirk, which must have given him a worrying few hours at the count.

So passed one of the great missed opportunities of Lever's life. Though it was not the end of his political career, his decision to put business before legislature probably deprived Lloyd George of one of the best cabinet ministers he could ever have had. Who knows what effect a voice within cabinet that favoured the practical involvement of workers in the running of business might have had on the all-but-total eclipse of the Liberal party by Labour over the next fifteen years? Certainly Lloyd George could have done with someone to remind him that principles were more important than power in the later stages of his career. But it was not to be.

The soapmaker was not entirely silent for the rest of his time in Parliament, however. In March 1907 he made a lengthy and eloquent speech on the contentious topic of payment for MPs. These days controversy surrounds the massive salaries that politicians award themselves for their part-time jobs in the heavily subsidized gentlemen's club of the Palace of Westminster: then the debate centred on whether they deserved to be paid at all. MPs had always been drawn from the gentry and it was simply assumed that they could support themselves from their family fortune while they generously deigned to run the country. In theory this made for an admirable tradition of voluntary service; in practice it meant that anyone without a rich daddy was barred from entry, and government after government was selected from an inbred in-crowd. Working-class candidates, dependent on their wages, could barely scrape together enough to make it to selection meetings and hustings, let alone give up five years' salary to represent others like them. Ramsay MacDonald lived off his wife's inheritance: he achieved his position in the cash-strapped Labour party largely because he was able to offer to work for free.

'Payment of members,' Lever argued, looking round at the few MPs who had managed to remain upright after lunch and into the evening sitting, 'was required to maintain the dignity and prestige of the House,' and he believed it would enormously raise its efficiency . . . 'It is urgently required, in order to give to every constituency an equal, free, and unhampered selection of parliamentary representatives.' His supporters went further, accusing the Conservatives of trying to maintain 'the existing conditions as obstacles to prevent the introduction of undesirables into this House'. This was exactly the sort of thing that Campbell-Bannerman (who supported the motion) needed Lever around for. His wealth and what he did with it was so famous that it was impossible to accuse him of getting his snout in the trough. As a colleague who spoke in support of the proposal pointed out, 'it could not be said that my honourable friend had any special interest in bringing it forward'.

MPs got their salaries, though not until after the next election, when Lever had left the House. They were set at £400 a year, roughly equivalent to £25,000 today. Naturally, politicians' egos are subject to a higher rate of inflation than the national economy, and our elected representatives now pocket a minimum of £55,000, supplemented by innumerable allowances, and, for many of them, with as many directorships as they can cram in without falling foul of the register of members' interests.

Lever was far from the first to propose the payment of MPs – indeed, he quoted the recommendations of a Commons committee in 1780 in his speech – but his final proposal for Westminster was entirely his own. The amateur architect in Lever was always looking for ways to express himself: it didn't take him long to decide he could improve on the work of Charles Barry and Augustus Pugin. While he thoroughly approved of the retro theme-park vision that had been imposed on the Palace of Westminster after the fire of 1834 – 'in the National style of Gothic or Elizabethan' was the brief the designers had been given –

he felt that the building was let down by one important detail. It wasn't the lack of offices that bothered him, or the fact that there wasn't enough room on the benches for every MP to sit down. Lever had a problem with the view that has graced a billion tourists' photos over the years – the appearance of the Houses of Parliament from the river side of Big Ben.

'I should not venture to make the suggestion, if I believed that it would do other than improve the architectural effect as seen from Westminster Bridge,' he wrote to the first commissioner of works, proposing the addition of a veranda running the length of the building above the existing terrace, supported by columns and topped with a groined roof. He offered to have the plans drawn up at his own expense – he would probably have been happy to pay for the whole thing himself – but his offer was politely declined.

It's such a wonderfully Leverish thing to do. To arrive in Britain's most imposing and pompous institution, a monument to centuries of ancestor worship and solemn tradition, and cheerfully point out that it's a bit rubbish and offer to give it a makeover. It's like turning up to a reception at Buckingham Palace and telling the Queen she ought to do something new with her hair. When the place was bombed by the Luftwaffe in 1941, MPs unanimously decided to rebuild an identical version, backing Winston Churchill's declaration that 'I cannot conceive that anyone would wish to make the slightest structural alterations in the House of Commons.' Even New Labour stopped modernizing for a moment when Lord Irvine decided he needed new wallpaper in 1997.

But if you should find yourself in central London any time soon, wander across Westminster Bridge and have a look at the Houses of Parliament for yourself from the other side of the river. The terrace Lever was talking about is covered by a couple of tatty marquees, put up years ago to shelter the assorted sixth-formers and constituency irritants that MPs have to entertain to afternoon tea. The white stripes that alternate with green and red on their canvas display the filth of years of exposure to the capital's smog. The statue-strewn splendour of the Parliament Square side peters out on this side of the building: there's nothing to see but barbed wire and spikes and the jetsam spewed up by the Thames. What the place could do with is a decent veranda, with maybe some pillars and a nice bit of groining. That would sort the country out.

15

EMPIRE BUILDING

LATE IN 1906 A LETTER ARRIVED AT THE GENERAL OFFICES IN Port Sunlight in a battered and tatty envelope. It had made its way across half the globe, forwarded on from the company's office in Sydney, where it had arrived thanks more to the determination and lateral thinking of the Australian Postal Service than anything approaching a proper address.

Misi Lever
Sunlight Soap, in Sitne

4 day in Seiptemba, 1906

Misi – Do you want buy plentee Copra. How much you pay one ton. Brittania man say you pay very good price. You got stemah, and pay money, no give paper on store. When you boss come look out Copra.

Nathaniel Mou
Native Chief of Pepsie
Rotuma Island
Oceania

Chief Mou timed his offer well. Lever was desperate to get into the raw materials market, and extend the control he now had over the selling of soap in the UK to the other end of the process. He was sick of budgeting for the wildly fluctuating prices the company paid for copra and tallow, tired of being held to ransom by plantation owners and slaughtermen. And he knew that things were not going to get better. 'The large soapmaker in ten or twenty years from today who has not behind him a raw material scheme must go under no matter what be his advertising,' advised Joseph Meek, the head of Lever Brothers in Australia, who sourced much of the company's ingredients. 'Mere investments in planting schemes will be no use; the soapmaker must own the raw material scheme and have it as a background to their business.' Scientific advances – the introduction of hydrogenation – meant that vegetable oils could now be used instead of beef fat to make margarine, and vast food companies like the Dutch Jurgens had begun snapping up the oil stocks that Lever Brothers regarded as rightfully theirs.

'The recent use of Copra oil for edible purposes increases our difficulties,' Lever explained to his directors. 'There is no corresponding increase in production. To leave the production of Copra in the hands of natives, who stop producing as soon as they have supplied their own limited wants, will not give the world the Copra it wants.'

This was imperial arrogance at its most basic, but as Chief Mou's letter demonstrates, the copra producers were just as keen to embrace capitalism. For hundreds of years the islanders of the South Pacific had been robbed, abused and infected by white visitors, from the conquistadors of the sixteenth century to the black-birders who raided the islands and enslaved their inhabitants as cheap labour for

Australian sugar plantations in the nineteenth. The precise rituals and complex traditions that had bound together their communities for generations – the passing down of tribal histories from grandparent to grandchild, the desiccation of corpses in canoe-shaped coffins within the family home, the hunting of heads from rival villagers to ensure one's own comfort in the afterlife – all had been ridden over roughshod by legions of interlopers who brought with them the dull, soulless but insistent cult of Christianity. Now, with black-birding outlawed and newly installed sympathetic British protectorates committed to ensuring that commercial development of the islands benefited the indigenous people as well as themselves, the islanders were determined to grab any chance to be players rather than pawns in this brave new world that had so far brought them nothing but trouble.

As usual, Lever emphasized the commercial benefits when outlining his plans to his fellow directors. 'The inducement to Lever Brothers has been that in times of scarcity when Copra is high, the islands may make a profit, and it is just at such times that such profit will be welcome.' But, as ever, his interests were far from solely financial. He had seen for himself the pointlessness of the main white presence in the South Pacific: the missions which steadfastly ignored the inhabitants' earthly problems in favour of forcing a spiritual U-turn that might guarantee them a better time in heaven. When he visited Fiji and Samoa in 1892 he had lamented this 'prayer for the souls of the dying, a sending of the chaplain previous to the execution'. 'If we really wish to give to native races the blessings of our civilisation and religion, so that they may become a happy and prosperous people, let us first teach them to make for themselves and their families the best use of their lands,' he had written in his diary as his boat chugged southwards across the Pacific. 'Let us make them into planters, cultivators and manufacturers of such articles as can be made out of the raw materials their lands produce; let us in short act as would wise guardians and trustees during the infancy and development of a ward. In this direction there is an enormous field for missionary effort.' Now he had his chance to put his plans into action, taking the word not of the King of Kings but his practical cousin the King of Sunlight out into the world.

Meek was charged with the task of finding suitable plantations in the South Pacific for the company to invest in. On the Florida Islands he met with the Chief Commissioner of the British Protectorate in the Solomon Islands, Charles Woodford, a career diplomat and thoroughly good egg who was delighted to receive him. 'It is not every day that we find a millionaire tenant in the Solomon Islands, and I think we may assume that the rental he pays is the lesser part of the advantage the Protectorate will derive from him,' Woodford reported to Lord Ripon, his political master at the Colonial Office in Whitehall. With Ripon's full blessing, he offered Lever Brothers a 999-year lease on a group of islands north of Santa Isabel: the Russell Islands, virtually flat and offering 300,000 acres of perfect plantation land.

Potentially perfect, that is: there was a great deal to be done before the company would see a return on its investment. The islands were covered in thick bush which had to be cleared away: once planted, the coconut palms needed tending for six to ten years before they would surrender up a usable harvest. Recruiting labour was not a problem. In 1896 the New South Wales government had introduced the infamous 'White Australia' policy, banning 'all persons belonging to any coloured race' from the country (much to their chagrin, they had to exempt the Aborigines whose land they had stolen a century before). The thousands of Solomon Islanders who had been dragged from their homes in the 1860s and 1870s and sold to plantation owners for a few pounds a head now found themselves making the return journey, often under as much duress. After thirty or more years in Australia they returned ill-equipped and unwilling to resume their old lives. Many were housed in specially built compounds on the Floridas while Woodford tried to work out what to do with them.

Hundreds were engaged by Levers' Pacific Plantations, the new company that had been formed to report back to Port Sunlight, 10,000 miles away. They signed two-year contracts at an annual salary of £8, more than anyone had received for similar work in Australia. They would be housed on site. The original plan was that they should be supervised by white plantation managers who would take a life-long lease on their plot of land, and share in the profits that would roll in with each year's harvest in the Lever Brothers' approved style. But this proved impracticable: Europeans were unwilling to sign away their lives and commit to an untried venture in such a remote and wild part of the world where, despite the best efforts of Woodford's staff and the missionaries, islanders continued to collect the heads of both rival villagers and Europeans in occasional hunting parties. Instead LPP were forced to offer salaries to plantation managers and accept almost anyone who applied; mostly they ended up with bushmen from the Australian outback. Lever was delighted with the calibre of the men he employed. 'They are sober and hard-working and used to a solitary life far from town or city,' he told colleagues as the reports began to roll in from the other side of the world. 'They can live in comfort, not to say luxury, where a city man from most places would grouch and grumble, sulk and starve.'

That might be true. But they were also violent, un-principled rednecks, who took every opportunity to abuse those under their command. These were the disaffected bigots for whom even a white Australia was not enough, men who had failed to make a go of things in the new world and were determined to take their frustrations out on the old one. They treated the Solomon Islanders with the same casual brutality that they had meted out to the 'Abos' back home; new recruits were advised by old hands that only one rule applied: 'treat them as muck. Remember that a white man's the only human being here and that there isn't any other kind.'

Conditions on Lever's plantations shocked A. W. Mahaffy, Woodford's second-in-command, as tough and unromantic a man as you could find anywhere in the Empire. He toured the plantations in 1908 and reported back that the managers were 'for the most part unable to deal with native labour, and it is not surprising when it is remembered that they have every opportunity to manifest their dislike of "niggers" . . . It is not denied that floggings take place upon the estates, and to put such power into the hands of ignorant and prejudiced persons constitutes a real danger . . . The mere absence of a policeman from the next corner does not justify him acting in a manner which would not be tolerated for a moment in a civilized community. They should remember that respect for honesty and sobriety is not confined to either place or colour.' The plantations were dispersed over such a large area that the company itself had difficulty supervising them: the protectorate was so short of resources and staff that policing them was simply impossible. Woodford had a small victory the following year when he succeeded in deporting one manager, P. C. Munster, who had shot and killed a worker. The state of the islands, Mahaffy concluded, would 'amaze and horrify the proprietor of the model town of Port Sunlight'.

They certainly would have done – but there is no evidence that he ever got to hear about it. Lever did not visit the Solomons until 1913, when the beauty of his surroundings seems to have blinded him to what was really going on. For the most part he relied on reports from Meek in Australia, who relied on reports from the local headquarters on Gavata Island, who relied on the managers on the ground, who were not stupid enough to confess to half of what really went on. Besides, Woodford suspected Meek and his colleagues of colluding in the cover-up: reporting on one Lever employee who had resigned and applied to join his own staff he wrote: 'If I may be permitted in an official despatch to express my strictly private opinion, it is that Mr Berneys was too honest and not sufficiently unscrupulous to satisfy the requirements of Messrs Levers' Sydney Directorate.' Whatever the case, what filtered back to Port Sunlight was still racist bile, but diluted to an acceptable contemporary level: like the Indians Lever had visited in Utah, the Solomon Islanders were 'lazy', they simply couldn't be bothered to work.

Lever's early comments on the fledgling operation have an indulgent air; he is a patient teacher willing to gently lead his people by the hand. 'In a land where a bountiful soil and climate provide for all his wants the native fails to see the logic of work as a substitute for head-hunting and fighting. The comforts and trappings of civilisation interest him much less than they do the African native, and his trading instinct is not as strongly developed,' he wrote in 1906. By 1911, when he addressed his army of sales representatives, an impatient jingoism had taken over: it was time to understand a little less, condemn a little more. 'The South Sea Islander when he tears off a palm leaf has supplied himself with a full dress suit; and when he knocks down a coconut he has provided himself with his Table d'Hôte dinner. But the South Sea Islander stagnates. He invents nothing, he plans nothing – he merely vegetates, and existence to him knows little variety, each succeeding day. Now that which has made England, and the people of England, is the fact that soil and climate are hard and stubborn, only yielding food, clothing and shelter in response to strenuous and persistent effort.'

It was this strenuous effort that, as he understood it, the Solomon Islanders were not willing to put in. In fact, it was more a case of lack of incentives. In his book *The White Headhunter*, based largely on the oral history passed down by the Solomon Islanders themselves, Nigel Randell recounts the objections of those who found themselves working for Levers' Pacific Plantations:

They were housed in airless huts built of corrugated iron, their beds flat pieces of wood. The work was dull and repetitive and the bulk of what they earned was retained by Levers and only handed over at the end of the contract when deductions had been made. Nothing could be purchased except from the company store which charged exorbitant prices – or 'native prices' as Levers euphemistically put it. There was no social life as there were no other islanders, male, or (more importantly) female. The place was a wasteland and when they had completed their two years in the fractious, bored, single-sex community they discovered that there were no firearms that they could purchase with their hard earned cash, only tinned meat, cheap watches, mirrors, razors and the inevitable beads. Above all there was no kudos. They had not been to the white man's world, and they had no stories to tell except of an island prison less than one hundred miles away.

Previous plantation owners had been baffled by the islanders' unique work ethic: they worked single-mindedly, sometimes for years at a time, until they had earned enough money to buy a gun, the most powerful symbol of the white man's power – and then they stopped, and showed no interest in extending their contracts, whatever pay rise they were offered. Money as an end in itself held little attraction for them – like so much else, it was a new and little understood concept on the islands. For centuries trade between villages had been a simple matter of bartering: the traditional currency of porpoise teeth rarely came into play. Throwing cash at the islanders only encouraged pointless spending, as Lever himself found when he visited the village of Faisie to negotiate the purchase of their own copra crop in 1913:

> The chief of the native village came out to meet us and we afterwards went into his hut. There I noted a wardrobe, three sewing machines, chairs, table, gramophone, thermoflask and other items of civilisation amid general dirt and disorder. Mr Woodford states that the natives are making so much money out of copra at present that they have no idea what to do with their earnings or profits, and either waste them on useless purchases or hoard them in some hole in the ground.

But no matter how much you paid people, they could not harvest a crop that did not exist. From the start Levers' palm trees were blighted by insect infestations and disease.

Frogatti beetles devoured the budding leaves long before the trees had the opportunity to bear fruit. The company imported a flock of mynah birds from India to tackle them but they 'in no way distinguished themselves': the birds were more interested in repeating the swearwords they had heard from the sailors on the voyage than in consuming the beetles. Lever had hoped that his 300,000 acres in the Solomons would give him the lion's share of the world-wide copra market: their yield was so bad that they could not even fully supply his mills in Australia.

The blame for this failure, however, was placed squarely with the indigenous labourers. Assured by a management desperate to safeguard their own jobs that it was only the workers who held the venture back from certain success, Lever hit upon an unusual solution to his problem: if Solomon Islanders couldn't get the job done, he would simply import a race who could. The answer lay several thousand miles away, in the powerhouse of the British Empire: India.

'Kulumbangra is quite an ideal spot for Hindoos, and from there as time went on they would spread all over the Solomon Islands,' Lever told his fellow directors, announcing that he had dispatched Meek to Calcutta to offer plots of free land as an incentive to come and work in the Solomons. 'We should have an increasing population instead of as at present a decreasing population. Land is valueless without men and women to live on it. It seems a pity that such good fertile rich land, as far as my knowledge goes the best in the Pacific for coconut growing, should be unused in this way.'

The Colonial Office did not see the matter in quite the same way. It was not the first time they had been approached with such an idea – for years the High

Commissioner of Fiji had been trying to persuade his political masters that 'the only possible agent of development seemed to be European capital coupled with imported Asian labour', while the islanders themselves were 'pensioned off in their own areas, protected against liquor, firearms, and land grabbers'. Indian labour had saved the sugar plantations of the Caribbean after the abolition of slavery, and Woodford himself strongly supported Lever's plan. But the scheme was riddled with diplomatic pitfalls: in Whitehall the Indian Office objected that the Solomons 'did not appear to be a suitable field of employment for Indians', in Westminster the nationalists on either side objected in strong terms to any kind of 'trade in human muscle', while the Australian government threw a spanner in the works simply because their own racist migration policy prevented them doing the same thing on their own South Sea island of Papua. After lengthy negotiations a compromise was offered. Levers would be allowed to recruit workers from India, but they could not offer them contracts: in other words, having paid to transport them 6,000 miles across the ocean, the company would have no guarantee that they would not go off and work for one of their rivals, or just sit on the beach all day and top up their tans. This was completely unacceptable to Lever: he demanded the right to contracted workers. The reply was a perfectly phrased diplomatic put-down: the Colonial Office was 'not concerned with the private interests of private individuals' but rather 'the revenue and the general prosperity which is the result of successful planting and settlement'. To Lever, whose planting had been anything but successful, it felt like a smack in the mouth.

'I cannot understand the attitude at the Colonial Office, but these interlacing Government departments such as the

Colonial Office and the India Office are very difficult to influence for the good and progress of those portions of the Empire where they feel a little in conflict,' reported Lever, as usual convinced that he knew best. He continued to push to be allowed to recruit in Calcutta for the best part of a decade, despite a policy from 1910 by the Indian Office to automatically reject 'all schemes that involve contractual periods of work overseas'.

Part of Lever's frustration was fuelled by a simple inability to understand how people could not wish to live and work (for him, the two words meant pretty much the same thing) in the Solomons. When he finally made it out there himself, in 1913, the place seemed a paradise on earth.

'Imagine you can stand on the deck of this steamer,' he wrote to Sydney Gross from on board the *Kulumbangra*, the specially adapted boat that LPP had purchased for travel between their widespread plantations.

The captain tells you that you are approaching 'so-and-so' island. Gradually it rises from the azure blue of the Pacific. Larger and larger it grows, until you can see every tree and palm clearly, and you drop anchor in a land-locked bay.

The launch is lowered to take you ashore. On rising ground you see the manager's bungalow, with a well-kept garden in front and line upon line of coco-nut palms in serried masses for hundreds of thousands of acres in the background. You land at a small jetty made of coral, of beautiful and fantastic form. You walk up to the red-roofed, white-sided bungalow and note the generous and ample width of the veranda all round. From this vantage you get a panorama of bay and palm-clad shores, with the good ship that brought you lying at anchor. You also get a bird's eye-view of the garden, and here you see gorgeous-hued tropical foliage, plants and brilliant white flowers such as are grown at home only in hot-houses and with difficulty and anxious care, but which here you see growing with little care and less attention, vigorous and strong. In the kitchen garden you see pineapples, oranges, limes, lemons, bananas, grapefruit, mangoes and all manner of tropical fruit. At the back you see a well-stocked poultry farm with the promise of an ample supply of eggs and chickens and ducks. You see pigs and dogs, horses and cattle, and of the horses, a bunch are waiting saddled and bridled to take yourself and party over the plantations.

Off you start, the estate manager explaining the year when each paddock was planted – some very forward, precociously forward, like human children, others backward, some very backward. Here a grove heavy with 140 nuts per tree, there patches of trees suffering from bud-rot, or root-disease, or leaf-disease, or ravages of beetles.

. . . As you return you pass a bullock-team at work, and stop to examine the steam-plough which did such good work in pioneer days before it was known that bullocks would thrive and prosper, but which is little used now, for it costs double in the Solomons per acre to plough by latest up-to-date steam power compared with the old-fashioned bullocks. And so you return to the bungalow, calling on the way at the dispensary where simple medicines are given out to the natives, and to have a look in the sheds provided for native quarters.

The air in the Solomons is bracing, and you do not feel fatigued, and after a bath and a good dinner enjoy the circle on the upper deck where, with the captain as central figure, anecdotes of sea and land, storm and stress, canoes and head-hunters, beach-combers and black-bird runners, test your credulity almost to breaking point.

It sounds as if the managers had done a very good clean-up job before he arrived. Naturally, he saw no evidence of the beatings that were regularly administered to the workers, and the plantations he toured were specially selected as those suffering the least from the various blights that were busy destroying his crops. But the iron sheds distressed him: before leaving he drew up ambitious plans for better quarters which suited his own preference for altitude and fresh air: 'my own idea is that at 3,000 feet we should meet with a cool climate and most healthy conditions'. And to focus on the abuse that was part and parcel of Levers' Pacific Plantations neglects one important improvement they brought to the Solomon Islanders' lives: in a country where white diseases like tuberculosis, dysentery and influenza were decimating the population, those simple dispensaries had already reduced the sick rate among his workers from 5.56 per cent to 3.18 per cent. By 1925, the year of Lever's death, it was steady at just 1.6 per cent.

But Lever's Solomons dream was never to come to full fruition. Bogged down in Whitehall intransigence and riddled with parasites, the plantations would never pay their way. His mission to rule the world – or at least that part of it that produced soap-making materials – would have to begin elsewhere.

16

A GOOD MAN IN AFRICA

IN THE ANNALS OF THE AGE OF EMPIRE, WITH ALL ITS attendant horrors, it is hard to find a people who have suffered more than those of the Congo. The heart of the Dark Continent, gateway to Africa, adopted home of Stanley and Conrad's Mr Kurtz, it was also a scene of genocide: between 5 and 8 million people were slaughtered in the jungle by the Europeans to whom they had been persuaded to sign away their land in the 1880s. The killing has not stopped: the vast land has continued to tear itself apart into the twenty-first century, independence giving way to civil war and military dictatorship before the season of blood in Rwanda spilled over its borders in the 1990s. A Democratic Republic in name, the country remains a bloody mess of opposing factions locked in a state of endless conflict.

Who is to blame? The Belgians. Europe's most over-looked nation, for centuries the tiny pawn of its belligerent neighbours, quietly adopted this vast swathe of central Africa at the end of the nineteenth century: a private colonization, undertaken by one man demented with the desire for a kingdom overseas. Leopold II, King of the Belgians, was an awkward, disagreeable, cold fish of a man who had to be taught the basics of sex by Prince Albert while Queen Victoria gave a similar tutorial to his young wife during a state visit. He so disliked the resulting three daughters that he attempted to ban them from inheriting his fortune, and was in fact an active paedophile, spending millions of francs on the services of child prostitutes throughout his life. From childhood he had been obsessed with extending the tiny kingdom that he would one day inherit. 'Petit pays, petit gens' was the theme of his acute inferiority complex, and as a young man he toured the globe filling notebook after notebook with figures, ideas and calculations which might one day show him a way to achieve his desire. He found a way in the borrowed clothes of philanthropy; promising to stamp out the 'Arab slave trade' that explorers like David Livingstone had identified in Africa, a trade which took men and women from the mainland to be sold in the Omani-controlled markets of Zanzibar. In fact Leopold's interest was much more selfish: he wanted an army of slaves of his own.

He was helped by Henry Morton Stanley, the Welsh-born celebrity explorer who in 1871 had been sponsored by the *New York Herald* to go in search of the long-lost Dr Livingstone, I presume. Stanley's talent for self-publicity was matched only by his talent for killing: he boasted that the Anglo-American Expedition for the Exploration of Africa in the mid-1870s 'attacked and destroyed 28 large towns and three or four score villages'. Despite the hundreds of inhabitants he slaughtered along the way (or perhaps because of them), he was happy to declare Africa the 'Unpeopled Country!' and he proved the ideal partner for Leopold's mission to claim the vast territory around the 'river that swallows all rivers' as his own. He was employed by the International Association of the Congo to help set up a 'confederation of free negro republics': privately, Leopold assured him that 'there is no question of granting the slightest political power to negroes . . . The white men retain all the powers.'

He was not wrong. In return for second-hand clothes, bottles of gin, and a few intimidatory tricks played with electric batteries and magnifying glasses to demonstrate the white man's intimacy with the gods, chief after chief promised 'freely of their own accord, for themselves and their heirs and successors for ever . . . to give up to the said Association the sovereignty and all sovereign and governing rights to all their territories . . . and to assist by labour or otherwise, any works, improvements, or expeditions which the said Association shall cause at any time to be carried out'. With the stroke of a pen – an instrument whose function they did not even understand – the people of the Congo signed away their lives in their entirety.

A full account of the horrors endured in the Congo is given in Adam Hochschild's brilliant book *King Leopold's Ghost: A Story of Greed, Terror and Heroism in Colonial Africa*, published in 1999. He tells how women were taken from villages to serve as concubines to state officials and traders. Men were forced to rape members of their own family, or killed for sport, the victims of wagers between soldiers as to who was the better shot. Children were taken from their families in their thousands and forcibly recruited into the military, a process that was aided and approved by Catholic missionaries, who were eager to save their souls by baptizing them before they were sent out to attack their own people. Often, instead of clearing the jungle, the difficult and time-consuming way to create space for plantations, inhabited villages were simply burned to the ground and rubber trees planted in their ashes. Most hypocritically, the Congo Free State (it was recognized as a Belgian colony in 1884) ran an active and immensely profitable slave trade, buying men and women for a few pounds from collaborating chiefs, or simply kidnapping them and forcing them into labour. Their children disposed of – those too young to march were simply abandoned in the jungle to die – they were whipped regularly and made to work in chain-gangs, shackled so tightly by the neck that their skin wore away and flies fed in their open wounds.

The European staff employed in the Congo Free State neatly absolved themselves from all guilt or independent thought by adopting the reductive thought-process common to mass-murderers from the Crusaders to the Nazis: the blacks were stupid, lazy, sub-human, worse than animals. Holding that as their central belief, there is little that human beings are not capable of. One man, Léon Rom, had trained as a book-keeper for a firm of customs brokers in a provincial town in Belgium: as station chief at Stanley Falls he decorated the flower-beds at his home with the severed heads of African women and children from the surrounding area. This was truly the heart of darkness.

Since its publication in 1902 Joseph Conrad's novel has been regarded as a brilliant work of fiction; it is not, it is journalism. The writer spent six months in Leopold's Congo in 1890 as an officer in the British merchant navy. When *Heart of Darkness* was published, he described it as 'experience . . . pushed a little, and only very little, beyond the actual facts of the case'.

The truth about the Congo under Leopold emerged only through the courageous efforts of a handful of whistleblowers: journalists who bothered to make the journey all the way to Africa or investigate the records of trade statistics put out by the company rather than rely on Leopold's excellent PR machine and hospitality in Brussels; Presbyterian missionaries shocked by the piles of corpses and severed limbs they found in the jungle; the members of London's Aborigine Protection Society, so heroically ahead of their times. Outrage began to spread in the new century: in 1903 the British government dispatched their consul in the Congo, Roger Casement, to report on the situation. Casement, a notorious figure who would be martyred in 1916 as much for his homosexuality as his Irish nationalism, had spent twenty years in Africa and was no stranger to white brutality there, but the state of the 'poor unhappy souls' he met in the country's interior drove him to a fury. The 'infamous, infamous, shameful system', he wrote, was 'hopelessly and entirely wrong . . . Instead of lifting up the native populations submitted to and suffering from it, it can, if persisted in, lead only to their final extinction and the universal condemnation of civilized mankind.'

Casement's vocal condemnation and the tireless work of campaigner Edmund Morel turned the Congo Free State into an international scandal. Eventually even Leopold realized he would have to do something. In 1908 he agreed to hand control of his personal fiefdom over to the Belgian government, though he made them pay dearly for it: the territory no one in Belgium had wanted or benefited from except the King ended up costing them more than 200 million francs. One year later he was dead, and the new king, his nephew Albert I, was left to sort out the vast and bloody mess he had left behind in Africa.

Albert was as different a man from Leopold as it was possible to find. Charming and likeable, he possessed two things that are fairly rare in the heads of royal houses: a happy marriage and a genuine desire to understand how ordinary people lived their lives. As a young man he had travelled around Europe incognito, posing as a common tourist in order to get closer to the real life that he knew would be kept at a distance on state visits. Unlike his uncle, who ordered his atrocities from afar, he had travelled to the Congo himself and met people whose hands had been cut off as punishment for refusing to work on the rubber plantations. He came back firmly opposed to forced labour, promising his full support to the government and the new Belgian Colonial Ministry that had been set up to ensure human rights within his country's territory.

First, however, they needed investment. Leopold had bequeathed the Congo's debts to Belgium but carefully squirrelled away all its profits and bequeathed them to his favourite teenage whore, whom he had married on his deathbed. The country was badly in need of a millionaire, but the continued press and public focus on the country now to be called the Belgian Congo meant that it had to be a millionaire with a conscience. King Albert's thoughts turned to an extraordinary village he had visited during his anonymous tour of Britain in 1903: the wide boulevards he had walked down, the light and airy factory he had toured, and the stories he had been told about the benevolent boss who had built this place for his workers.

Dr Max Horn arrived in Port Sunlight towards the end of 1909, bringing with him the cordial greetings of the Belgian Colonial Minister Jules Renkin and a bulging dossier of facts and figures which he hoped would persuade William Lever to take an interest in the 'vast and almost unexploited palm forest of the Upper Congo'. The various concessions that Leopold had granted had concentrated on the rubber and ivory trades: in terms of oil-palms, Lever Brothers were being offered fresh and virgin territory of nearly 2 million acres. The strict conditions which were attached to any deal – investors had to agree to build hospitals and schools for their workers and pay a minimum wage of 25 centimes (two shillings) a day to every black employee – would have discouraged most businessmen, but they were music to Lever's ears.

Besides, he was by now tiring of his ventures in the Solomons. The yield was way below expectations and his own country's colonial administration were flatly refusing to give him the support he requested. Now here was the Belgian Colonial Office so keen to work with him that they were prepared to send one of their top men over on spec. What better way could there be to demonstrate his pique than to simply take his money elsewhere?

He had his doubts about Horn's offer, however. The five areas that Horn pointed out on the map he spread on his writing desk were widespread and deep in the interior of the country. Leopold's railway stretched only 240 miles into the country, much of it supported by metal bridges over the uneven land. With a gauge of just two-and-a-half feet, it was unsuitable for carrying any kind of heavy freight. Otherwise, the only transport was by the river itself and its many tributaries. He was also concerned that he might face the exact same problems that bedevilled his Solomons enterprise. He devoured books on the tropics and remembered well Stanley's opinions of the Congolese as idle and lazy in his book *The Congo and the Founding of its Free State*.

Nevertheless, he agreed to send a party of surveyors out to Africa to see the territories for themselves. It would be a difficult and arduous task, and he picked two men who were quite spectacularly unsuited for it: L. H. Moseley, who had experience with the Bank of West Africa in Nigeria (but mostly at its headquarters in Liverpool), and the engineer Henry Beckwith. They arrived ill-equipped, not unlike the typical white visitor that Stanley had described three decades previously:

> He has heard that it is slightly warm on the Congo, but in Europe he smiled at this; thought he could well endure that heat, since Europe in summer was 'ever so much hotter'. Still, after the ship drops anchor, an uncomfortable quantity of perspiration exudes through the pores of his skin, and the flannels that were endurable at sea become almost intolerable. On stepping ashore this warmth increases; the flannels absorb the perspiration until they are wet and heavy, and cling uncomfortably to his body. The underclothes are full; the outward clothing has begun to be damp, and dark streaks along the seam of his coat show that they are actually wet, until in fact he represents a water-jug covered with wet flannel such as we string up in the tropics as a water-cooler.

The five sites that Horn and Renkin had picked out as most suitable for palm plantations lay hundreds of miles apart. Between them was endless jungle, much of it impenetrable, passable only by way of the great river that stretched through the land and gave it its name. 'Going up that river was like travelling back to the earliest beginnings of the world, when vegetation rioted on the earth and the big trees were kings,' wrote Conrad in his own fictionalized account of the same journey. 'The broadening waters flowed through a mob of wooded islands; you lost your way on that river as you would in a desert, and butted all day long against shoals, trying to find the channel, till you thought yourself bewitched and cut off forever from everything you had known once – somewhere – far away – in another existence perhaps ... this strange world of plants, and water, and silence.'

Bitten by insects and highly alarmed by the stories of cannibalism and terror that their steamer's crew spun to pass the time, Moseley and Beckwith agreed that their survey need not be as extensive as they had originally planned: they were sure they could get a good idea of the place by walking just a few miles around the five sites that the Belgians had proposed. In the end they made it to three, and barely explored those. 'It was on this evidence, and some unreliable information given by the government officials and the agents of trading concerns that the position of the circles to be granted was fixed,' writes David Fieldhouse in *Unilever Overseas*. 'Nevertheless, Moseley and Beckwith wrote a generally favourable report, recommending acceptance. Their main reservations were that social conditions were bad; that Africans, particularly in the Lusanga region [the largest site] appeared to have been alienated by the harsh treatment they had received during the previous twenty years; and that Belgian officials and private firms were likely to be obstructive because they feared foreign intrusion.'

Less enthusiastic was Albert Thys, a Belgian business-man who had been invoved in the Congo since 1886, whom Lever wrote to privately for advice. 'My dear sir, form a company to exploit the wild oil palms in the Upper Congo?' replied the incredulous Thys. 'Hopeless, there aren't any palms there worth mentioning, and I know my Congo.'

Most of the European businessmen in Africa appear to have agreed with him. 'The West African business world as a whole was sceptical, and looked on the venture more as a philanthropic undertaking than as a sound commercial proposition,' wrote Hulme Lever in his account of his father's life, 'but, undaunted by these doubting Thomases, amongst whom were some of the most experienced men in the African trade, Lever remained convinced that the undertaking would in the end be successful.' In 1910 he instructed Max Horn to begin drawing up the paperwork. La Société Anonyme des Huilières du Congo Belge, a company jointly owned by Lever Brothers and the Belgian government, came into being in April 1911, with a starting capital of 25,000,000 Belgian francs – around a million pounds. To justify such a massive investment, each of the mills that were to be built to serve the five plantations would have to process no less than 6,000 tons of fruit per annum.

'If we fail, the "wiseheads" will wag their beards gravely – "they always said so" – and if we succeed, the same "wiseheads" will attempt to rush in through the gap in the wall we have made,' wrote Lever to Horn. 'The inrush of a herd of wild elephants would be trifling to the inrush there will be to the Congo if we prove a success.'

The truth was that Lever would simply not allow the venture to fail. Having watched from afar as his Solomons enterprise petered away to nothing, he was determined to give all his personal attention to ensuring that the Congo plantations succeeded. Thirty years earlier he had proved that sheer force of personality alone was enough to turn a business idea into a worldwide phenomenon. Now, at the age of sixty, he was determined to do the same again.

'Not a palm area was selected nor a sight chosen, except on his authority,' recalled his son, by now firmly installed within the business himself. 'Not a building was erected unless the plans had been passed by him, and very often these plans were largely his own. Not a piece of plant or machinery, nor a craft on the river, from the largest stern-wheeler to the smallest launch or barge, was ordered until he had carefully examined and passed the specifications. It is no exaggeration to say that the organization which came into being, from the shipping base at the port of Matadi and the administrative headquarters at Kinshasa to the farthest area of Elizabetha, over a thousand miles from the Congo mouth, was his personal creation.'

Lever pored over the reports from the ground with almost boyish enthusiasm. A description of one of the sites, near Lusanga, was printed in full in the company's in-house magazine: 'The appearance is park-like – bright, grassy, spaces on undulating hills, with clumps of palm and wood . . . it rises in a slight slope from the river toward the interior, and is covered with magnificent palm trees, laden with fruit . . . a beautiful corner of nature.' Having already read every book he could find about Central Africa, Lever invited explorers with first-hand experience of the region to Port Sunlight to lecture the villagers. After a 'new cinematograph film to a piano accompaniment by Mr Easley', the African veteran E. Thoday informed his astonished audience that 'the Northern Bambala, though addicted to cannibalism, were, on the whole, rather nice people', and concluded with a stern warning to Lever, who sat enthralled in the front row. 'While new industries would be a blessing to the natives, new wants, imported from Europe, would be a curse. Strict regard must be paid to local conditions, and no attempt be made to impose on the natives a mode of life utterly unsuited to the genius of their race.' In reply, Lever demonstrated an empathy that had been horribly absent in the generation that preceded him: 'the Congo natives,' he assured Thoday, 'although regarded as savages, nevertheless possessed the fundamental attributes of humanity – love of home, children and so forth – and the methods which brought out the best that is in ourselves were equally applicable to the dark-skinned people.' It was sentiments like this, so loudly and publicly expressed, that ensured the support of such vocal opponents of Leopold's atrocities as Emile Vandervelde, the leader of the Belgian opposition. He told Parliament that 'had the suggested concessions been offered to any other firm, he would have opposed them, but he was aware of the conditions which existed at Port Sunlight', and so gave Lever his whole-hearted support.

Out in the jungle, things moved with breathtaking speed. The first machinery was dispatched from Ostend – it was a condition of the treaty that half the supplies and white staff must be Belgian – in August 1911. A few months later Huilières du Congo Belge's manager in Lusanga, Harold Greenhalgh, was passing enthusiastic reports back to Port Sunlight. 'We have cleared fifty acres and roads have been laid out. We are building our first mill and houses both for the natives and our European staff. It is an ideal spot for a town. On one side there is a small hill on which the Europeans can live in health, and we have deep water and a very fine navigable river right in front, and an ideal spot also for the native population. It is embedded in extensive areas of palm-trees stretching for miles upon miles.' In March 1912 the first consignment of palm oil arrived at the Lever Brothers factory near Brussels, and on 27 March Lever himself presented the first bar of Congo-created Sunlight to King Albert, not in its usual parchment and cardboard packet but an inlaid cabinet of ivory. He also announced the names he would give to his five new plantations: while the biggest, near Lusanga, would be named Leverville, the others would be Alberta, Elizabetha, Brabanta and

Flandria, in honour of the King, his wife and their children.

While this swift progress, and the positive reports he received from Greenhalgh, delighted Lever, he knew there was no substitute for seeing the plantations for himself. Smaller investments in Nigeria and Sierra Leone had faltered when he relied on the opinions and experience of others: this time he was determined to get in there himself. He made the first of two trips to the Congo in the winter of 1912–13. As ever, he was accompanied by Elizabeth, who could no more have stayed behind than he could have survived without her for four months. She was the first European woman to tour the Congo – under Leopold, it had been the ultimate boys' club, staffed by those fleeing their family responsibilities or, like Stanley, running scared from the female sex altogether. The presence of Elizabeth and her redoubtable maid Dulston, their elaborate dresses spotless and their parasols always at hand, must have been as disconcerting to the steamer crews, plantation managers and missionaries they encountered on their travels as it was intriguing to the Congolese, but the ladies took everything in their stride – including their brief adoption of 'a native girl of five years of age' who claimed to have been sold as a slave by her parents, and who travelled up the river with them as far as the Jesuit mission at Womballi. On their return, Elizabeth was rewarded with an honorary fellow-ship of the Royal Geographical Society, on the motion of Lord Curzon of Kedleston, her travelling companion from the *Australia* on her first world tour two decades previously.

They travelled in a large party which included Dr Horn, now on the board of the HCB, and Doctor William Prout, an expert in tropical medicine who doled out regular and enormous doses of quinine to his companions in order to combat the threat of malaria. In four months the party covered over 15,000 miles, half of them by river in a specially adapted steamer, the *Lusanga*, with which the Levers were delighted. 'Edkins has rigged up a special cabin for us in front of the saloon deck just under the captain's cabin,' wrote William in his diary. 'This saves my wife going up and down steps, and also gives us a larger and better arranged room. The saloon is large and airy, fitted with mosquito-wire gauze to windows and doors. I had a screen of the same wire gauze fitted all around the front of our cabin, so that we now have a veranda eight feet deep – cool and insect proof.'

Such domestic comforts seem to have banished the looming doom and gloom that Conrad perceived in every leaf along the banks of the river Congo. The 300-page diary that the sixty-one-year-old Lever kept during the journey contains not one jot of introspection, exuding instead the puppyish enthusiasm of a *Boy's Own* adventure. 'We were told we might perhaps see an elephant, but we saw nine elephants!' he recorded on 29 December. 'Mr Moseley had his gun and a few cartridges and wounded one, but it got away.' Two weeks previously he had been delighted by another encounter with the local wildlife. 'Shortly after six a.m. I heard a great shouting . . . we were passing close to a dead hippo floating on the water. The black crew were very excited, yelled and shouted, and no doubt were greatly disappointed that the captain would not stop the boat to secure this supply of food for them, to their idea just in the best condition for eating – blown up with the gases of decomposition. I understand that if the captain had stopped and the dead beast had been cut up and brought on board, no white man could have survived the smell.'

Even here, far beyond the limits of what most of his

contemporaries would call civilization, he managed to maintain his strict daily routine. 'We are now settling down to our life on board,' he reported on 11 December. 'Rise at five a.m, shave, cup of tea at 5.15, cold bath at 5.30, breakfast 6.30, lunch 12, afternoon tea 4, dinner 6.30, bed 9.' Only one thing discomfited the great washday revolutionary, though he recorded it with his tongue wedged firmly in his cheek. 'Our greatest hardship whilst "roughing it" on the Congo appears to be that there is no starch on board. What is life without starch? How can we maintain our self-respect amidst the more than half-naked cannibals we see when our linen fronts, collars and cuffs are limp and starchless!'

They enjoyed many of the other blessings of civilization, however. Lever took with him a new invention, Everready's tungsten-bulbed 'pocket electric torch', which he used to look in the houses of the villages where they moored along the way, concluding that 'no respectable dog would have fought for one of these huts as a kennel'. From the safety of the boat they used a larger electric searchlight to torment a tribal gathering they passed:

> As its rays reached each group round the fire, the natives bolted in terror into their huts. In the case of the Capita, or chief man, who was dressed in trousers, waistcoat and straw hat, he bolted first, and left his wives and children to jam themselves in the door trying to follow him . . . Edkins asked one what he thought of it, and he replied 'White Man Palaver Moon'. Anything about the white man – such as railway, steamboat, etc – that the native finds beyond his comprehension is very often called 'white man's palaver'.

It is difficult to decide what is more objectionable about that paragraph – the casual bullying, or the use of that singular 'the native' to describe the 200 or so separate and enormously diverse communities that inhabited the Congo area. But horseplay with a spotlight is in a different league to shooting holes in the inhabitants' ears or smearing their faces with excrement, favourite pastimes of station commanders under Leopold. Ten days later, when he reached Elizabetha, Lever was impressed to find that 'the reputation of "the ship that carried the moon" had travelled 200 miles into the interior in a few days', and his account of negotiations with those he hoped to persuade to work for him shows that he recognized and respected the intelligence of the Africans in a way that was far from common:

> The Commissaire told the Chief that I was a great Chief from the White Man's country, that I wanted his village clean and sanitary, and that I was willing to help to build him a village on the new site . . . and that, in addition, I would give presents to himself and his headman . . . The Chief asked for time for himself and his head-men to talk it over, which was, of course, accorded. I watched closely the faces of both men and women, and they were set in a critical, non-committal, intelligent way, which showed they knew well all that was said and had no intention of giving themselves away by too hasty grunts or nods of approval. At night we received word that they had assented.

I am making no attempt to rehabilitate colonialism: the system that existed in the Congo was exploitative and Lever, like all his staff, was, by today's standards, deeply racist. But by the standards of the day he was exemplary. He made good on all his promises: ten hospitals, two schools (with teaching in the native languages as well as one of the almost equally diverse languages of Belgium), and a generous wage for every one of his 17,000 employees. Best of all, just six years after New York's Bronx Zoo had exhibited a member of an Ituri tribe of pygmies from the Congo in the same cage in their monkey house as an orangutan from Sumatra, Lever was doing his best to understand his employees as human beings capable of making perfectly valid lifestyle choices.

> The native has few wants: a little salt and a little cloth are his indispensables; after this, beads, brass rods and other luxuries. Chief Womba, at Leverville, can be taken as an example. Twelve months ago he and his people were poor and few in number, and were keen to bring fruit. After twelve months or less of selling fruit, he is rich and lazy, has ten wives, and his village is about four times the size it was; but he gathers little or no fruit. The palm-tree is in these parts the banking account of the native, and he no more thinks of going to his bank for money when his wants and ambitions are supplied than a civilised man would.

The Belgian authorities were rather less indulgent of this cashless economy: they imposed new taxes on their subjects in order to force them to accept paid employment with the company. The taxes worked on a sliding-scale: the more wives a man had, the more he paid. Since the tribal chiefs had the most wives, they owed the most, and it was they who had the power to sign employment contracts on behalf of their entire communities. Many tried to get round this by sending their slaves to the plantations and taking the wages for themselves, a practice which Harold Greenhalgh was disgusted to discover in 1915 and did his best to stamp out.

In this, as in everything, he received the full backing of Lever, who continued throughout his life to take a close, almost obsessive interest in the African business. 'It was his readiness to investigate and decide even minute problems that took Huilières du Congo Belge past the early disasters which wrecked so many contemporary African ventures', according to David Fieldhouse in his study of the business, *Unilever Overseas*. It was Lever who drew up the plans for the station managers' homes on each of the five plantations; it was Lever who laid out the street plan for the new, brick-built villages, who recruited nuns to run a child welfare service to reduce the rate of infant mortality and even designed a special crêpe-rubber boot to protect the feet of his workers as they shinned up the palm trees to harvest their fruit. And it was Lever who in 1924 was followed from village to village by a great crowd of children, 'yelling and shouting, jumping and clapping their hands, and I am told the words were *Mukende Munene, Na m'Bila*, "the Big Chief of the Palm Tree Company"'.

Lever could not have been happier than he was travelling the Congo with Elizabeth by his side. Even as they sailed from Africa on the SS *Leopoldville* in February 1913, he was planning their return. 'My only regret is that I did not make the journey twelve months earlier. If I have another regret it is that I am not yet certain I can come again this year. I ought to come out again in November. It is the most important service I can render to the business, and, if at all possible, I intend to come. We have much to do, and we may have many more difficulties than we can foresee today, but we hold winning cards if we play them rightly.'

It felt, he told Elizabeth, as if he had been given a new lease of life. The future, it seemed, had never looked more rosy.

17

ASHES TO ASHES

THE PRIME MINISTER ARRIVED IN PORT SUNLIGHT ON THE morning of 20 July 1912. He was in desperate need of a holiday: the last twelve months had seen the greatest constitutional upheaval the country had ever faced as the House of Commons went into open battle with the House of Lords, a diplomatic face-off with Germany over the Moroccan port of Agadir, a miners' strike, riots on the streets of most British cities and increasingly aggressive demands by Irish protestants for a separate state in the north of the country. Nevertheless, he remained grateful to William Lever for his support in the last parliament and felt he owed him an official visit. Lever had already been rewarded with the title of Baronet in George V's Coronation honours list the year before – he was now Sir William, though he instructed the Sunlighters that they should continue to refer to him just as they always had done. Now, however, Asquith wanted to make a more personal gesture. As well as giving the works and village at Port Sunlight a very public endorsement, he would also visit Thornton Hough and meet some of the villagers Lever had helped out of his own private pocket.

He was fulsome in his praise. 'Here you live, side by side, having a common interest, common spirit, pursuing common ends, and feeling, those of you who are workers, that you are not creating wealth which your labour helps to produce for the selfish enjoyment of others, but that you are participators in the fruits of what is earned,' he told the crowd which assembled beneath the bunting at Port Sunlight to cheer him on. 'It is a splendid monument, it is a noble example, and I venture to congratulate you, one and all, from Sir William Lever down to the humblest of those who are co-operating with him, on the enormous contribution which you have made towards the solution of one of the most serious and formidable of our social questions.'

Unfortunately, his carefully stage-managed stroll round the gardens at Thornton Manor was less successful. We will let Sir William's son, who was present and correct in his Sunday best, tell the story:

> Two militant looking women had managed to effect an entrance, and were seen advancing from the farther end of one of the garden walks. An elderly lady, standing not far from the Prime Minister, stepped forward with an open umbrella to protect him, at the same time exclaiming, 'how dare you do this to the Premier of all England!'

The women, and tens of thousands like them around the country, were enraged by Asquith's failure to keep his promise to introduce legislation that would give votes to women. He had already bottled out of supporting a Labour motion on the matter in 1910: that decision had led to riots on Downing Street by what *The Times* called 'demented creatures ... some of them quite young girls, who must have been the victims of hysterical rather than deep conviction'. When the 1912 session came and went without an Enfranchisement Bill, events took a nastier turn. Christabel Pankhurst, who broke away from the Women's Social and Political Union founded by her mother that year in favour of a more violent campaign, described her followers' methods in her book *Unshackled*:

> Many militants had been restive for some time, considering that it would be more dignified to anticipate the sorry outcome of the Government's now broken pledge than await it passively. As leaders, we had felt bound to restrain this eagerness, but now there was no reason for delay. The ingenuity and the pertinacity of the Suffragette guerillists were extraordinary. Never a soul was hurt, but the struggle continued.
>
> Golf greens suffered on one occasion by the carving on the turf of 'Votes Before Sport' and 'No Votes, No Golf'! The editor of Golfing complained on the plea that 'golfers are not usually very keen politicians.' 'Perhaps they will be now,' said the Suffragettes.
>
> The damage done to property was more spectacular than serious. Museums began to be closed, here and there, with preventive caution, to the vexation of American visitors. Mr Lloyd George's house at Walton Heath paid the price of its owner's deed.

What actually happened was that a holiday home which was being constructed for the Chancellor was blown up by a home-made bomb just a few minutes before a crew of builders arrived for the day, part of a nationwide arson campaign targeted at empty properties. Bricks were thrown through the windows of Downing Street. Most famously, Emily Davison threw herself beneath the hooves of the King's horse on Derby Day in 1913, dying a martyr to the suffragette cause four days later. Protests were becoming more and more spectacular.

Lever abhorred such violence, but he was a long-time supporter of the women's cause. He had been hosting meetings in favour of female suffrage at Hulme Hall as far back as 1903, the very year that the Pankhursts formed their Union, and he had continued to speak out in favour of women having a political voice throughout his various electoral campaigns. He extended both the pensions and co-partnership schemes to women from the outset, for he believed that 'when ladies do their work as faithfully as the Port Sunlight girls do, I don't see why they should be left out'. 'The old idea of woman has got to go,' he told an audience of schoolchildren in 1916. 'Woman has to be the companion and helpmeet of man, as was originally intended, and it can only be done if she receives an equal education in every way and an equal equipment with man.'

It wasn't enough to save him.

On 7 July 1913, not long after their return from the Congo, Sir William and Lady Elizabeth were invited to dine with the King and Queen. They were making a royal tour of industrial Lancashire, which, naturally, involved them meeting with a lot of very rich businessmen and aristocrats rather than the people who worked in their factories. That evening the Levers were part of a group invited to dine with the royal party at Knowsley Hall, seat of the Earl and Countess of Derby. It lay on the other side of the Mersey, and they set off from Thornton Manor by car early that afternoon.

At the same time another car was making its way southwards from Preston and beginning the steep climb up on to the moors. At Chorley it branched off up one of the macadam roads that Lever had built when he first took over the Rivington estate. It stopped outside one of the great barns at the very foot of the Pike, and its occupants went inside to order tea. Edith Rigby looked like any other day-tripper who had decided to take advantage of the good weather and go for a stroll around Lever Park with her husband. The staff noticed that she seemed unusually interested in whether Sir William was in residence up at the Bungalow that night, but that was not so unusual; he was a famous man. Her further questions – did the staff sleep in? Did he employ a night watchman? – were dismissed as the normal curiosity of a tourist. Perhaps she too owned a remote property, or hoped to one day – she certainly wasn't short of a bob or two, judging by the uniformed chauffeur who remained outside in the car. Because of his presence, none of the staff got close enough to notice the odd smell of paraffin that hung around the vehicle.

The car continued up the hill as evening began to fall. A few hundred yards short of the Bungalow grounds, it stopped, and Mrs Rigby and her companion got out and continued by foot. The man was not her husband, a respectable doctor with a practice in Preston's Winckley Square. He was Albert Yeadon, a strapping man who had been recruited to carry the containers of paraffin which filled the car's boot. Rigby herself carried a small cardboard suitcase.

Yeadon helped Mrs Rigby to climb over the railings around the Bungalow's gardens, but not without injury: she slipped and cut her hand on one of the iron spikes, staining her grey suede glove with blood. She did not cry out. They were barely more than 100 yards from one of the gardeners' cottages: to make a sound would be fatal to her plan. She waved away Yeadon's concern and indicated to him that he should pass the paraffin containers over the fence one by one; that done, she whispered to him that he should return to the car. Settling down beneath the canopy of a rhodo-dendron bush, well out of sight, she waited for night to fall.

Rigby was nothing if not thorough. It took her hours to lug the paraffin containers up to the Bungalow one by one, and longer to inspect the entire property to ensure that no one was inside. She peered through the windows at the antique furniture, the tapestries and paintings, some of them dating back to medieval times, and she planned the best points to pour in the fuel and burn the whole place down. Around midnight she lit fires at four places, using a rolled-up copy of the *Suffragette* newspaper as a taper; subtlety was not her strong point. She waited until the wooden building was well aflame, and then walked back down the hill, panicked birds swooping out of the nearby pigeon tower and flapping about in the smoke above her head. She tied the suitcase to the railings after checking its contents: a message she had tapped out on her husband's surgery typewriter the day before:

LANCASHIRE'S MESSAGE TO THE KING FROM THE WOMEN:
VOTES FOR WOMEN DUE

Message to the King, Liverpool: Wake up the Government.
First give us reason to be loyal, and then try us.

As an afterthought, she tossed in her bloodstained glove as well.

The alarm was raised by the watchman for Liverpool's reservoirs, who saw flames licking the horizon at half-past one. He ran to the office of the residential engineer, one Mr Adamson, and raised him from his bed. As Adamson dressed, both men heard Mrs Rigby's car pass along the road outside. Neither of them made it to the door before it had gone around a corner and out of sight. Rather than give chase, the men headed up the hill. They told the *Bolton Journal* what they found at the top:

> The bungalow burning fiercely in three or four places on all sides of the building. It was then very evident, said Mr Adamson, that the fire had been started at each of these points, and that each had taken hold securely. When Mr Adamson arrived the whole residential part was evidently doomed, for very soon afterwards it was one huge mass of flames. Mr Jonathan Simpson, who was architect for the whole series of buildings, told our representative that the residential part was chiefly a timbered structure, and that the flames and the heat must have been intense. Some idea of the terrific nature of the heat may be gathered from a view of the huge iron beams which were constructed in the building. These are twisted and bent into all sorts of grotesque shapes. One huge iron girder which had spanned the residential part had bent almost double. Indeed, the interior of the place whilst the fire was raging must have been very much like a huge furnace.

The height at which the Bungalow was built was its downfall. The wind that blew in unimpeded from the Irish Sea turned it into a towering inferno, while the Horwich and Chorley fire brigades, both of whom Adamson telephoned, squabbled over whose patch the top of the mountain was in. In the end only one fireman – Chief Officer Semple of Horwich – would attend, unofficially, and without the equipment that was needed to fight such a huge fire. 'A length of hose was brought into service, and one jet of water was got into play upon the flames,' reported the *Journal*. 'This was entirely insufficient to extinguish the fire, but was made excellent use of to save the garth and outbuildings. These outbuildings are largely constructed of stone.'

The Levers did not arrive back from their royal dinner-date until the early hours of Tuesday morning, and had barely gone to sleep when they were roused by the telephone at Thornton. It was 4 a.m. James Lawrence, a Rivington resident and local councillor, told them that their home had been entirely destroyed.

Jonathan Simpson arrived at Rivington as dawn broke. It was a scene of utter devastation.

All that are left behind are bent and twisted fire grates, radiators, and a huge cistern which had crashed down from its supports. The place had been completely razed, walls, and interior, to its very foundations ... Beautiful old furniture, exceedingly valuable tapestry, needlework and pictures which had been objects of so much admiration by visitors to the cottage have been totally destroyed. Of the tapestry nothing remains but pieces of wire netting. The lovely veranda which had overlooked the gardens, is no more. Charred timber is lying about in the shrubbery, and lead has flown all over the place on to the surrounding stonework. The peaceful scene in the garth, where pigeons fluttered unconcernedly about and around the lawn and gardens, was in striking contrast to that on the site of the former cottage, adjoining though they be.

Back at Thornton Manor, a shell-shocked Lever received two telegrams from his dining companions the night before. Lord Derby's upper lip was so stiff you could have cracked eggs on it:

Please accept sincere sympathy with you at the loss you have sustained by the burning of your house. A most deplorable thing to have happened.

The King, who had enjoyed his conversation with Lever far

more than the usual platitudes he had to rattle out on such occasions, was more compassionate (or perhaps he could just afford more words).

> Much regret to hear from the newspapers that while you were here (Knowsley) last night your house at Rivington and its contents were destroyed by fire. I sympathise with you in your loss. – George R.I.

Edith Rigby gave herself up to the police in Liverpool that Thursday. As well as the arson attack on the Bungalow she admitted putting a pipe bomb full of stones and pieces of iron in Liverpool Cotton Exchange the previous weekend: though it exploded at night when the building was empty, it did thousands of pounds' worth of damage. From the dock she made a personal appeal: 'I want to ask Sir William Lever whether he thinks his property on Rivington Pike is more valuable as one of his superfluous homes occasionally to be opened to people, or as a beacon lighted for King and Country, to see that here are some intolerable grievances for women.' Later that year she would join the hundreds of other women jailed across Britain for 'suffragist outrages', many of them continuing their campaign in prison through hunger strikes, but by then Lever had already given his emphatic answer. Within a few months a new, bigger, better bungalow was taking shape on the site of the old one: 'This time I shall build something they cannot burn,' declared Lever, and Jonathan Simpson constructed the new, luxurious Bungalow entirely of stone, and roofed it with reinforced concrete. It took the form of two interlocked L's, stamping the presence of Lever definitively upon the landscape, proof against fire, flood, storm or any of the vicissitudes life might throw at him. It sent a defiant message out to the world: he was unstoppable.

She lived long enough to become a grandmother. That was one of the few things that William had to console himself with in the dark days after the funeral. A month after they had got back from the Congo, Hulme's wife Marion had given birth to a beautiful baby girl. They named her Elizabeth after her grandmother. And now that grandmother was dead.

The worst of it was that he had been away. He had long been due to visit the associated companies on the Continent that July, to tour his factories in Switzerland, Germany and France. She should have come with him. She would have come with him – she always came with him, she accompanied him everywhere – but she had been feeling under the weather for a few days: a slight cold, nothing more, probably just the shock from the fire a fortnight before, but she didn't feel up to the travelling. So he kissed her goodbye at Thornton Manor on the 19th and drove off to the station, and she soldiered through the rest of the day and went to bed as usual that night in the open-air bedroom, the room where she had woken up so many times next to her husband soaked to the skin or covered with an extra blanket of snow. This time it was a fine summer night, but she missed the usual warmth of her husband's body beside her. The next night they moved her inside and wrapped her up warm, but it was too late. By the time the doctor arrived on the morning of the 21st there was little he could do but agree with the housekeeper's diagnosis: it was pneumonia.

Elizabeth Lever died on 24 July 1913. William had sped back from Europe as soon as he received Hulme's telegram: he got to Thornton just in time to say goodbye. 'He found my mother sufficiently conscious to know that he was present, but her strength was too far spent for recovery to be possible,' recalled Hulme. 'She passed away only a few hours after his return.'

They had said they were unable to remember a world without each other in it. Now William had to face spending the rest of his life alone. 'During the whole of our married life of 40 years, however early business called me, I never breakfasted alone; she was always up and saw that the breakfast was properly prepared, and I always knew that whatever might happen in the course of the day the great event for her would be my homecoming in the evening.' Now all that remained to wake him was the electric buzzer that his night-watchman sounded each morning. He would rise from a cold, empty bed and breakfast alone, and all he had to look forward to was another evening spent among the antiques and works of art that cluttered up every one of his three homes.

'Without the gracious influence of my wife I doubt whether there would have been a Port Sunlight; I doubt whether there would have been a firm of the dimensions of Lever Brothers,' he told the crowd who gathered for the opening of the gallery he named in her memory, which housed those very antiques, a decade later. 'She was essentially a womanly woman, and her knowledge of business was nil. But a wife need not be an inspired genius in guiding and directing her husband – genius might be a handicap and not a help – but she can be an inspiration and a source of confidence.'

Now that inspiration and confidence had abandoned him. And his troubles were only just beginning.

18

MAKING A KILLING

EBENEZER HOWARD WAS JUSTIFIED IN FEELING PROUD AT
the first congress of his International Garden Cities and
Town Planning Association at Port Sunlight in July 1914.
The 'marriage of town and country' he had detailed in his
book all those years ago was proving to be a happy one:
his own Letchworth, now more than a decade old, was
thriving, and a gradual greening was taking place throughout Europe, from Henrietta Barnett's 'beautiful green
and golden scheme', Hampstead Garden Suburb, to
Margarethenhöhe, the steelworkers' village near Essen in
Germany. Even the new capital of the world's youngest
country, Australia, was to be a garden city: the architects
Walter and Marion Griffin were designing Canberra with
homes for 75,000 citizens centred not on the grey political
or industrial districts but instead on a vast ornamental lake.
It was his vision writ large, carrying the world into the new
century: 'town and country married, and out of this joyous
union will spring a new hope, a new life, a new civilisation'.
But the congress was far from the only international

talking-point in the summer of 1914. Two weeks earlier, Archduke Franz Ferdinand of Austria-Hungary had fallen to an assassin's bullet in Sarajevo. His death would be far more significant than anything he had achieved in life. As the delegates at Port Sunlight discussed the finer points of sanitation and population density, the diplomats and warlords of Europe were manoeuvring themselves into position for conflict. Some of the 150 representatives of more than a dozen countries who gathered at the Auditorium that day had already played a part in the rush towards war: for all their benevolence, the Krupp family had built Margarethenhöhe on warships and guns – their steel empire, born in the railway boom of the last century, had been revitalized and expanded courtesy of the Kaiser's lust for military might. Others would have vital parts to play in the coming conflict, including William Lever. The production lines that his guests toured that sunny afternoon would soon be churning out not soap but munitions, and many of the boys who manned them would soon lie cold in the mud of the Western Front.

War was declared on Germany on 4 August. That same day the Kaiser's troops had flooded into Belgium, seizing control of Albert's kingdom and, with it, the Lever Brothers' business in Brussels and the Huilières du Congo Belge. As news spread of the approach of the German troops, A. L. Webster, Lever's enterprising works manager in Brussels, took matters into his own hands. Every day vast amounts of glycerine were drained from the boiling pans in his factory, to be refined and used to make emollients and laxatives. But glycerine could also be used as an ingredient for explosives, and he was not prepared to let such a source of weaponry fall into the invaders' hands to be used against his own people. Methodically he toured the factory dismantling and sabotaging every piece of machinery; when he was sure that the soaperies were beyond use, and with the Germans almost at the door, he melted away into the suburbs of Brussels, leaving his identity behind. But Webster's work was not over: a couple of weeks later the German soldiers who had been stationed to guard the factory and attempt to get it working were surprised to find a bearded Frenchman by the name of René Oriens at the gates, offering his services. He was an experienced soap-maker, he told the guards, and he had heard that they were having trouble restoring the plant: could he be of help?

Webster's craftiness was only outshone by his bravery: he remained at the Brussels factory in the guise of René Oriens for most of the war, supervising the reconstruction of the machinery and consistently finding new faults and problems which, he sadly reported to his German bosses, meant that no glycerine could be produced. Fluent in four languages, he kept up his pretence brilliantly: no one suspected that the conscientious Frenchman's efforts at repairing the machinery were exactly what ensured it stayed broken. What little glycerine could be produced was of poor quality; the army requisitioners soon gave up and looked elsewhere to supply the ravenous guns of the Western Front.

Back in Britain, the pointing finger of Earl Kitchener was appearing on every public wall:

Your King and Country Need YOU.
A CALL TO ARMS
An addition of 100,000 men to his Majesty's
Regular Army is immediately necessary in the
present grave National Emergency
God Save The King!

The war minister desperately needed to create a new army to take on the Kaiser's 4 million troops: unlike Field Marshal Sir John French, the leader of the British Expeditionary Force which had immediately headed across the Channel, he had little confidence that the war would be over by Christmas. In the event, 300,000 men heeded his call before the month was out. Many of them had little choice but to seek a new living in the army – half a million men were made redundant in August 1914, jettisoned by businesses terrified of the effect that conflict would have on their bottom line. It was not so at Lever Brothers. William Lever guaranteed not only to keep the job open of any man who signed up to fight for his country, but to pay the difference between his army wage and his usual salary directly to his wife back at home. To lead the way, he even joined up himself as a private in the local volunteer training corps: at the age of sixty-three he donned the grey-green Norfolk jacket that formed the corps uniform to march alongside men half his age, sworn to defend the Wirral from the Hun.

Seven hundred Sunlighters signed up in August 1914, filing through the Gladstone Hall which had been cleared and turned into a temporary recruiting office, staffed by clerks on secondment from the General Offices down the road. There were enough of them to form an infantry unit in their own right. The army gave them the title of the 13th Service Battalion of the Cheshire Regiment, but to everyone at home they were simply the Port Sunlight Pals.

Lever himself marched the Pals through the streets of Chester on 13 September and handed them over to the command of General Sir Henry Mackinnon. 'We are much indebted to Sir William Lever and his colleagues for the splendid example they have set to all employers of labour,' the soldier told the cheering crowds, 'and when I see this fine body of young men, I have no fear whatever as to the result of this war.' He was optimistic. The Pals were a ramshackle lot, with no uniforms or weapons: they marched with their overcoats slung over their shoulders, some with caps and some without, each man trying to keep in step with the beat of the Port Sunlight boys' brigade band who led the parade. The War Office was so short of supplies that they gratefully accepted Lever's offer to provide 'his' battalion with food and drink during their training. With uniforms they were less lucky: khaki dye had traditionally been imported from Germany, so the bulk of the new recruits wore 'Kitchener Blue' outfits that had been hastily assembled in specially commandeered textile factories. The 13th Battalion had to make do with a set of red jackets left over by the household cavalry, enough for about half of them, which they wore over their own scruffy civilian shirts and trousers to perform their training manoeuvres at Salisbury and Aldershot. They practised the daily cleaning and cocking and firing and naming of parts with broom handles, for they did not receive service rifles until August the following year. Nevertheless, spirits were high when the battalion was presented to Field Marshal Earl Kitchener for inspection on 12 August 1915. They finally got their chance to fight for their country the following month, when they were shipped to Dieppe as part of the 25th Division, proudly wearing the regimental symbol, a red horseshoe, on their spotless uniforms.

The Port Sunlight Pals were slaughtered in the endless battle of the Somme, which claimed the lives of more than a million people, dragged on for months and achieved precisely nothing. Twenty thousand men were killed in the first half-hour of fighting alone. The tattered survivors of the battalion were left holed up in the Ypres salient, bombarded from three sides by the enemy, hemmed in by mud, barbed wire and the constant stench of death. Many were torn to pieces by machine-gun fire, others were simply sucked in and drowned by the festering, bomb-churned quicksand of the battlefield. Forty-eight thousand men of the 25th Division died, one of the heaviest losses in any part of the army. By the beginning of 1918 the 13th Battalion was so decimated that army commanders decided to disband it, and split the few remaining Pals between other brigades.

The effects of war were not limited to the battlefield. The improving collection of art and antiquities that Lever had installed in Hulme Hall was carefully packaged up and put into storage in October 1914 to make room for Port Sunlight's newest residents, 111 Belgian refugees who had fled before the German invasion, taking only what they could carry. Thornton Manor was turned into a Red Cross hospital under the command of Marion Lever, Hulme's capable young wife. The Hill, Lever's London mansion on Hampstead Heath, was also given over to the use of the Imperial nursing service, housing hundreds of servicemen who had been lucky enough to suffer a 'Blighty wound' that would take them away from the hell of the Western Front. Lever also offered his brand-new concrete home at the peak of Rivington Pike for use as a hospital, but the offer was gratefully declined – the building was just too remote, the weather conditions too unpredictable for the shell-shocked casualties to cope with.

In 1915 part of the works at Port Sunlight was turned over to munitions manufacture, producing on average 320 shells a week. Scientists in the Lever Brothers laboratories also put aside their research into scourers and detergents to concentrate on chemical weapons. One of the most effective gases used in the trenches prior to the introduction of mustard gas in 1917 was known as 'PS' after the peaceful village where it was created. Port Sunlight even housed soldiers on active duty in 1916 when the 2nd Battalion of the Cheshires were billeted in the Auditorium, evicting the volunteer training corps who had just been put on high alert to defend the village from enemy Zeppelin attacks.

Lever himself did not take part in the defences. Despite his show of marching alongside the other volunteers in 1914, he had reluctantly had to accept that in his sixties he was no real use to them. Apart from anything else, he had become profoundly deaf. The massive doses of quinine that had been prescribed to him by Dr Prout in the Congo had kept him safe from malaria, but they had destroyed what remained of his already fragile hearing. While he experimented with every kind of primitive hearing-aid then available, he found it almost impossible to follow conversations in noisy rooms, or to comprehend anything that was not spoken clearly and directly to him. Increasingly he was cut off from what was going on around him, and inevitably he became more self-centred. Issuing orders and having them accepted without question had always been a habit. Now it was a necessity.

None of this stopped him from doing his bit for his country, however. Private Lever left the volunteer corps, but Captain Lever – Hulme – remained, and, as he put it, his father found 'forms of service more suited to his experience, abilities, and age'. The first of these was in Whitehall, as a member of the Central Board of Military and Civilian Members to Control Contract Prices and Administration Generally, a title which even Kitchener had to concede was less than snappy – it was later renamed the Navy and Army Canteen Committee.

His particular speciality – sourcing the raw materials for soap-making – had become a national priority, for the guns of the Western Front were devouring shells at a rate of 10,000 per mile per hour of bombardment, and a constant supply of glycerine was desperately needed. Lever was co-opted on to the standing advisory committee to the Controller of Oils and Fats in the Ministry of Munitions headed by Lloyd George, and the government requisitioned at cost price every ounce of glycerine that his factories could produce. 'We should proceed imagining that the sale of soap is a secondary consideration, the production of glycerine being the main consideration,' Lever instructed his staff, but the new by-product hardly went to waste. In a neat quid pro quo which was no doubt eased by Lever's influence in Whitehall, the government agreed that Sunlight should be the brand which was supplied to every soldier in the British army, one of several deals which ensured that Lever Brothers could boast during the war years of 'the highest output in our whole history'.

One negotiation which was less successful was Lever's attempt to gain permission to continue exporting Sunlight into enemy territories. His novel argument – that the more soap their military opponents bought in from Great Britain, the less glycerine they would produce for munitions in their own factories – did not wash in Whitehall. 'It would make the Germans clean, but it would not make them better fighters,' Lever blithely assured officials, but his request was declined. Besides, if the newspapers were to be believed, the Germans had come up with their own in-genious and infernal methods of producing glycerine. In 1917 *The Times* dutifully reported a story cooked up by Sir

John Charteris, the head of British Military Intelligence, that the enemy had set up a gruesome 'corpse factory' in occupied Belgium for 'distilling glycerine from the bodies of the dead'. The tale added to a public hysteria already stoked by stories of babies being bayoneted and priests lashed to the bells of their own church towers and rung to death. Anti-German feeling was running so high that businesses with even vaguely Teutonic-sounding names had been looted, and dachshunds and German shepherd dogs attacked in the street. German connections were to be played down at all costs: even the royal family had sussed that Windsor was a wiser choice of surname than Saxe-Coburg-Gotha, while doctors across the country were forced to rebrand German measles as Belgian flu before anyone would admit to suffering from it. For Lever Brothers to be identified as trading with the enemy would have been commercial suicide. It is extraordinary that Lever should even have considered it.

The government did, however, open up a new area of trade for Lever Brothers. Attacks by German U-boats meant that imports of all kinds ended up at the bottom of the North Sea. The country's supply of margarine, which came almost entirely from the neutral countries of Denmark and Holland, was particularly threatened, while price increases and shortages at home meant that butter was beyond the reach of many. Lever Brothers had long been considering margarine production as an obvious sideline – it would be a more cost-effective use of the better-quality oils produced on their overseas plantations, and Port Sunlight already had its own oil refinery on site – so the Food Ministry's request in 1914 that they begin manufacturing their own brand as soon as possible was a welcome one. The Planter's Margarine Company came into being that November, and the first blocks of the new spread rolled off the production line in a specially purchased factory in Cheshire not long afterwards. There was just one problem. Plate, as the margarine was rather uninspiringly called, was foul stuff. Almost as soon as it appeared in shops, letters from dissatisfied customers began arriving at Lever Brothers' HQ.

'I have been waiting for these complaints ever since I received samples,' Lever glumly admitted to his colleagues, 'and also from the ominous silence by many of the friends to whom I have sent samples.' At least he was willing to suffer loyally alongside his customers. A 1916 letter to a friend bemoans downstairs strife at Lever's London home: 'I have had a mutiny in the domestic staff at The Hill because I lay down the rule that we must eat Plate margarine ... I had to interview the whole staff in the dining room yesterday morning before leaving. Several of the maids had told the housekeeper that they would rather leave than eat the margarine, and of course I have to insist upon the margarine being eaten.' At this point he might have thought ruefully of one of Sydney Gross's earlier ads, which depicted a rosy-cheeked housemaid stalking out with her belongings: 'Yes, I've left! Because I must have SUNLIGHT SOAP.'

Despite Plate's unpalatability, the business became a success. Partly this was simply through lack of choice – despite the optimistic instructions by Lord Devonport in 1917 that British households should eat more meat, 'bread and scrape' was all that many working-class families could afford, and the bread itself was scarcely better, bulked out as it was with maize, barley and even potatoes. By 1917 Planter's was producing more than 27,000 tons of margarine a year, and Lever felt confident enough in the product to spend over a million on a second factory close to Port Sunlight. By early 1918, when rationing was finally introduced in Britain, margarine was one of the items that was restricted. This followed reports the previous December of more than 3,000 people queuing outside a shop in London in the hope of buying some margarine for their families.

The government might have held off regulating people's food consumption for as long as possible, but their drinking habits were a huge concern from the outset. Lloyd George famously declared that 'drink is doing more damage in the war than all the German submarines put together', and one of his first acts after war was declared was to hike the beer duty from 7s 9d a barrel to 25s in the war budget of November 1914. The tax went up again the following year, the Chancellor declaring that 'we are fighting Germany, Austria and drink, and so far as I can see the deadliest of these foes is drink'. But Lloyd George and his cabinet colleagues still felt that more needed to be done in order to sober up the nation. Lever was invited to join the Central Control Board (Liquor Traffic) which helped to implement some of the least popular parts of the Defence of the Realm Act, an all-encompassing piece of legislation which banned everything from Guy Fawkes' Night (to save fuel) to bad news (reporting of which was 'liable to cause alarm and despondency'). But – and this was the committee's concern – it also regulated opening hours for the first time, forcing pubs near ports or munitions factories to shut their doors by 11 p.m., and banning them from opening in the morning at all (depriving workers of the frequently taken opportunity to turn up to work already drunk). Even as the government were putting prices up, they were putting the permitted alcohol level of beers and spirits down. And as if that wasn't enough, in October 1915 it became a criminal offence to get your round in – buying alcohol for other people was punishable by a fine of up to £100.

One of the most persistent arguments made by the temperance campaigners – including King George V, who declared Buckingham Palace a booze-free zone in April 1915 – was that women, deprived of the 'controlling influence' of their husbands, were turning to drink. The idea that a great many of them might be justified in drowning their sorrows after the arrival of form B.104-82B – the standard notification of death sent out by the War Office – seems not to have occurred to the prohibitionists. But this was just one of a number of new prejudices which the women of Britain were facing alongside many new opportunities.

The First World War was not the beginning of female employment in this country, as it is sometimes depicted. More than 5 million women already worked before 1914 – Lever Brothers had employed plenty of women from the outset – and the proportion of women in the labour force increased only marginally during the next four years. The difference was in the jobs that they did. From their most common roles in domestic service, a tradition which was all but killed off by the war, women moved into all areas of employment. There were women bankers, women drivers, women clerks, women doctors, and, of course, women munitions workers. Many of the more macho jobs remained a male preserve – Liverpool dockers threatened to strike in 1916 when they were forced to work alongside women, and even Lever Brothers preferred to train up adolescent boys rather than let the 'girls' loose on their more complicated machine tools. Lever himself was enormously supportive of a greater role for women both in the workplace and society. In a 1916 address to the Bolton School, a co-educational establishment to which he was a major donor, he nailed his colours firmly to the mast:

> This war has discovered woman. Women are in evidence everywhere, engaged in hundreds of useful and honourable occupations, and discharging their duties excellently. It was never imagined prior to the war what women could accomplish in other work than was then open to them ... Women are working side by side without affectation – easily and naturally – in munition factories ... taking care of the sick and wounded, a work which is being well discharged by delicate girls, and by matrons, and those who are no longer young. The war will clear out all preconceived ideas on this question. And the Bolton School will, without doubt, take a prominent lead in the good work of Education, and of nationalising a clearer, more definite, and wiser recognition of woman's true position and equal right with men to full opportunities for useful, intelligent, efficient and honourable service for the Empire and Humanity.

He went on to forecast the arrival of a welcome day when women would head multinational businesses of their own – a day which, sadly, has yet to arrive nearly a century later. But despite the blows he had recently suffered, Lever was ever the optimist. In an address at the Oldham Art Gallery in 1915, when anti-German feeling was at its height, he outlined a truly international vision:

> Let us cease all wild talk of capturing German trade ... Let us concentrate on improving the conditions of life for our people with friendly rivalry in thoroughness and efficiency with other nations. Let us begin by capturing German ideas and American ideas of broad, airy, direct and convenient roads and streets, beautiful public buildings, fine and well-centred railway stations, with well laid out

suburbs, with cheap and comfortable rapid transit facilities . . . in
short, substitute salubrious suburbs for squalid slums.

In the midst of the greatest slaughter and inhumanity
known to mankind, Lever was battling to keep his dream
alive. And when the war finally dragged to its bloody end,
he made its remembrance the centrepiece of his vision.
The war memorial at Port Sunlight stands at the foot of the
village's central green, looking down a peaceful avenue
flanked by roses to the art gallery he built in memory of his
wife at its head. Designed by the sculptor Sir William
Goscombe John, it is a quiet masterpiece. A granite cross is
flanked by eleven bronze figures representing the 'defence
of the home': not only the soldiers with their bayonets at
the ready, the airmen and the fusiliers huddling beneath the
might of their great field gun, but a nurse tending to
the wounded and a mother and children left behind
on the home front, every one of them ready to stand and
fight for what they believe in. And every one of them has
something else in common. Though defiant, they all look
absolutely terrified. It is the least jingoistic, most honest
and moving memorial I have seen.

The monument was unveiled by two of the surviving
Pals in December 1921. Beneath it was buried a book containing the names of their 481 comrades from the village
who died in the fields of northern France. Their widows
and children, and hundreds of their comrades who had
been injured on the battlefield, looked on. Standing beside
Sergeant T. G. Eames, who had lost his sight at the Somme,
Lever made a heartfelt plea for the future.

The result of victory is not a reward but a new task – a task only
yourselves can perform. Your and our nobler task is to win and

consolidate the peace. The foundation of war is hatred of our enemies. The foundation of peace is brotherly love and the banishment of all hatred, even of those nations who so recently were our enemies. Trade and commerce must be turned to their normal channels, or we endure the agonies of unemployment with attendant hunger, sickness, and suffering beyond mortal strength to endure. We must restore trade and commerce to its accustomed channels with our former enemies. We must forget they ever were our enemies. Let us all now, at this Christmas season, consecrate ourselves to the nobler task of restoring peace and goodwill, love and fellowship, trade and commerce with all peoples – with our former enemies no less than with our sorely tried and true and trusted Allies. That is our nobler task, and the best memorial to our Glorious Dead.

19

PICTURE THIS

IT IS A TRUTH UNIVERSALLY ACKNOWLEDGED THAT A famous man in possession of a good fortune must be in want of a portrait. Lever had several done in his lifetime. Luke Fildes flattered both him and Elizabeth in 1897, ironing out paunches and wrinkles to present them as a thrusting, modern young couple all set for the new century (despite the fact that they were approaching fifty at the time). George Hall Neale also produced a slimmer, trimmer Lever in masonic regalia in 1918, his eyes warmer, his face calmer, his expression more dignified than it often appeared in real life.

Now, however, there was a new Lever to be recorded: in the birthday honours list of 1917 King George had topped up Lever's baronetcy and made him a full member of the peerage. For his territorial designation the new lord chose his birthplace, in its ancestral name of Bolton-le-Moors, and for his name he chose Leverhulme. Elizabeth, who professed not to care about such things, had not lived long enough to be made a baroness, but with her family name,

Hulme, bound to his own she would always be with him. The College of Arms were sniffy about it, claiming that there was no precedent for such a joining of names, but William was insistent. His coat of arms featured two nice spotty elephants, for no reason that I know of other than that he rather liked them.

The grocer's son was at the peak of his achievements, and fêted at the highest levels of society – his celebratory dinner at the House of Lords was attended by one current, and two future, prime ministers, Lloyd George, Andrew Bonar Law and Churchill. By 1920 he felt the time had come to commission a new work from the best-known portraitist in Britain, the man *The Times* called 'the most famous of living English painters'.

Augustus John was already past his best when he came to paint Lever. Never quite fulfilling the early promise he showed as a student at the Slade, the forty-two-year-old had nevertheless cornered the market as society's favoured portraitist: subjects from Lloyd George to Lawrence of Arabia sat for him. Just a year before he had attended the Versailles peace conference as Britain's official artist. A prototype Damien Hirst, he oscillated between periods of monastic solitude in the Welsh countryside and well-publicized drinking binges in Soho – he ran his own drinking club in Greek Street where fashionable artists boozed, brawled and boxed in the small hours, and founded the Allied Artists' Association, an anti-establishment rival to the fusty Royal Academy that Lever so loved.

The two men's characters could not have been more opposite, but they rubbed along well enough during the sittings that were scheduled at John's Chelsea studio in June and July. At the end of August John put the finishing touches to what he considered one of his best pictures:

standing back from the canvas, he admired the way it seemed to 'breathe with life and self-satisfaction and only lacked speech'.

Lever did not agree. The portrait arrived at his Rivington home on 7 September, safely trussed up in a wooden packing-case. He unwrapped it in the privacy of his glass-walled study with its view out over the moors, and gasped in horror. The picture looked nothing like him. A watery-eyed, weak-faced, languid old man looked back at him, or rather, seemed to gaze aimlessly into the distance, a foolish, simpering smile on his lips. The picture's composition drew the eye to a set of long, grasping fingers which curled greedily around the arms of his chair. This was a man who loved money, and was happy to sit back, stupefied, as he watched it roll in. It was hideous. An insult. He was damned if he would let anyone see it.

He opened his private safe and attempted to stuff the canvas inside: it would not fit. Quickly he went to the kitchen next door, fetched a knife, and with it beheaded himself, slicing a ten-inch square from the canvas around the portrait's face. This he rolled up and stuffed deep in the safe's dark interior, locking it and returning the only key to his breast pocket. That done, he crammed the remains of the picture, now loose on its frame, back into the packing-case and departed the house to pace out his anger in the gardens.

'That this portrait wounded my father deeply there can be little doubt,' wrote Hulme in his own biography of his father, published not long after Lever's death. 'He spoke to no one about it at the time; indeed it was not until some time afterwards that I could persuade my father to show his old friend, Jonathan Simpson, and myself the square containing the head.' Privately, William admitted that the picture was 'chastening' and 'humbling to his pride'; on a more practical level he objected to the size and informality of the picture when he had requested a formal portrait fit to be hung in the boardroom at Lever Brothers or installed in the gallery at Port Sunlight when it opened. He did, however, pay John's fee in full, and there, he supposed, the matter would end.

So it would have done, were it not for an over-zealous housekeeper at Rivington who went into the study to tidy up after Lever's departure and, spotting the canvas replaced in the packing-case, assumed it was meant to be returned to John for improvements. Back it was mailed, and barely had the artist banked his cheque than he received his own canvas, mutilated and contemptuously thrown back at him with no explanation.

John fired off an angry letter to Lever by return of post. 'I am intensely anxious to have your Lordship's explanation of this, the grossest insult I have ever received in the course of my career.' Lever immediately drafted a full and honest reply – too honest in fact, for his blunt mercantilism only added further insult to injury. 'I am extremely distressed at the blunder that has occurred; I assure you it is entirely a blunder on the part of my housekeeper,' he explained, neglecting to apologize for his own act of vandalism that had so enraged John. He explained that he had tried to hide the whole thing in the safe, but 'there were internal partitionings and other obstacles that prevented me doing this, so I cut out the head which is the most important part of the portrait'. If John was not enraged enough by such philistinism, the cack-handed offer of a date with Lever's sister to make up for it sent him over the edge. 'I was urgently requested to keep the matter dark, and invited to dinner in Hampstead,' he recalled in his own autobiography, published in 1952. 'My answer to this was to inform the Press of the matter: the story was then published, with photographs of the work, before and after treatment.'

At least John did not go to the *Daily Mail*: this time the story broke in the rival *Daily Express*, which was owned by his close friend Lord Beaverbrook, but every other paper was quick to pick up on the dispute. It was a hell of a story. 'Telegrams and cables now began to pour in from artistic bodies all over the world, including if not China and Peru, certainly Japan and the USA,' recalled John, 'eloquent expressions of indignation, scorn and ridicule.' Gratifying as this was, he swiftly regretted involving the press: his house was besieged by reporters eager to prolong the scandal by squeezing further juicy quotes from him when all he wanted to do was be left to paint. He retreated to the home of one of his mistresses in the seaside town of Broadstairs, but the press pack followed and camped on the doorstep. When he refused to give in to their entreaties to sue Lever, they just wrote that he was going to anyway. The *Manchester Guardian* printed one of those sanctimonious leader columns in which, long after moving south, they still specialize: 'The common fairness of mankind cannot assent to the doctrine that one man may rightfully use his own rights of property in such a way as to silence or interrupt another in making so critical an appeal to posterity for recognition of his genius.' Anyone would think Lever had marched into the National Gallery and put his foot through one of the canvases on the wall rather than commissioning his own portrait and deciding he didn't want to display it. He compounded his new philistine image by refusing to enter into debate on the topic: 'All I am impressed by,' he told journalists, 'is that Mr John can get his advertising perfectly free, whereas the poor soapmaker has to pay a very high rate for a very bad position in the paper.' Had William Frith of *New Frock* fame still been alive he could have had a field day in the papers. Fortunately for Lever he had passed away in 1909, but W. T. Stead of the *Pall Mall Gazette* had gone down with the *Titanic* three years later, and this time around he had no one in the press to fight his corner.

Soon things got really silly. The students at the Chelsea School of Art had a tradition of making their own guy and parading it through the streets each 5 November before burning it in Hyde Park: this year it was Lever's turn to go up in flames. In Italy he was the cause of the first and only art strike in history – painters, models and everyone in any way involved in the painting industry were reported to have laid down their brushes for twenty-four hours, and gathered to burn a giant effigy of 'IL LE-VER-HUL-ME' made of soap and tallow in the Piazza della Signoria in the centre of Florence, where it must have made a horrible mess for someone else to clear up. The papers probably made both events sound more impressive and popular than they actually were, but the results of a moment's madness with a carving-knife (at least one in which no blood was spilled) have rarely been so spectacular.

In the end neither man had the stomach to prolong the fight. John exhibited the doughnut-shaped remains of the portrait under the title of *Lord Leverhulme's Watch-Chain*, a joke which signalled the end of hostilities. Lever failed singularly to learn his lesson, erupting into the papers again a year later after an abortive attempt at haggling with Sir William Orpen over another portrait (he claimed that since he was shown sitting down, he should only pay for a three-quarter-length canvas rather than the full-length one he had ordered), but he clawed back his reputation as a patron when Victoria's youngest daughter Princess Beatrice visited Port Sunlight to open the Lady Lever Art Gallery in 1922.

The elderly Beatrice was book-ending a process begun by her nephew George V eight years previously in 1914, when he laid the foundation stone of the gallery during an official visit to Port Sunlight. The village, the offices and even the works themselves had been draped with union flags and floral bunting in preparation for the royal arrival. 'Honour to our King & Queen', read the inscription on a temporary triumphal arch that had been hastily erected outside the Technical Institute at the entrance to the village from the New Chester Road. At Hulme Hall, in the midst of the cramped collection of art and antiquities that Lever had loaned from his personal collection, King George pressed a button beside a bird's-eye view of the village. It set in motion both a crane at the north end of the diamond and a scale model in the hall itself: both lowered inscribed stones into place in the foundation blocks beneath them. The completion of the task was announced by an illuminated sign – 'Stone Well And Truly Laid' – which delighted the monarch and relieved the technophile Lever. The rest of the royal trip went exactly to plan, bar an unscheduled visit to the home of a Mr and Mrs Percival, who were astonished to find the King and Queen of England on their doorstep after Queen Mary announced her desire to look inside one of the poor people's dinky little houses.

The completion of the gallery had been long delayed by the war, but it remained true to Lever's original vision, an educational showcase for the arts of the world rather than his own preferences. 'I have to cater for all tastes at the gallery ... for those who do not particularly admire pictures, statuary etc.,' he announced, and indeed, the collection seems to have had practically everything covered: from masonic regalia to medieval altarpieces, African head-dresses to Grecian urns, musical instruments, swords, death-masks, tapestries, statues, commodes and four-poster beds: so much that the gallery cannot keep it all on show at one time. There are works by Turner, Constable, Reynolds and Rossetti; works in marble which range from Rome in the first century BC to the scandalous 'New Sculpture' of the end of the nineteenth. But Lever's own eccentricities were also indulged: an entire room was devoted to furniture and personal items once owned by the emperor Napoleon; another is decked out incongruously in Robert Adam-style panelling, despite being far too small to carry off the intended effect. The gallery became a national museum in 1986; it remains an exceptional collection, every room yielding new and unexpected treasures. When Lever's collection of antique clocks all chime together, on or around the hour, the place feels truly magical.

Ironically, it is here that the John portrait now hangs, restored towards the end of the artist's life through the efforts of the Royal Academy and Lever's grandson Philip, who kept the missing segment safe until it was reunited with its surround in 1954. You can still see the join, a rect-angular halo that seems to hang around our hero's head. And you can still see two other things: it really isn't a very good picture, and it doesn't look anything like William Lever.

20

UNWANTED UTOPIAS

LEWIS AND HARRIS LIE AT THE OUTERMOST LIMITS OF THE British Isles, connected to the mainland only by the spider-web of CalMac ferry routes which string together the ragged archipelago of north-west Scotland. The co-joined islands – they are one piece of land, divided near its middle at a seemingly arbitrary point – are the outermost of the in-habited Outer Hebrides. To get there you have to island-hop: the toll bridge will take you as far as Skye, but beyond that, you're on your own.

Harris is the sort of place that makes you realize exactly what islands are: lumps of rock jutting up from the ocean floor which just happen to have the misfortune to break the sea's surface. The vegetation in this part of the island is minimal; soil itself is a rarity. This is a land of stone; not stones scattered like hundreds and thousands by playful glaciers as you might see in the picturesque glens of Skye, but solid, unrelenting hard, grey rock, tempered only by the scantest covering of lichen and heather. This stuff is gneiss, the Ur-rock, formed 3 billion years in the past, before babies like limestone and sandstone dared show their faces. In the dips lurk still, glassy lochs, dark water impassively reflecting dark sky. At times grey sky and grey stone seem to meld into one vast, colour-swallowing, life-sapping whole. It is like walking on the moon.

But it is also a land of surprises: every so often the road will turn and you will find a little corner of the Caribbean. Harris has the most perfect beaches you will ever see, with acres of golden sand – real, rich, retina-burning yellow – bordered by wave after wave of bright turquoise surf. Bounty-advert perfect, they are a slice of the tropics that have somehow drifted fifty degrees too far north and attached themselves to one of the most forbidding land-scapes on earth.

It is these beaches that gave life to Harris, that allowed people to set up home and scrape a living on this stark rock in the North Atlantic. Their golden sands are made up almost entirely of seashells, the gneiss being simply too hard to break down into grains as less hardy rocks do else-where. Shells are rich in calcium. Calcium limes soil. And the wind that flows in unimpeded from the Arctic Circle takes enough of this magical stuff and hurls it far enough inland to create machair, a miraculously verdant grassland which provides nourishment enough for crops and beasts.

Not that the bulk of Harris's population live around the machair. Their homes are mostly grouped along the island's Nordic east coast, a landscape which seems to be unsure whether to exist in a solid or a liquid state. Houses are hidden in nooks and crannies in the rock, or huddled on the shores of the freshwater lochans that saturate the interior. The people of Harris didn't ask to be here; they used to live on the west coast as logic (and survival) demands, but like most of the inhabitants of the highlands and islands they were turfed out of their homes when eighteenth-century landlords realized that sheep were more profitable and less demanding tenants than people.

This was the land of contradiction and necessity where William Lever finished up his life. Here, at the southern-most point of the island, is the last unfinished utopia to bear his name, testament to ten years of hostility, mis-understanding and desperately inappropriate dreams that found no home in these islands. The man who had tamed the Congo and turned the Empire on which the sun never set into a vast machine working in efficient harmony to create and market his products, finally came unstuck much closer to home, the blind passion that so much success had instilled in him all but guaranteeing his failure. The town of Leverburgh still bears his name, but these days the sign-posts have reverted to the original Gaelic, An T'Ob. The last traces of his work here are vanishing, swallowed up by the unchanging bleakness of the Western Isles.

Why did William Lever return to Lewis and Harris? He had first seen the island from the deck of a Langland's Shipping Company cruise ship back in 1884, with Elizabeth young and happy by his side. He had threatened to retire then, telling Jonathan Simpson he had 'never felt more dis-inclined to return to business in my life'. Now, alone, and past the age at which he had urged his parliamentary colleagues to introduce a compulsory old age pension, per-haps his mind returned to the idea. Nineteen-seventeen was his fiftieth year in business, an anniversary which he celebrated with a dinner party at Rivington for all the surviving staff of the Lever Wholesale Grocery Company. There were depressingly few. At Port Sunlight too, many of his erstwhile colleagues had moved on. It was twenty years since his brother had left the office for the final time.

Sydney Gross had retired in 1906. John Tillotson, director of the Imperial and Foreign departments, died in 1915. The board of directors was made up of a new generation – literally, for his son Hulme and nephew James Ferguson were now members.

The war, and the new directions in which it had pushed his business, had exhausted William. His work in Whitehall, among those who did not know his ways or appreciate the problems and embarrassment his deafness caused him, had been arduous. When Winston Churchill, newly installed at the Air Ministry, requested that Lever stay on and sit on the committee that would develop a civil air service for Britain, he declined. He was, he told the minister sadly, too deaf to be much use to anyone.

So it was time to move on. But Lever was constitutionally incapable of taking a quiet retirement. If he was to spend more time away from Lever Brothers – and he was, in theory, determined to slacken the reins, having already expanded the board in 1914 to take some of the weight off his shoulders, though he still insisted that everyone report personally to him – then he would need a new project with which to fill his time. He found it in the small ads which in those days filled the front page of *The Times*.

Lieutenant-Colonel Duncan Matheson had inherited Lewis from his great-uncle Sir James, the last in a long line of abusive landlords who had been more bothered about the animals he could shoot on the island than the humans who lived there. In 1887 the islanders, sick of being forcibly evicted from the crofts which provided them with enough grazing and growing land to feed their families in favour of Matheson's deer and grouse, had risen up and rioted against him. His great-nephew had been trying to get rid of the estate for four years – the government's Scottish Office had been dithering over whether to buy it since 1913 – and he was all too happy to accept Lever's offer of £143,000. He splashed out a further £25,000 on necessary accessories – boats, farm stock and some rather nice tapestries that suited the castle in Stornoway – but got the 30,000 inhabitants for free.

'His idea was to improve the lives of the crofters while no doubt incidentally improving his banking account,' wittered one Mrs Stuart Menzies at the time. Menzies was a sort of groupie for captains of industry, penning the 'Romantic Life Stories' of such titans as Lords Beaverbrook and Northcliffe during the first two decades of the century. She turned her pen to Lord Leverhulme in her 1921 book *Modern Men of Mark*, and found him to be the original ragged-trousered philanthropist. 'There are only two things I should like to see altered about him,' she wrote. 'The first and most important is his neck. I should have liked to have seen that fine head on a longer neck. The second concerns his nether garments. I do not think it is so much the cut of them as the care of them that troubles me.'

Trouser-press problems aside, Lever was still a vigorous man with enough energy to contemplate the complete transformation of Lewis. Harris was always part of his plan too: he added it to his portfolio in 1919, paying £56,000 to Sir Samuel Scott and the Earl of Dunmore for their estates there. In his departing note to his residents Scott wrote, 'after long talks with Lord Leverhulme I was convinced that in him you would have a proprietor who would further your interests and do all in his power, far more than I could ever do, to help you'. All were agreed that the new land-lord's intentions were good, though there were plenty who questioned whether he was making a wise decision. It didn't matter. With three decades of almost boundless success behind him, Lever wasn't in the mood to listen to anybody, even if he could have done. 'An advantage of being deaf is in business you can form your own plans and need not listen to anyone's advice,' he liked to joke to his friends, and he resolutely ignored the concerns of his fellow board-members, who regarded the purchase of the islands as a potentially disastrous distraction for their Chief. As far as Lever was concerned, it was nothing to do with his colleagues anyway. 'If it had been a good purchase in a financial sense, Lever Brothers would have had it. But it was not, so I kept it for myself.'

Lord Leverhulme first set foot on his new property on 30 June 1918. The people of Lewis were waiting for him on the harbourside in the island's capital, Stornoway. Speculation about his intentions had been rife in the Scottish and local press since he had visited anonymously the year before. Some reports claimed he intended to use the islands only as a 'residential retreat'. Others quoted him as saying, 'if there are any economic problems, I shall be glad to work with the people for their solution'. Whatever the truth was, he was a millionaire, and therefore definitely worth making friends with.

Things didn't work out quite as intended. Leverhulme was due in Stornoway late on Saturday evening. Hundreds of the town's inhabitants thronged the quayside, beneath bunting and a huge banner that read 'WELCOME TO YOUR ISLAND HOME'. They had even called out the local pipe band to welcome him ashore. But there was a problem. Lord Leverhulme's boat didn't appear over the horizon till just before midnight. He wasn't going to get there till the first few minutes of Sunday morning. And while sucking up to soap-producing millionaires is all very well, there's one benefactor you absolutely don't get on the wrong side of in the Western Isles. If there's one rule that is unquestionably followed out here, it's that God doesn't want you to do anything on Sundays.

So it was that when Lord Leverhulme arrived on his new island, he was greeted by a group of men holding silent bagpipes and several hundred guilty-looking people just standing and staring at him. It wasn't the best start, but it was a fairly good indication of what was to come.

Sundays in Stornoway are extraordinary. The town is hardly a hip metropolitan centre at the best of times, but on the Sabbath it's something else. I visited one summer Sunday in 2002, and the place was like the second reel of a zombie movie. It was deserted. Not just quiet in a big-football-match-on-telly-and-it's-a-bit-cold-out kind of way, but utterly, disturbingly devoid of any signs of life. The shops were shut. The pubs were closed. The bus station and the ferry terminal were completely empty.

What was doubly disturbing was the absence of people doing Sunday things, the sort of things you do to prove to yourself that you're not doing anything. The gardens were all perfectly tended, with spotless lawns and weedless beds, but not one single person was out working on them. No one was even sitting out in the sunshine. The eighteen-hole golf course in the grounds of Lews Castle was immaculate, unsullied by anything as messy as players. A couple of crows picked over the fairway on the seventh hole, but apart from that, not a single thing moved.

For a significant part of the British population, golf is what Sundays are for. People get up at dawn to tee off before the course gets crowded out. But here there was nothing. A large sign by the clubhouse lists the green fees, the dress code and contact details for the club secretary, and then mentions as a tiny afterthought that the course isn't open on Sundays. Round here you take that for granted.

And apparently, the Sabbath rules aren't nearly as strict as they used to be. In his book *Hebridean Connection*, Derek Cooper writes about ministers in the 1970s who refused to change their church clocks for twenty-four hours after the beginning and end of British Summer Time, because it was sinful to do so on the Lord's day, and who instructed house-bound parishioners not to tune in to church services on the BBC because 'all the preparation of a studio service on the Sabbath is quite contrary to God's teaching'. One minister of the Free Church, the majority faith on the island, even banned his parishioners from going out for a walk on the Lord's day unless they could produce a doctor's certificate saying it was essential for their health.

So what do all the locals do on Sundays? They go to the Kirk, of course. One church on Kenneth Street in Stornoway has the largest congregation anywhere in the UK, with around 1,500 people attending every Sunday evening. It's the sort of crowd the Church of England would give its Right Reverend for. The Free Church, formed by a breakaway group of Church of Scotland ministers in 1843 after a dispute over reforms to the parish appointments system, is the key to Lewis and Harris's identity. Fiercely Gaelic, intensely devout and theologically plain silly, it has held the community of this island and those that surround it in an iron grip for the last 150 years. This is the Hebrides. They do things differently here. It was a point which William Lever found very hard to grasp.

A few miles from Stornoway, at Arnol, you can experi-ence the conditions under which virtually all of Lever's new tenants lived. At some point in the first century AD people built the first houses here, directly above the beach. They fished from the sea and nearby Loch Arnol, grazed animals on the hillside, and cut peat for fuel from the boggy area behind their houses. Seventeen centuries of coastal erosion later, the inhabitants got tired of bits of their village dropping off into the sea, and when the peat finally ran out they simply upped sticks and built new houses further inland. It was virtually the only change the community had undergone in all that time. Building methods hardly changed in Lewis between the birth of Christ and the coronation of the current Queen. They didn't need to. They'd found a method that worked.

One such house still exists here, restored and run by Historic Scotland. Number 42 Arnol (there's only one street to choose from) is a wide, squat building that looks from the outside like four dry-stone walls surrounding a haystack. In fact there is a mass of peat-mould and earth behind the walls, almost six feet thick, backed by another internal stone wall, with only a few tiny porthole-like windows punched in it through which you can peer into the gloom of the interior. The outer wall is topped off with turf, which lends the house an oddly Tellytubbyish feel; the roof is thatch weighted down by stones strung together with rope woven from heather gathered from the surrounding land. Nothing was imported, nothing was wasted, in fact hardly anything needed to be paid for. It's an environmentalist's wet dream, an almost organic structure, a living, breathing part of the landscape.

The house was heated day and night by a single peat fire which was kept burning on the chimneyless kitchen hearth; the smoke was absorbed into the thatch above, and the resulting mineral-enriched silage was stripped off and spread on the fields every year as fertilizer. It may have ensured that the lungs of the inhabitants were equally carbon-enriched, but the natural cycle was essential to the very existence of the building. When Historic Scotland turned the place into a museum in the 1970s, they replaced the peat fire with storage heaters. Within two years the damp had seeped through the floor, and the thatch was falling to pieces. The fire was quickly restored.

The stifling smoke of the peat fire and the absolute silence that the six-foot-thick walls create give the building an almost otherworldly atmosphere. Sitting inside, you truly feel like you've travelled back through the centuries. But this house was occupied, in exactly this state, by an entire family along with their cattle and chickens (who had a slightly larger part of the house to themselves than the humans), as late as 1964.

It beggars belief. Lever was astonished to find people still living like this in 1917. Fresh from the Congo and the airy, brick-built and sanitary houses of Leverville, he pronounced the houses on Lewis 'not fit for Kaffirs'. But they were the standard way of life on Lewis and, as such, the people were deeply attached to them. When the family from number 42 moved into their own mainland-style 'white house' fifty years later, they returned to the dwelling they'd abandoned within months. The concept of rooms with right angles in them was just too luxurious for them to cope with.

Lever and the people of Lewis were all but guaranteed not to get on. Even if they had spoken a common language – they didn't, and the good lord was forced to take a Gaelic translator around with him wherever he went – their outlooks, their frames of reference, their methods of living, were utterly alien to each other. The people of Lewis lived lives that were ruled by the wind and the rain, and tried to block the unruly elements out of their homes as best they could. Lord Leverhulme inherited a perfectly good castle in the centre of Stornoway and spent thousands of pounds ripping out windows and walls to invite the weather into his bedroom.

That's not to say they didn't try. Lever was no stand-off landlord, more concerned with the hunting, shooting and fishing on his estate than the lives of his tenants, like so many others in the highlands and islands. Yes, he entertained English high society lavishly at Lews Castle, stocking the shooting lodges and importing his two unmarried sisters, Emily and Alice, from Thornton Hough to play host to a glamorous guest-list which included the future King George VI. But he also held frequent balls and garden parties to which the islanders themselves were warmly invited; before long everyone in Stornoway had supped at the castle. The luckiest got to see Lever indulge his latest hobby: since his deafness had denied him the pleasures of social conversation, he had become a passionate ballroom dancer. 'I spend the day entirely surrounded by men, and I don't want to spend my evenings also in ponderous conversation with men,' he told his son, explaining why he had had lavish ballrooms installed in all four of his homes. 'I like to have a few young friends about me whom I can chaff. It keeps my mind young, and prevents me becoming dull and heavy.'

He was always the last man on the dance floor – usually because he couldn't hear the end of the music, and often continued to mercilessly waltz an embarrassed partner round the room long after the final notes of the tune had faded away. Ever the egalitarian, he maintained his strict policy of dancing with 'the plainest women first', and then working upwards.

Still, as throughout his life, pleasure came far below business in his list of priorities. He came to this two-in-one island determined to transform a poverty-ridden backwater into a model of offshore prosperity. 'Lewis and Harris have too long been the Cinderella in the government pantomime,' he thundered to the Philosophical Institution of Edinburgh in 1919. He was determined to be their fairy godmother. 'I wish to introduce a higher scale of living and greater opportunities for happiness and well-being to the fine people of the Western Isles. I have travelled all around the world, and I find Lewis and Harris men honoured and respected and filling the highest positions . . . throughout our colonies. It is only in their native island that they are living under conditions of squalor and misery.' He was determined to tug them up by their bootstraps. It is a very hard thing to do with people so poor they cannot afford shoes.

Stornoway had never seen anything like it. Within a year of Lever's arrival, the tiny fishing boats in the harbour were dwarfed by three new factories which would produce ice, process fish offal and can the herring they brought in for export around the world, with further factories, and squads of shoal-spotting aircraft, planned for the smaller ports all around the island. The town had a new gas works, electricity plant, dairy and steam laundry. Every man and woman who worked in these new enterprises would receive wages 'not a whit inferior to those paid elsewhere'. But the transformation was not limited to the islanders' working lives. New roads were snaking out from the capital to all four corners of Lewis. Lever even presented the town council with plans for a complete redesign of Stornoway along Port Sunlight lines, complete with wide boulevards and public buildings, parks, an art gallery and (something completely new for the Hebrides) its own railway station. He called it the 'hub of the universe' or 'the Venice of the North'. It involved demolishing a substantial portion of the town that had stood there for centuries and rehousing half its citizens in spanking new homes, but he was certain they would not object.

And, to be fair to him, he was quite prepared to put his money where his mouth was. The cost of this proposed Venetian blinder would be met entirely by Lever himself, and he had already expressed his willingness to spend up to £5 million of his own cash in the long-term transformation of the island. He didn't have much choice, because at every juncture the government politely declined his invitations to become involved. The Ministry of Food told him his cannery was 'not clearly in the national interest', and the Ministry of Transport informed him that railways in the Hebrides were not a priority. Lever was undaunted, happily stumping up the cash from his own fortune, and, ever the wise businessman, setting up three new companies to make good the return on his investment. The Stornoway Fish Products and Ice Co. Ltd and the Lewis Island Preserved Specialities Co. were based on the island, while MacFisheries, a chain of fishmongers set up to promote the sale of Lewis fish, quickly multiplied across the mainland. 'I am convinced that there is no reason why Lewis should not be one of the greatest centres of fishing in the whole world,' he announced. There were actually several fairly sound economic and geographical ones, not least the fact that for two out of seven days God had put fishing off limits: overnight trips on either Saturday or Sunday encroached on the Sabbath, and any catches that were landed late on Saturday afternoon were routinely left to rot on the harbourside rather than risk the wrath of the big fisherman upstairs.

'It may be fairly said that before the first year was over, public opinion both in Stornoway and the hinterland was entirely in my father's favour,' wrote the second Viscount Leverhulme in 1927, in the most apologetic chapter of an otherwise triumphant biography. Observers noted that he was 'in danger of being saintified' for all he had done for the island. But even the remote islands of the Hebrides could not escape the ruinous effects of the war to end all wars, and its aftermath. One sixth of Lewis's population had signed up to serve their country between 1914 and 1918, the men overseas with the Seaforth Highlanders, the women in munitions factories on the mainland. It was the highest proportion of volunteers from any part of the Empire. Now, with their new laird barely settled in to his new home, the survivors were on their way back. And they were still in fighting mood.

One of the reasons for the massive turnout from Lewis in 1914 was a promise from the government that each man who signed up to the armed forces would be rewarded with something more valuable than gold: his own plot of land. The crofting system was the very framework of life in these islands, unchanged for thousands of years. The land was divided into small, regular plots, each one farmed by a different household. Each family ate what they could produce on their croft, their diet supplemented by the fish they could catch locally. They made their own clothes from the tweed that they spun, and scraped by in an almost entirely cashless economy, wanting for nothing, because there is no point thinking about what you can't have. But what should be yours by right, you have to be prepared to die for.

Perhaps the government gambled that the army's brilliant tactic of sending troops to walk slowly into machine-gun fire would polish off so many Lewis men that they'd need only about an acre of land to share between those that remained. Or maybe they really had intended to buy the island from Matheson, and it was merely red tape that had bogged down the negotiations for so many years before Lever came in with his better offer. Whatever the reasoning, at the end of the war there were 2–3,000 applications pending for crofts on Lewis, most of them from young men who had been prepared to make the ultimate sacrifice in return for the chance to start making a living of their own. Even if the government took over the seven large farms on the island (which it announced its intention to do in 1918), there would only be enough land to create an extra 140. However you looked at it, the maths didn't work.

And it was Lever, the newcomer to the island, who was left to deal with the fallout. He was unlucky enough to inherit centuries of bad relations between the islanders and landlords infinitely less well-meaning than himself. He did his best to make his good intentions clear – 'my instincts lean towards men and women, and not to salmon and grouse and deer,' he assured the Scottish Office in 1918 – but the harder he tried to explain this, the more suspicious the islanders grew.

Lever was more than happy to guarantee homes to everyone on the island. Part of the idea behind the Venice of the North was that 'every man who wants to live in Stornoway can have a house in Stornoway, and every man who wants a croft can have a croft'. But he had his own plans for the farms that the government had promised to the islanders. They were to be centres of agricultural excellence, producing milk, meat and cereals for the workers on the boats and in the factories of the new super-ports he had planned for every corner of the island. 'The new Lewis and Harris must be full of thriving and prosperous cities, towns and harbours, and of happy, rich, contented men and women, ten, twenty or one hundred times in number that of the present population,' he declared in 1919. Crofting, in the form it had existed since the Stone Age, had no part in his plans. He thought it a 'wholly impossible' way of life. Instead, those islanders who didn't work in the expanded fishing industries should find work in his jam factories, his willow-basket factories or his tweed factories or linen mills. Their primitive houses should be exchanged for 'what I might call Villas', with 'a nice porch to keep the wind from blowing in'. What more could anyone ask for?

He might as well have tried to explain the concept of surrender to the Japanese, scruffiness to the Swiss, or tell jokes in Germany. There was a problem of understanding here that went way beyond Lever and the islanders' mutually exclusive language.

Things came to a head in the spring of 1919, when the would-be crofters took things into their own hands. In the wake of the tragic loss of 208 returning servicemen who drowned that New Year's Day when the boat commandeered to bring them home sank within sight of Stornoway harbour, and perhaps spurred on by news of a general strike and riots over working hours in Glasgow, the islanders' demands had taken on a new militancy. All across the island, locals raided farms and began to dig up their fields and divide them up as their own. As in Zimbabwe in recent years, the dispossessed were returning by force to the land they regarded as their own. Farmers stood by and watched as their fences were pulled up, their grazing lands ploughed and their cattle set loose on the moors.

Lever confronted the raiders on 12 March 1919. Almost 1,000 men and women gathered near the village of Griais to hear their landlord try to restore law and order. He did well. He talked of 'a new era in the history of this loyal island of

Lewis that you love above all places on earth, and that I too have learned to love'. He talked about all the money he was willing to invest in the island, and he talked about fishermen returning to land with light hearts and heavy boats. All of this his interpreter put into Gaelic, and the crowd cheered every phrase. But they cheered louder for one of their own when he shouted Lever down in their own tongue:

> Come, come men! This will not do! This honey-mouthed man would have us believe that black is white and white is black. We are not concerned with his fancy dreams that may or may not come true! What we want is the land – and the question I put to him now is, will you give us the land?

Or at least, that's how Colin MacDonald, an envoy from the Scottish Board of Agriculture and, one suspects, a frustrated poet, put it.

The anonymous crofter had hit the nail on the head. Lever had no intention of giving them the land at all. He was quite prepared to give them a thousand other things they didn't know they wanted, but the part they had to play was as grateful tenants, going along with his vision like so many worker ants. Since Elizabeth's death his control freakery had been allowed to reign unmitigated. Lever Brothers had been forced to buy out at least one company from a joint enterprise because of their chairman's inability to work with its directors, and a court case that Lever had insisted on launching against his old Warrington rivals Crosfield's had been thrown out by a judge who 'failed to understand what the claim was'. Port Sunlight remained Britain's perfect garden city only because the Village Estate Department ensured that every lawn was clipped to regulation length and planted only with flowers from the official list. The fussiness of Lever's strictures over every aspect of its inhabitants' social lives had not decreased during his extended absences in the north.

But there was an important difference between Lewis and Port Sunlight: Lever had created the latter from nothing, and it was his to engineer in any way he saw fit. What seemed to escape him was that Lewis and its people had got by without him for thousands of years, and even if that was all they were doing – getting by – they didn't want anyone else to come in and tell them how they should be running their lives.

Even the very silly Mrs Stuart Menzies grasped it. 'We all looked at one another and said, "What a splendid idea! Why have we never thought of that before?" . . . Unfortunately . . . the inhabitants prefer arranging their own lives, their own fishing, by their own rules and regulations, to be happy and comfortable, in their own way,' she tutted disapprovingly. The *Scotsman* newspaper put it even more succinctly. 'He can't expect to graft a new civilisation on top of the old one all at once.'

Except that that was exactly what Lever had managed to do in the Congo, subsuming not just the ancient traditions of the jungle but thirty years of horror and mistrust with his brave new world of universal healthcare and the minimum wage. The early schemes and dreams that his critics had mocked as indulgent follies had taken root and spread throughout Britain, transforming its society from top to bottom. Every elderly man and woman in the land now received the pension that was rightfully theirs. Workers who had once lived in fear of their bosses now demanded the eight-hour day as a right. Women had a voice not just in industry, but since 1918 – as long as they were over thirty and did not live in rented accommodation – in the running of the country.

His magic touch had not entirely deserted him. Lever was cheered and applauded at every meeting he held with the crofters, and while many of the raiders continued to defy the landlord they contemptuously referred to as 'the old soapie-man', in several cases he managed to turn whole communities against the trespassers in their midst and persuade them to abandon the farms. But back on the mainland, the government took one look at the lawless mess that their land promises had resulted in, listened to Lever's pleas for help, and decided to wash their hands of the whole affair. The Scottish Board of Agriculture refused to evict the raiders from Lewis's farms, and, when he offered to do it himself, told him that they would not support him. The police on the mainland declined to do anything. So Lever, whose intentions were never anything less than admirable, was abandoned and cast as the villain of the piece.

About ten miles north of Griais, there is a perfect monument to Lord Leverhulme's period in charge of the island. He struck a compromise with some of the raiders in Tolstadh, promising them other employment in the area if they pledged their support for his plans. He commissioned a new road that would link their village with the port of Nis at Lewis's northernmost point, where the inhabitants had unanimously voted to 'strongly repudiate the short-sighted action of a few fellow-crofters in raiding and breaking up the farms and thus jeopardizing the bright future ahead'. The road would run across several miles of bleak, un-inhabited moor at the top of the island. It was work for work's sake. The new route would shave just two miles off the journey from Nis to Stornoway by the existing roads, and besides, the only motorized vehicles on the island belonged to Lever himself. The fact that he was willing to spend many thousands of pounds of his own money on the project is testimony to his boundless benignity as much as his sheer bloody-mindedness. He still honestly believed it would be needed for the fleets of delivery lorries that would roll out of Nis when he had turned the island into the centre of Europe's fishing industry.

The road, along with every one of Lever's other grand projects, was abandoned in May 1920 after the Scottish Secretary, Robert Munro, had warned him in a heated meeting that he would release any raiders whom Lever succeeded in having imprisoned. All that remains now is a vast arched bridge spanning a narrow gorge through which the Ghearadha river tumbles down to the sea. It is a masterpiece of engineering, a cantilevered triumph in concrete, dropped in the middle of nowhere. No road leads to it, and none leads away.

The intransigence of the raiders was not the only reason for the stoppage of works. As the Chief busied himself with the finer details of his industrialized utopia, far away a time-bomb had been set ticking. It had the potential to bring down the whole edifice of Lever Brothers, jeopardize the living of tens of thousands of employees across the world, and destroy everything that William Lever had worked so long and hard for. And it was about to explode.

21

THE FEAR

LEVER HAD DONE HIS BEST TO TAKE A BACK SEAT IN THE running of the company after he started spending more time in the Hebrides in 1918. He realized that it was time to let a younger generation take control, however much it went against his nature. 'The danger in good old England is that we are inclined to belittle the young men, and the young women also,' he had said in a speech a few years previously, 'and you know that lack of encouragement is the greatest stimulus that a young man can have applied to him.' So he had let the extended board make more decisions, and he had allowed his senior managers to make their own recommendations about which 'young men who had out-standing capacity' should be promoted within the company. But Lever could not let go. During the seven years in which he spent much of his time in the Hebrides, he exchanged around 50,000 letters with his colleagues back at head-quarters, concerning some of the minutest details of the company's business. Some praised the way things were run in his absence. Others displayed all the panic of a new mother who has unwillingly employed a babysitter for the very first time. 'What steps is the Control Board taking with Associated Companies that are either making losses or below datum profits?' he demanded of James Ferguson, the experienced head of the Imperial and Commonwealth division, in one handwritten blast. 'If merely noting "same" then where does control come in? If you are not taking action then tell me and I shall take hold myself. I feel very hurt at the placid calmness of nerve under circumstances that mean ruin.'

Part of the problem was that Lever simply had too much on his plate. The peaceful retirement he had planned on Lewis and Harris had descended into a mess of feuds and difficulties. The European businesses needed careful rebuilding after the conflict of the last decade. The Congo, though successful, was always a worry. Sales of Plate margarine had nosedived when the armistice brought choice back to consumers. And he was incapable of giving less than his all to any enterprise he was involved in. In 1918 he had been offered the Mayoralty of Bolton, an honorary position which required him to do little more than dress up in robes and press the flesh with the odd dignitary on special occasions. Instead he insisted on chairing every monthly council meeting in person, and drawing up his own spectacular plans for the redevelopment of the city (the council gratefully rejected the vision he presented in a self-published book, *Bolton: As It Is and As It Might Be*, though they did accept the gift of Leverhulme Park, which still stands in the suburb of Darcy Lever to the west of the city).

During a whirlwind tour of Lever Brothers' US interests in January 1920 Lever received a telegram from the board back in Port Sunlight, requesting the go-ahead to invest in a business in the British colony of Nigeria. The Niger

Company had played a big part in the unification of the country only a few years previously, and it handled around 100,000 tons of oilseed a year. It was now up for grabs, but a number of prospective purchasers were interested. His fellow directors were 'anxious to buy', though they thought they would have to offer a high bid of £6 per share.

Lever was in a good mood: under the leadership of F. A. Countway and with a number of new brands on the market, the US business was going from strength to strength. Together, the two men were negotiating a move into the US margarine business with the purchase of shares in a major American producer. He sent back a telegram to the UK giving his wholehearted approval to the Niger deal. 'Congratulations. Price high but suicidal if we had let opportunity lapse.'

'High' was an understatement. At £6 10s a share, the price the board ended up paying, the Niger Company cost Lever Brothers more than £8 million. It was eight times as much as they had invested in the entire Congo enterprise. And no one appeared to have properly thought the deal through.

'When I returned from New York I found all my colleagues cheering and hurrahing over the Niger purchase and not one thought being given to what it meant to raise and provide £8 million by July 1st,' grumbled Lever. His ungraciousness can be excused by what he discovered with only the most perfunctory of enquiries. Not only had Lever Brothers agreed to allow control of the Niger Company to remain in the hands of its current management for a further five months, but they had made no investigation of the company's accounts. And when they did get hold of the books, they contained a few surprises. Not least an undisclosed overdraft of £2 million, which the company's bankers were demanding back.

It was, in the words of the company's official historian, an 'astonishing transaction', and it seems to have amazed Lever as much as anyone. He carpeted Clarence Knowles, the head of the raw materials department who had handled the deal: 'What I should like you to do is write myself what answer I must make when I am challenged by shareholders (and I am almost certain to be) as to why Lever Brothers did not give instructions to the company's auditors to make a full investigation of the Niger Company's books before completing the deal.' It was a very good question. Part of the answer is probably that the senior staff at Port Sunlight had got so used to their chief taking decisions and negotiating business over their heads that many of them actually did not have a clue how to conduct business themselves. And now, once again, they desperately needed him to sort the mess out. But this time, it was beyond him.

As threats of legal action from the Niger Company's bankers increased, Lever announced his plan. His business had a capital of well over £100 million: it had been expanding at a breakneck speed for more than thirty years. They could easily raise the purchase price by an issue of company stock, while an overdraft from their own bankers would take care of the £2 million debt. But the massive unemployment that followed demobilization, and the runaway inflation which resulted from the relaxation of the economic controls imposed in wartime, made this a time of financial crisis. The market for Lever Brothers' soap had gone into decline, and their vast stock of raw materials, so rich a resource while international shipping was threatened, had plummeted in value. Even worse, it meant that their brokers were not prepared to underwrite a new flotation. The final blow came when the bank declined his request for a loan. 'I do not think anybody feels that your great company is not perfectly good, the assets being what they are,' came the careful reply from Barclays, 'but that a good many of us feel that you have gone ahead too quickly in view of a difficult financial situation. The truth is that there is not enough money to go round, and it has to be strictly rationed as, say, sugar or any other commodity.'

It was a devastating blow for Lever. 'Candidly, I don't consider that you are using an old client of over thirty-four years connection with that consideration he ought to receive,' he whined to the manager. He had grown accustomed to getting what he wanted. Back in 1914, on the last occasion that the company had issued capital, his finance director J. K. Greenhalgh had resigned in protest at the chairman's decision to publicize their past profits rather than the current ones. Lever had been bemused by the man's reaction. Did he not understand that shareholders and the public alike ought simply to have *faith* in him? Now, it seemed, that faith was gone.

'He was never nearer disaster and the sacrifice of all his plans for the future than at this moment,' writes the company's official historian, a man not given to over-exaggeration. At Port Sunlight, a state of emergency was declared. Several departments had to be closed for a day or more each week. Scourging himself for his complacency, Lever found fault and decay throughout his empire. With an almost manic fervour he devoted himself to 'combing out inefficient men, and too highly paid men, elderly men, and men past their work'. Four decades of smiling generosity had rendered the company bloated and over-comfortable. And now, in his rage, Lever turned upon his creation. 'If a man had been with us for twenty years, he leaned upon us and thought he could come-a-day, go-a-day, God save Sunday, with his eye on the clock, and that was quite enough.' No longer. Over the next five years, three thousand Sunlighters were given their cards. When they were sacked from the company, they lost their homes in the village. The many privileges to which they had become accustomed were torn away.

'I am confident that this has produced a state of fear in the minds of the remainder that if they were not efficient their turn would come next,' wrote the new, ruthless Lever. But no one felt that fear more than he did. He instructed his servants to wake him even earlier, determined to put in more and more hours at his desk. And night after night he would lie awake in his cold bedroom, lashed by the wind and the rain, a black terror eating away at his heart.

> I ask myself what has caused me to begin work at four thirty in the morning during the last two or three years, and to work laborious hours, and to have only one absorbing thought, namely my own efficiency and the maintenance of my own health for the task I had to perform; and I am bound to confess that it has not been the attraction of the dividends but fear, merely cowardly fear. I could call it by lots of high sounding names, but if I must be perfectly candid with myself I am convinced that it has been the gnawing fear in my heart that Lever Brothers would have to pass their dividends. I had placed myself in this position by accepting money from all classes of investors, including widows, spinsters, clergymen and others – all subscribers for Lever Brothers shares from the confidence they had in the business and myself, and these might possibly have to forego their dividends, which would mean probably curtailment of what they depended upon for their day-to-day food, clothing, rent etc. Candidly, this has been my great fear.

But even as the seventy-year-old laboured to try to save the hundreds of thousands of people who depended upon him across the globe, everything else he held dear seemed to be crumbling around him. The fine industrial relations he had cultivated at Port Sunlight collapsed in 1920 in a messy and damaging strike which put the soaperies out of action for twenty-one days. The Warehouse and General Workers' Union, which had for years enjoyed a monopoly at the works, demanded that the rival Liverpool Shipping Clerks' Guild be banned from recruiting at Lever Brothers. Lever refused to do so – 'the question of which union an employee should belong to is the private concern of the man or woman concerned' – so the Union called its members out. At the same time, the secretary of the Engineers' Union publicly denounced the very conditions that had once made Lever so praised an employer. 'No man of an independent turn of mind can breathe for long the atmosphere of Port Sunlight. That might be news to your Lordship, but we have tried it. The profit-sharing system not only enslaves and degrades the workers, it tends to make them servile and sycophant, it lowers them to the level of machines tending machines.'

His anger probably had more to do with the increasing mechanization of the soap-making process and the ensuing redundancies than it did with the village itself, but Lever was wounded, partly because he knew there was truth in the criticism. Binding the village so tightly to the works had bred resentment alongside his cherished sense of community. 'You couldn't leave work behind,' recalled one resident, Jim Edwards, in Sue Sellers' book *Sunlighters*. 'Whatever club you went into you were rubbing shoulders with people who were working in the same place. The village was a competitive community.' Angus Watson, a colleague of Lever's, wrote that 'the whole village was dominated by the spirit of soap ... You could no more escape from its influence than from the odour (not at all an unpleasant one) permeating it from the great factory plant.' The village had existed for too long in splendid isolation: its inhabitants stewed alongside immediate neighbours they had to deal with night and day, and were ostracized by those from beyond its boundaries. 'I'd never build a second Port Sunlight,' Lever confided in Andrew Knox in the early 1920s. 'It was a mistake. People who work and live together always quarrel.'

The happy atmosphere that had once reigned in the offices was also gone. Knox, then a junior member of staff, recalled that 'just after the First World War, people came and went with considerable rapidity. The general feeling at my level was that one could understand better why they went than why they came.' Part of the problem was the lack of firm leadership since Lever had focused his efforts elsewhere. Undisputed leaders of the national soap market Lever Brothers might be (they had even taken over the giant of their early years, Pears, in 1915), but they had also diversified in several half-hearted and ill-thought-out directions. By 1920 the company was the owner of a sawmill in Plymouth, a colliery near Durham, a Welsh limestone quarry and a paper mill. Of the £50,000 purchase of the engineering firm J. G. Jackson, Lever pronounced himself as ignorant as anyone else. 'I have never myself understood why this business was purchased. I have never seen that it could possibly be of any interest to Lever Brothers.' The King of Sunlight had lost control. He desperately needed help.

The end of his reign came not with a bang but a whimper. It was contained in a telegram that winged its way back to Port Sunlight from Lever early in 1921.

Suggest you call in D'Arcy Cooper for assistance if he can help.

In that single sentence William Lever surrendered the absolute power with which he had ruled an extraordinary empire for the best part of four decades, and handed over his crown. Francis D'Arcy Cooper was an accountant whose company had worked with Lever Brothers for years. He had followed his father into the accountancy business, and he was a rationalist through and through, with none of Lever's capacity for dreaming. A tall man, prematurely balding, his eyes had none of the fire that Lever's displayed. 'We are trustees for some 200,000 shareholders, and we have no right to spend one penny unless we are absolutely certain we are going to get an adequate return,' he coldly instructed the managers of Lever Brothers' overseas businesses when he arrived to take the reins that year. Though he did not officially join the board until 1923, from that moment on D'Arcy Cooper was the man in the driving seat. The first thing he did was go back to Barclays, promising 'an undertaking from the Company that further developments by the acquisition of new businesses would cease'. Lever gave one last gasp of defiance – 'the business can well rest after I have gone to view the daisies from the underside ... expansion may not be so rapid after my death, consolidation may take its place' – but he knew when he was beaten. The final deal struck with the bank in February was for a loan which would stave off the threat of legal action and inevitable bankruptcy, but only on condition that a large proportion of debenture stock was issued to them in return. The issue of debenture was a move that Lever, still the sole owner of all the ordinary shares, had long and passionately resisted. In effect he had now handed over a significant part in the running of the business to Barclays bank. The rest of it lay very firmly with Francis D'Arcy Cooper.

The accountant's transformation of the company was rapid. He hacked through the web of interrelated businesses that had been allowed to multiply around the company's core by Lever's policy of 'competition within the family'. To the distress of the chairman, who hated the idea of 'scrambling eggs' that he had spent so long laying, D'Arcy Cooper restructured Lever Brothers along clear and logical lines. Associated companies which 'showed no prospect of profit' were simply shut down. Others were stripped of every asset deemed not absolutely essential. Land and factories were sold off as far afield as Canada, India and Japan. Within a year, he had saved the company one and a quarter million.

Part of this was done by reducing wages across the board, a move which Lever himself vehemently opposed. Sadly, he had to accept the inevitable. 'What can a union do to keep back the tide?' he mused in the summer of 1921. 'Labour leaders may mimic King Canute, but they cannot be more successful than he – let us treat all men justly and sympathetically under all circumstances. Soap may have its bad times to face, but today soap makers' wages are above (and we rejoice) the average labourer of the United Kingdom.' He was placated by the introduction the following year of one of his long-standing dreams, a company unemployment benefit scheme that, along with sick pay and life insurance which came in at the same time, helped to ease some of the pain on the factory floor. But it was not only the workers who suffered. Thousands of pounds were saved by the axing of inefficient managers throughout the business, and D'Arcy Cooper even filleted the board of directors. From now on, everyone answered to the Special Committee on which he sat with Lever, his son, and just two other directors. 'Its immediate function was to ensure that Lever acted only on proper advice and after mature consideration,' writes David Fieldhouse in his study of the company. 'The underlying assumption was always that the Committee now had full executive authority even in his absence, and even more important, that all decisions must be collective.' As if to ram the point home, the company left its spiritual home. In 1921 the senior management of Lever Brothers moved from the general offices at Port Sunlight to a new headquarters by Blackfriars Bridge in London. They would never return to the village again.

Lever was a broken man. Attempting to adjust to the new regime, he veered from peevish outrage to almost simpering subservience. 'I can assure you that yourself and the other members of the Special Committee are of the greatest help to me, and I am anxious to avail myself to a still further extent of this help,' he wrote to Harold Greenhalgh in the spring of 1923.

It is not that I am feeling in any way unequal to this work at present, but that I am conscious that very often after 70 changes come very suddenly and I am anxious to consider the business first, foremost and all the time. It is always a great pleasure to me to fulfil all the duties I perform but I have no right to indulge in my preferences. It was for this reason that I bought the island of Lewis thinking that I could then be at a distance and yet sufficiently near to be reached immediately by cable and in a couple of days by post.

A year later, his communications had become even more pathetic:

> On many occasions I am asked as to my views on matters. If, after I have expressed these views, no comment is made upon them I take it for granted that we are united on the subject, but it often happens I am certain that on further consideration other points of view occur to some one or all of my colleagues which would modify their previous assent. This is greatly to the advantage of the business that it should be so, but what I want is that when on after-thought a modification of the original idea is thought advisable, I should be informed of that forthwith, because I might have other views to put before my colleagues that I did not bring forward at the time because we were all agreed but which I ought to have the opportunity of bringing forward if further thought on the matter gave to any of my colleagues or all of my colleagues a changed opinion . . .

Once, he had wielded absolute power and dismissed dissent with a curt, 'We won't argue: you're wrong.' Now he was reduced to penning these rambling, unpunctuated pleas and sending them off to London in the hope that somewhere, someone would listen.

But no one seemed to be taking much notice of him any more. Up in Lewis all his elaborate schemes had been stalled for years as the deadlock continued over the occupation of the farms. By now some of the raiders had gathered two harvests from their illegally held land, and still the government stonewalled over whether or not they could be evicted. Powerless to stop them, and determined not to reward their defiance by carrying on with his grand schemes for the island, Lever described himself as 'a bird with one wing broken'. The great canning and icing plants on the harbourside in Stornoway lay silent, trading conditions too risky for the launch of such an ambitious venture. As the stalemate dragged on, everything from the widespread unemployment that affected the island as much as the mainland to the failure of the potato crop was blamed upon the landlord who had promised such miracles, and delivered so little.

Worse, Lever was felt to have added insult to injury when in November 1922 he was made a viscount (which allowed him to pass his noble title down through his family), and he chose as his title Lord of the Western Isles. He intended only to pay tribute to his new home, just as he had to his birthplace with the title he had chosen for his baronetcy. 'I viewed Bolton in the position of a mother, and I viewed the Western Isles in the position of a wife.' But, unwittingly, the Englishman had usurped a name that was steeped in Highland legend, traditionally royal, and intimately associated with Scottish nationalism. Though the stoic residents of Lewis pronounced themselves largely unmoved, the outcry could be heard right across the mainland. The *Scotsman* reported 'a blast of indignant protest against what is regarded as a specimen of gross Saxon presumption and invasion', and *The Times* in London reported the outrage of the Duke of Atholl, expressed in the presence of the Prince of Wales himself. 'The men of the north honour their Prince as "Lord of the Isles", a title, or even its semblance, the right to which they yield to no other person. If any meaner subject claims it, we resent it in Scotland. From 1503 the title has been absolutely associated with the Scottish Crown.' The Gaelic Society of Inverness even appealed to the Prime Minister, Bonar Law, to strip Lever of the name.

The scandal redoubled the criticism of Lord

Leverhulme's presumption in trying to transform the Hebrides, which had already seen him denounced on the floor of the Commons as 'taking it upon himself to tell these people that their future lives are to be guided along the lines laid down, not by themselves, not in accordance with the traditions of their ancestors, but according to the dictates of a successful soap-boiler who happened to buy up that island'. By contrast, the citizens of Harris, the southern part of this recalcitrant island, were welcoming him with open arms. They had embraced his plans for a vast Atlantic fishing port and a whaling station which would work the waters off the coast of Norway. So enthusiastic were they that the inhabitants of Harris's largest port, Obbe, had even agreed to rename their town in his honour (though memories differ over just who came up with the idea). Leverburgh offered him more joy than he could ever expect to receive from Lewis. Though it went against every instinct that he had, he knew it was time to give up.

On 3 September 1923, Lever called a meeting with the Stornoway Town Council, the Lewis District Committee and the parish council. Rather than relying on the joke-filled prompt cards he usually used, he had typed out what he wanted to say in full. He was determined to get this right.

> I never had a more uncongenial burden laid upon myself than the one that devolved on me today, which is to explain fully and without reserve the position I find myself placed in with regard to my relationship with the island of Lewis. As I explained to you at our first meeting, I was not attracted to Lewis by any love of sport, but entirely by the possibilities of doing something in a small way for the permanent benefit of its fine people . . . I am really now left

without any object or motive for remaining here. For me to come each year as an ordinary visitor to the castle, and knowing that I could take no interest in fishing or sport, would be meaningless. I am like Othello, with my occupation gone, and I could only be like the ghost of Hamlet's father haunting the place like a shadow.

If he was laying the tragic heroics on a bit thick, he could be forgiven. He had come to Lewis with the very best of intentions, and he left in the same manner. He bequeathed Lews Castle and its estate to the town of Stornoway, on condition that they named its grounds 'Lady Lever Park' in memory of his wife, who had now been dead for a decade. Every house he had bought to demolish in Stornoway in preparation for his perfect city was offered back to its previous owner at ten per cent less than he had paid for it. The town was welcome to all his factories and any income they could make from them. Every farm on the island was to be gifted to the people. And every croft was to be handed over for free to its occupier – except for those that had been seized by raiders. All he kept was a few uninhabited off-shore islands – the Shiants, the Flannans, Rona and Sula Sgeir. In total they were worth less than £500. Five years previously, the island had cost him £143,000. He had sunk well over a million pounds into his increasingly desperate attempts to keep his dream alive. And now he was kissing it all goodbye.

Other responsibilities continued to gnaw at his mind. The fear was still with him. At four every morning the jarring burr of an electric buzzer would sound out through the darkness, its volume high enough to penetrate his almost complete deafness, and, unimpeded by walls or ceiling, to wake his neighbours for miles around. He would be at his desk in the neighbouring 'sanctum' within half an hour, obsessively poring over notes and reports on the business that was conducted in his name, desperate to offer opinions that might help his colleagues. At meetings of the Special Committee he strained to catch everything that was being said: for all D'Arcy Cooper's drastic action, the outlook was still far from good. The Niger Company was recovering from years of shambolic management, most of it imposed from afar, for its directors had never seen the need to leave the comfort of their desks in Britain when deciding the best policy for Africa. A complete change of staff had done much to stop the rot, but none of the company's raw material schemes were bringing in the sort of returns that they needed. So Lever decided to do what he had always done in these situations: he would go and sort the situation out himself. There was little that he could achieve stuck in Britain, especially now that every decision had to be made in triplicate and interfered with by so many others. He needed to be at the heart of things. He needed to go back to Africa.

D'Arcy Cooper opposed it. His son opposed it. Even his doctor advised against the trip. But this was one thing the old man could decide for himself. 'We urged him to reconsider his decision,' Hulme recalled, 'not to lay himself open, at the age of 73, to the strain and risks of such a long and arduous journey in tropical Africa, but in vain. He considered that he would be failing in his duty to his shareholders if he did not visit these colonies and study on the spot the problems which confronted him.' Lever declared that he would make his way south 'even if the path was lined with machine guns, poison gas and undermined. We are simply fiddling in Western Africa while Rome is burning and something very extreme has got to be done.'

So he went. He took with him Andrew Knox, the young

clerk whom he had known since he was a child in Port Sunlight. Knox served, he recalled, 'as a sort of equerry – to look after the tickets and luggage, to pay all out-of-pocket expenses, to take notes on meetings'. It was an unenviable job. 'My immediate predecessor had distinguished himself by leaving the old man's battered but precious black brief case on the Bergen–Newcastle boat. The captain of the boat was radioed to enquire if his Lordship's black brief case containing important papers had been found. The reply came back that a black brief case had been found, but it contained only a clean shirt and two lemons: was this the one? It was.'

Lever's behaviour on the 1924 trip was no less bizarre. Every night, aboard ship and in the hotels and homes that they stayed in on their journey, he requested two lemons and a bottle of soda water to be delivered to his bedroom. Knox simply assumed that this was what he liked as a bedtime tipple – until 'one night after he had retired, which he usually did fairly early, and I was sitting in the hotel lounge with the rest of the party, I was astonished to see the Old Man coming down the stairs and marching towards me. He was a notable figure with his old-fashioned grey-worsted morning coat and head of curly white hair, so that by the time he reached me everyone in the place was looking at him. He placed in front of me eight quarters of lemon and said, in his best Lancashire accent, "They're no good to me, they're cut." And marched off again.'

Despite his increasingly erratic habits, Lever's appetite for work was in no way diminished by the demands of the 15,000 mile journey. In the space of five months he wrote nearly nine hundred letters concerning the business, and another six hundred to friends and relations. 'He attended to his private mail every afternoon when he was free to do so, and privately, I was to make sure he was awake at 4.00 p.m.,' Knox confided.

The first stop for the party was Leverville, which had been transformed since Lever had visited the fledgling enterprise with Elizabeth a decade previously. A thousand kilometres of road threaded their way through the once impenetrable jungle. Nineteen steamers and seventy-two barges chugged their way up and down the Congo and its tributaries, carrying the 54,000 tons of palm fruit that were collected every year from the plantations to the seven mills that had been built to turn them into precious oil. Seventeen thousand natives toiled here, many of them living comfortably in the hundreds of brick houses that had replaced the mud huts into which he had peered during his negotiations with the tribal elders years before. Ten hospitals, each staffed by trained European doctors, cared for the medical needs of the workers, while their children were educated at two huge schools. And everywhere the old man went, he was hailed: *Mukende, Munene, Na m'Bila*, the Big Chief of the Palm Tree Company. Lord Leverhulme looked upon his works, and he saw that they were good.

Less satisfying was the situation in Nigeria, where Francis D'Arcy Cooper joined him to inspect the Niger Company's holdings. Depressed by the chaotic running of the trading stations and the poor quality of the palm-nuts that passed through them, Lever turned his mind instead to an enterprise whose future he thought was brighter, his new fishing business far away at Harris. That summer's catch had exceeded all expectations: so many herring had been landed at Leverburgh that hundreds of extra staff had to be brought in from the mainland to smoke them. His last task before departing for Africa had been to supervise preparations for the 1925 season, which would see operations extended to trawling for cod as well as drifting for herring, and much of the correspondence he had been sending home from Africa concerned these plans, which he outlined now to D'Arcy Cooper. To his shock, the accountant did not share his enthusiasm. D'Arcy Cooper had been distracted from his work too many times by this private scheme which he regarded as nothing more than a gross extravagance: he was sick of being dragged away from his desk in London at a moment's notice to journey to a wild and inhospitable island from which the company stood to gain nothing. Now, once again, with the Niger Company's problems staring him in the face, Lever was banging on about kippers. The two men's differences of opinion erupted into a blazing row in the cabin of a steamer as they made their way upriver in Nigeria; it ended with the younger man forcing his boss to sign a statement declaring his sole responsibility for the Harris venture, and guaranteeing that Lever Brothers would not be held responsible for a penny of the money he was spending there. An enraged Lever is said to have demanded to know what D'Arcy Cooper would like him to do with the people who were relying on him in the Hebrides; the accountant replied that the best thing he could do with the islands was to 'sink them in the Atlantic for four hours, and then pull them up again'.

Lever was subdued on the homeward voyage in the spring of 1925. Knox and his companions noticed that Lever 'rested far more than was his wont, sleeping very often through the morning and again later in the day'. He did, however, rouse himself to read the lesson at one of the ship's Sunday services. The captain gave him a free choice of texts, and just as at his brother's funeral fifteen years before, he turned to Ecclesiastes:

I made me great works; I builded me houses; I planted me vine-yards. I made me gardens and orchards, and I planted trees in them of all kind of fruits. I made me pools of water, to water therewith the wood that bringeth forth trees.

I got me servants and maidens, and had servants born in my house; also I had great possessions of great and small cattle above all that were in Jerusalem before me. I gathered me also silver and gold, and the peculiar treasure of kings and of the provinces: I gat me men singers and women singers, and the delights of the sons of men, as musical instruments, and that of all sorts.

So I was great, and increased more than all that were before me in Jerusalem: also my wisdom remained with me. And whatsoever mine eyes desired I kept not from them, I withheld not my heart from any joy; for my heart rejoiced in all my labour: and this was my portion of all my labour.

Then I looked on all the works that my hands had wrought, and on the labour that I had laboured to do: and, behold, all was vanity and vexation of spirit, and there was no profit under the sun.

William Lever arrived back at Port Sunlight on 19 March 1925. He spent half an hour in private contemplation in the Lady Lever Art Gallery before being driven to his office, where he was abashed to find a deputation of directors and senior managers waiting to receive him. 'Well, I am very glad to be back with you all again,' he told them as he shook each man warmly by the hand. 'There will be plenty for us to do, and I am sure it will all be well done.' His own first task was to prepare his speeches for the AGMs of his companies. The first, that of the Huilières du Congo Belge in Brussels, was a rousing success: travelling back with his son, the old man seemed in better spirits than Hulme could remember. 'The drive which I had with my father across London from Victoria to Euston will always live in my memory. In Brussels, every moment of his time had been busily occupied, but he had appeared to be in splendid health. At his hotel, scorning the lift, he had on every occasion run up the two flights of stairs to his sitting-room, two steps at a time . . . He spoke to me with almost boyish enthusiasm of the prospects of the Congo enterprise and of his plans for future visits . . . He then went on to talk of several other projects which he was hoping to carry out over the next ten years.'

At the Lever Brothers AGM the following week, Lever was able to deliver the happy news that the company had returned to profit for the first time in five years. They were not yet at a stage to make payments on the debenture stock held by Barclays, but with the help of D'Arcy Cooper they had clawed their way back from the brink. Lever Brothers now had 187,000 shareholders, and 85,000 staff 'living and working in almost every country in the world'. Their issued capital was some £57 million, but, and this was the fact that pleased him most of all, 18,000 of their staff were co-partners, ready to share in the rewards that the future would surely bring. Just the night before, he had hosted a dance in Port Sunlight for two hundred guests from the village, who were, the *Port Sunlight News* reported, 'delighted to see our Chairman looking so well and in such splendid health. He danced almost every dance on the programme, and remained until late in the evening.'

It was only when he arrived in London the following Monday, after a night in a sleeping-carriage on the train, that Lever started to feel unwell. He telephoned his apologies to the office at Blackfriars: he was not up to coming in, but if his secretaries could come to the house at Hampstead he would work from home. It was one of those secretaries who called Hulme on the Wednesday: it was obviously taking 'great effort' for his father to get through his paperwork; could he come down to London and do his best to 'keep business matters away from him'?

He lasted a week, during which his personal physician diagnosed him as suffering from pneumonia, like his wife before him. 'As the hours went by the end became inevitable,' wrote Hulme, who was by his bedside. 'On Thursday the 7th May, at 4.30 in the morning – the hour at which he had been accustomed to begin the work of each long and busy day – he passed peacefully away.'

A lone bell tolled out from Christ Church that morning as the Sunlighters hurried to the soaperies and the general offices. At Lews Castle above Stornoway, the flag was lowered to half-mast. And at Leverburgh, the whistle that hung from the side of the brand-new canning sheds by the quayside sounded a single, long blast. The first floral tributes started to arrive at Port Sunlight later that day, 'from every rank and class of life, private and business friends and associates, employees and former employees, both men and women pensioners among them'. They were stacked in the central aisle of the Lady Lever Art Gallery where later his body would lie in state as thousands of people queued up to pay their respects.

'That he would ever have relaxed of his own free will is doubtful, and the enforced inactivity of an invalid would have been intolerable to him,' wrote Hulme two years later. 'My mother had influenced his life's achievements in a way not easily to be explained to those who did not know her intimately, and the sense of loneliness which fell upon him after her death affected the future course of his life in a manner which possibly he himself hardly realised. I cannot help feeling that, in many of his added activities, he was seeking a means of escape from thoughts which inevitably forced themselves upon him unless his mind was occupied with problems which demanded nothing less than the whole of the energy and power within him.'

In death they were reunited. The tomb of William Lever lies alongside that of Elizabeth, in the cod-mediaeval narthex attached to the north-western end of Christ Church, Port Sunlight. Their bronze effigies, by Goscombe John, architect of the war memorial down the road, turn to each other slightly in their sleep. A smile plays on Lord Leverhulme's lips; his eyes are closed, freed of their burning intensity. His face is at peace. At the couple's feet sit two children, gazing out beyond the confines of the churchyard to the second family the couple created for themselves in the village, and far beyond.

Afterword

THE GARDEN ON THE HEATH

THE NINETEENTH OF SEPTEMBER 2003. IT IS WILLIAM LEVER'S 152nd birthday. Hampstead Heath is bathed in bright sunshine, patches of grass scorched to a dry yellow after one of the hottest summers on record. Despite the sun, this corner of the heath is quiet: the joggers and daytime dog-walkers tend to avoid the area behind the Jack Straw's Castle pub, and this afternoon there are only a handful of middle-aged men lingering among the trees, casting hopeful glances in each other's direction. The ground is littered with the detritus of furtive encounters: ripped condom packets, fag butts and the occasional tissue drifting stiffly in the wind.

The extra-curricular activities that this end of the Heath is notorious for are probably one reason for the obscurity of one of London's least-known public gardens, which lie here. The formal grounds which Thomas Mawson designed for Lever after he bought his Hampstead home are on his usual monumental scale: two neighbouring properties were knocked down to make room for the Pergola, a set of vast formal walkways high above ground

level, ramparts built from the stone excavated by the building of the local underground line in the 1920s. An 800-foot
labyrinth of classical colonnades is strewn with wisteria,
clematis and climbing roses: through cast-iron trellises
you can glimpse the vast fish pond which slices down the
middle of the great lawn in front of the huge mansion.
Climbing the steps to the Pergola you enter another world,
one for ever rooted in the formal decadence of the roaring
twenties. With each corner you turn you half expect to
encounter a group of masked revellers in black tie and ball-
gowns, but no, the best you can hope for is a couple of
twenty-first-century gentlemen practising their own particular kind of gay abandon.

The Pergola is now owned by the Corporation of
London, which restored it after it passed into their ownership as a ruin long after Lever's death. It is maintained
alongside the wild heath beyond as one of the great green
'lungs of London', the open spaces which the Corporation
safeguards for the capital's citizens to escape from the thick
smog that hangs over the most polluted city in Britain.

And what of the house behind it, The Hill, which Lever
purchased in 1904 and extended in his usual jackdaw
fashion, adding entire wings plucked from different
periods? A developer's sign outside the gates on North End
Way announces that this is now Inverforth House: The
Ultimate Hampstead Apartments, with Three Magnificent
Suites for Sale. Lever's mish-mash of styles has been
turned to the estate agents' advantage: if you have a million
or so to spare, the Jacobean or Georgian Suite could be
yours.

Thornton Manor, now The Hill. Is this how it all ends,
in luxury apartments? Even Port Sunlight is now desirable
real estate: by the eighties tied tenancy, limited to

employees at the works, was no longer legal, and the business had grown so much that less than 10 per cent of those who worked at Port Sunlight were able to be housed in the village. In 1980 estate manager Peter Hodson announced that houses would be sold off as they became vacant: 'The founder was always very aware of the forces of social change. We have started to give Port Sunlight a valid role in the modern world. I think he would approve.'

Sixty per cent of Port Sunlight's homes are now privately owned. They have not quite yet reached Hampstead prices – in 2003 a parlour-type cottage on Corniche Road would have set you back £86,500. But the Port Sunlight Village Trust, a charity established in 1999, retains ownership of a number of properties which it lets; it also retains full control of those front gardens, and keeps a close eye on alterations to the exteriors of the Grade II listed buildings, aiming to 'preserve and enhance the character of the village and retain the essential fabric of the community'.

Not that Port Sunlight is entombed in mothballs. In 2002 the construction company Bovis built Osbourne Court, a set of flats on a vacant site close to the old cottage hospital. Only the freshness of the paintwork and the developer's signs give away the building's modernity: it picks up on both the squat solidity and the eccentric detailing of its neighbours and looks for all the world as if it has been there since Lever's day. Thankfully, however, this time around the architect was not required to install the bathrooms next to the front door.

Lord Leverhulme's monument in the eyes of prosperity will be the noble work perfected by him at Port Sunlight and carried into the many other undertakings supervised by him. There could be no better claim to the honours of industry than the achievement of the man

who said many years ago, and never ceased to prove that he meant it, 'I would rather have a system that will produce the finest type of men and women than one that would produce the finest dividends.'
— Obituary, *Daily Telegraph*, 8 May 1925

Lever Brothers thrived under the leadership of Lord Leverhulme's successor – not, as he hoped, his son, but the man to whom he ceded his position as head of the company in 1925. 'The greatest memorial we can erect to my father is the successful carrying on of the business which he founded,' announced Hulme Lever, the second Viscount Leverhulme, in July that year. 'It is for us to show that my father was right when he founded the Co-Partnership scheme, that the scheme is not an idle theory but a practical commercial proposition which is reflected in the progress and the profits of the business.' And to that end, knowing that he did not have the talent for leadership that the task required, he stood aside from his birthright, taking a new role as 'Governor' of Lever Brothers, leaving the running of the empire in the hands of another man: Francis D'Arcy Cooper.

The first thing the new chairman did was to jettison the Hebrides. All development on Harris ceased only a week after Lever's death. By October the island was up for sale. The piers, fish-curing sheds, offices and staff accommodation on the harbourside at Leverburgh passed into the hands of a demolition company for a desultory £5,000.

> Lever started the heavenly climb
> He went up the stairs two at a time.
> St Peter said, 'Make room, make room,
> Here comes Viscount Leverhulme.'

St Peter said, 'Don't be cross with me
But this is a mere formality;
Have you any failure to confess?'
And Lever truthfully answered, 'Yes.'

'I left my programme incomplete,
The Western Islands had me beat.'
St Peter said, 'I'm not surprised;
To tackle Lewis was ill-advised.

The Scottish Islands are a rotten deal,
Those Celts are terribly difficile;
We find them unwilling to pull their weight
When we let them in at the Golden Gate.'
– from 'The Ballad of Lord Leverhulme', by Louis MacNeice, 1938

One lot was saved from sale: MacFisheries, the chain of
fishmongers that Lever had set up to sell the produce that
he was certain would soon be bursting from the nets of his
fleet in Harris. D'Arcy Cooper's policy was clear: all
ventures that had nothing to do with the company's core
business were to be disposed of, but it quickly became
apparent that he would get nothing like the £2 million or
more that Lever had invested if he went for a quick sale. He
decided to hold on to MacFisheries until he could get a
better price.

It was a lucky decision. MacFisheries was a success in its
own right, and would continue to be so. But it was also,
thanks to a shrewd investment by Lever, the owner of a
company producing sausages and ice cream by the name of
T. Wall and Sons, and it would eventually form the basis
of Lever Brothers' massive food division, which now
includes such brands as Bird's Eye, PG Tips, Marmite,

Hellmann's Mayonnaise and Pot Noodle. It paved the way for Lever Brothers' merger with their great rivals the Dutch margarine company Van Den Berghs in 1930, to create the multinational behemoth Unilever. Foodstuffs now account for more than half of the company's worldwide sales. Even as his colleagues whispered that William Lever was losing his touch, he was quietly laying the foundations for their future.

> Our regretted chief was a social reformer. He was a forerunner of better times.
> – M. Bertrand, Minister of State in the Belgian government, laying a wreath upon William Lever's tomb, 22 May 1925

The 1930 merger swept Lever's treasured co-partnership scheme out of existence. The Kingdom of Sunlight was now the Unilever Empire: to allow the financial share in the company to rest solely with a handful of the company's longest-serving workers in England would be unfair upon those who toiled under its flag elsewhere across the globe. But the founder's idealism was far from forgotten: a new pension scheme was rolled out across the board, and in 1936 the Short Time, Unemployment, Sickness and Accident benefits scheme was introduced to finally lay to rest the 'ghosts' that William Lever had devoted so much effort to exorcising from the lives of his workers. By now, however, the world at large was beginning to catch up with him. In 1942 William Beveridge launched his report on social insurance with words that could have come straight from the mouth of Lever: 'Want is one only of five giants on the road of reconstruction ... the others are Disease, Ignorance, Squalor and Idleness.' The revolutionary reforms which followed over the next decade, and rolled out the welfare state across Britain, came as nothing new to Port Sunlight: the village had quietly been getting on with looking after its inhabitants from cradle to grave for sixty years or more.

And Lever's part in this did not go unnoticed. In 1951 the left-wing economist Nicholas Davenport visited Port Sunlight to write a piece for *Progress* magazine. 'I was amazed to find that not only had he put into practice most of our principles of social welfare, but that he had anticipated many of our problems and had pointed the way to the proper solution of them. He seemed to me to be the embodiment of the epoch into which he was born – the hundred years of social reform . . . The Labour party in its pragmatic approach to the theory of the Welfare State owed much to William Lever.'

What would the man who described himself as 'a Liberal without restrictive adjectives' and slammed the 'Socialist cure-all' as an idiotic dream have made of this tribute? The theories he espoused were often so contradictory to his actions that it is hard to identify a place for him anywhere on the political spectrum. He rivalled that other disciple of Samuel Smiles, Margaret Thatcher, in his avowed belief in laissez-faire economics, bitterly opposing state subsidies and tariffs and insisting that 'without competition we cannot succeed. There is no growth, no life, no progress without resistance – merely stagnation.' Yet in the Commons he came over more like Tony Benn, castigating his colleagues for failing in their 'duty of doing something for those members of the community who were not in a position to do it for themselves', and demanding a higher rate of income tax on the rich to pay for the upkeep of those incapable of helping themselves. Those in his own employ were spoon-fed everything they could possibly need, but in return were obliged to sit through constant lectures on how they must 'sacrifice ease, comfort, and enjoyment' and 'pay the price of self sacrifice' if they wished to make anything of their lives.

'There was an almost quaint contrast between his theoretical passion for extreme individualism and his practical hostility to individualism in being,' wrote the journalist E. T. Raymond of the King of Sunlight three years after his death. Lever's own endlessly repeated favourite phrase when describing his beliefs, 'Enlightened Self-Interest', does not come close to bridging the gap.

Part of the reason for the dichotomy, I think, lies with Lever's flat refusal to waste time on discussion – even with himself. 'We won't argue: you're wrong,' was the phrase which characterized his debating style with colleagues, and he seems to have adopted the same approach to any doubts or contradictions in his own mind. He was not given to introspection: he had too much else to be getting on with. In Elizabeth he found the only person whom he could listen to, and the way she tempered his ideas and humanized their presentation was sorely missed from 1913 onwards. After her death he stood alone, deaf both to the thoughts of others and to the voices that crowded in his own head. 'If I decided everything twice I would double my work,' he was fond of telling colleagues. Once you had formed an opinion, you stuck with it for ever – even if it flew in the face of everything you did for the rest of your life.

Perhaps, however, Lever was just way ahead of all of us. T. G. Houghton, a member of the staff at Warrington in the earliest days, was drafted in by *Port Sunlight News* in June 1925 to pen a tribute to his old friend and colleague which makes him sound like an architect of New Labour, stranded a century before his time. 'One of his dearest ambitions was to help towards a complete reconciliation of Capital and Labour, and to bring both to a proper appreciation of their dependence on each other, and he has done much to remove reproaches that were levelled, not without reason, against earlier generations of capitalists.' Peter Mandelson would be proud of him. Lever was certainly always looking to the future. His first speech at the House of Lords in June 1918 was a proposal for decimal money to aid trade and commerce between nations. 'If we cling to our present coinage too long we shall find ourselves the weaker,' he warned the House, 'and we shall find the American gold dollar and not the British sovereign the dominant factor in international finance.' I wonder which side of the Euro debate he would find himself on now.

> By the death of Lord Leverhulme this age has been shorn of one of its biggest figures. It is given to few men to achieve as much materially as he did, and his career is a welcome witness that our English stock has not lost capacity to produce men on the heroic scale.
> – Obituary, *Morning Post*, 8 May 1925

In the summer of 2002, the BBC ran its Great Britons poll, which racked up all the usual suspects – Shakespeare, Elizabeth I, John Lennon, Churchill – in a top 100 which was put to a public vote. Lever was championed by Evan Davis, the BBC's own economics editor, who called him 'one of the great pioneers of modern consumerism', which would have delighted him, and 'one of the great Victorian philanthropists', which would have annoyed him no end. It is also the title awarded him by English Heritage in a blue plaque which commemorates him on the wall of his Hampstead home. A similar plaque decorates 16 Wood Street, in Bolton, and there is another on the side of the manse in Port Sunlight, where he stayed during construction work at Thornton Manor. It is as unnecessary as the tacky granite obelisk that was unveiled beside the Lady Lever Art Gallery in 1930: the village which surrounds them will always be tribute enough to his memory.

> My happiness is my business. I can see finality for myself, an end, an absolute end, but none for my business. There one has room to breathe, to grow, to expand, and the possibilities are boundless . . . I don't work at business only for the sake of money. I am not a lover of money as money and never have been. I work at business because business is life. It enables me to do things.
>
> – William Lever, 1924

That business goes on, one of the biggest in the world, and still, if their corporate PR machine is to be believed, true to the ideals set out by its founder all those years ago. In 2002 Unilever spent £69 million on community projects across the globe: it gave scholarships to the children of its employees in Ghana, funded reforestation projects as far apart as Kenya and Thailand, donated offices to HIV projects in Nigeria and provided a floating hospital on the rivers of Bangladesh, taking up-to-date healthcare out to the country's most remote communities. Staff at the company's London headquarters were encouraged to devote part of their working week to mentoring local primary school children and helping them learn to read.

And Lever's own name lives on in the Leverhulme Trust, a charitable foundation he created in his will, which donates around £25 million every year to academic research projects in all disciplines around the UK. In 2002 physicists, geographers, economists, biologists, archaeologists and geneticists benefited from the enduring

generosity of the grocer's son. Dr N. B. Rankor of Royal
Holloway University got £250,000 to look into 'Ship Sheds
in the Ancient Mediterranean', which is about as far from
soap-making as you can get.

BURIAL OF VISCOUNT LEVERHULME
IMPRESSIVE AND UNPRECEDENTED SCENES AT
PORT SUNLIGHT
FOUR MILE ROUTE LINED BY SORROWING CROWDS
3,000 CHILDREN SING AT GRAVESIDE
WONDERFUL CARPET OF WHITE WREATHS
– Headlines from the *Bolton Evening News*, 11 May 1925

The works at Port Sunlight were closed on the day of
William Lever's funeral. Francis D'Arcy Cooper had to
unlock the doors of the General Offices himself when he
arrived with the other directors of Lever Brothers shortly
after the burial. Together they made their way past the
silent desks and upstairs to the glass-walled sanctum above
the deserted offices, where the portraits of James, Eliza and
Elizabeth Lever still hung. Each man present gathered
around the writing desk to read over the resolution that the
chairman had drafted for them, and give their assent to it
being distributed among their offices and businesses that
were scattered across every corner of the globe.

> The board . . . desire to place on record their admiration of his life
> and work, distinguished by genius, courage, imagination, and
> devotion to duty. His career was inspired by the highest ideals of
> public spirit and service to his fellow men, and notably by his
> interest in the welfare, education, better housing, and amelioration
> of the conditions of labour of every rank of industrial worker, as
> evinced by his creation of Co-partnership, Life Insurance, Old Age

Pensions, Educational and other schemes for the benefit of his employees, and by his gifts to the communities of Port Sunlight and Merseyside, to his native town of Bolton, and the nation.

Each man nodded his assent, and signed his name. Then they filed out of the Chief's office, down the stairs and back into the spring sunshine. On Wood Street the trees were in full leaf; the flowers in the Diamond were as bright as the hundreds of wreaths which still carpeted the Lady Lever Art Gallery at its end. The men stood for a moment looking at the village, with its spires and turrets, domes and arches, the last of the mourners still making their way from the churchyard down the wide boulevards lined by immaculate front gardens. It was D'Arcy Cooper, who for all their differences had remained fond of the old man until the end, who best put into words what they were thinking.

'He's probably now arguing with St Peter about the architecture of the gates.'

ACKNOWLEDGEMENTS

Since I began working on this book I've been vaguely telling people it is a 'sort-of biography'. I never presumed to write the definitive work on William Lever, but rather to recount a personal journey through the world in which he lived, the world he created around himself, and the legacy that he has left behind. If you haven't yet visited the most vital part of that legacy, Port Sunlight, you should go now. I'm serious. You've finished the book, so put it down, get in the car and head for the M53. What's keeping you?

Readers of a more sedentary nature who wish to know more about the man and his works will find plenty of pointers in the bibliography that follows. This book could not have been written without reference to the second Viscount Leverhulme's 1927 account of his father's life and Charles Wilson's three-volume history of the company he founded. Both men did much of the legwork for me long before I was born. I drew much of my primary material from the various company pamphlets and magazines that Lever himself edited, or at least had a hand in, in particular *Port Sunlight*

News, *Progress*, *Square Deals* and *The Sunlight Year Book*, as well as the many examples of his own writing and speeches which he published during his lifetime, and interviews that he gave to various journalists. Where I have drawn from contemporary newspapers or periodicals I have acknowledged the sources in the text.

I'm grateful to the staff of the Lady Lever Art Gallery, the Port Sunlight Heritage Centre, the British Library, the Mitchell Library in Glasgow, Bolton Central Library, the House of Lords records office, and the Public Records Office and the British Library Newspaper Library, all of whom helped me in my research. And to Bill and Christine Lawson, whose conversation at their excellent Seallam! centre on the Isle of Harris inspired me to find out a bit more about this peculiar chap in the first place.

I would like to give heartfelt personal thanks to the following for (variously) their inspiration, information, remuneration and accommodation: Matthew Collin, Tina Jackson, Sam Hart, Ian Hislop, Andrew MacQueen, Olivia Coy, Wayne Parker, the late L372 NTW, Adrian and Emily Travis, my agent David Smith, Doug Young, Bill Scott-Kerr, Sheila Lee for her excellent work on the pictures, Dr Richard Singleton and Spike and Anna Golding. But most of all, for their help, love and support, I'm more grateful than I will ever be able to say to my mum and dad and to Michael Tierney.

PICTURE CREDITS

The Church Institute, Bolton. Courtesy *Bolton Evening News*; William and James Lever with their sister, Elizabeth Emma, from the Unilever magazine, *Progress*, April 1926; Wood Street, Bolton. Photo Nic Clews.

Bird's-eye view of Port Sunlight, 1898. Topham; Port Sunlight employees, 25 March 1914. Topical Press/Getty Images; house in Port Sunlight, 1903. Topham; Lord Leverhulme carrying the King's colours of the Wirral Battalion, 1922. Topham.

Mrs William Hesketh Lever by Luke Fildes. National Museums Liverpool (Lady Lever Art Gallery); open-air bedroom, Thornton Manor. Photo courtesy Sotheby's Picture Library; dinner at Thornton Manor, c. 1903. Photo from the family archive by courtesy of Sotheby's Picture Library; grounds of 'The Hill', Hampstead. Universal Pictorial Press/Topham; Rivington Pike on an open day. Courtesy *Bolton Evening News*.

The First Lord Leverhulme by Augustus John, 1920.
National Museums Liverpool (Lady Lever Art Gallery);
Girl with Dogs by Charles Burton Barber, 1893. © Lady
Lever Art Gallery, Port Sunlight, Merseyside, UK,
National Museums Liverpool/www.bridgeman.co.uk;
advertisement for Sunlight Soap, c. 1900. Mary Evans
Picture Library; 'The Patron, William, first Baron
Leverhulme, setting out on a long, painful, and certainly
unpremeditated journey adown the Ages', cartoon depict-
ing Augustus John and Lever by Max Beerbohm, 1920.
Photo National Portrait Gallery Picture Library, copyright
the Estate of Max Beerbohm, reprinted by permission of
Berlin Associates; cartoon, *Daily Mirror*, October 1916.

'Stornoway of the Future' by Raffles Davidson, 1920.
Photo © Comhairle nan Eilean Siar and the Stornoway Pier
and Harbour Commission; a crofter's cottage, Lewis. ©
The Trustees of the National Museums of Scotland.

SELECT BIBLIOGRAPHY

Auction catalogues:
  Collection at Rivington, Knight Frank & Rutley, 1926
  Furniture and Tapestries from Lews Castle and Cheshire, Knight Frank & Rutley, 1926
  Contents of The Hill, Hampstead, Knight Frank & Rutley, 1926
Best, Geoffrey, *Mid-Victorian Britain 1851–75* (Fontana, 1979)
Bryson, Bill, *Down Under* (Doubleday, 2000)
Cammidge, P. J., and Howard, H. A. H., *New Views on Diabetes Mellitus* (1923)
Camplin, John M., *On Diabetes and its Successful Treatment* (1858)
Cooper, Derek, *Hebridean Connection: A View of the Highlands and Islands* (Routledge & Kegan Paul, 1977)
Dickens, Charles, *David Copperfield* (Penguin Popular Classics, 1994)
Dickins, Shirley J., *Grenfell of the Congo* (National Sunday School Union)
Van Emden, Richard, and Humphries, Steve, *All Quiet on the Home Front* (Headline, 2003)
Engel, Matthew, *Tickle the Public: One Hundred Years of the Popular Press* (Victor Gollancz, 1996)
Fenton, Alexander, *The Island Blackhouse* (Historic Scotland, 1995)
Fieldhouse, David, *Unilever Overseas: The Anatomy of a Multinational* (Croom Helm, 1979)

Forty, Sandra, *The Pre-Raphaelites* (Grange Books, 1997)

Furtado, Peter, *World War One* (Andromeda, 1988)

Gardner, Brian (ed.), *Up the Line to Death: the War Poets 1914–18* (Methuen, 1964)

Gent, Leslie, *Bolton Past* (Phillimore and Co., 1997)

Gomez, Joan, *Living with Diabetes* (Sheldon Press, 1995)

Haythornthwaite, Philip J., *The World War One Sourcebook* (Arms and Armour Press, 1992)

Herries, Amanda, *Japanese Gardens in Britain* (Shire, 2001)

Hindley, Diana and Geoffrey, *Advertising in Victorian England 1837–1901* (Wayland, 1972)

Hochschild, Adam, *King Leopold's Ghost* (Macmillan, 1999)

Holroyd, Michael, *Augustus John: The New Biography* (Chatto & Windus, 1996)

Hope, Michael, *Lever versus Liverpool* (Anatole, 2002)

Horrie, Chris, and Chippendale, Peter, *Stick It Up Your Punter: the Uncut Story of the Sun Newspaper* (Simon & Schuster, 1999)

Hunter, Gavin, and Boumphrey, Ian, *Port Sunlight, a Pictorial History* (Yesterday's Wirral, 2002)

Jenkins, Roy, *Churchill* (Macmillan, 2001)

John, Augustus, *Chiaroscuro: Fragments of an Autobiography* (Jonathan Cape, 1952)

Jolly, W. P., *Lord Leverhulme: A Biography* (Constable, 1976)

Knox, Andrew M., *Coming Clean: A Postscript After Retirement from Unilever* (Heinemann, 1976)

Larson, Erik, *The Devil in the White City* (Doubleday, 2003)

Lee, Christopher, *This Sceptered Isle: The Twentieth Century* (BBC, 1999)

Lever, William, *Following the Flag: Jottings of a Jaunt Round the World* (Lever Brothers, 1893)

    address at AGM of Imperial Arts League, 1915

    address at St George's Road New School, Lever Brothers, 1915

    Art (Lever Brothers, 1915)

    Day By Day, That's All (Lever Brothers, 1915)

    Fast Asleep on a Gold Mine (Lever Brothers, 1915)

    Each Other's Burdens (Lever Brothers, 1916)

    Girls and Boys (Lever Brothers, 1916)

Lever, William Hulme, *Viscount Leverhulme* (George Allen and Unwin, 1927)

MacNeice, Louis, *I Crossed the Minch* (Longman, 1938)

May, Trevor, *The Victorian Schoolroom* (Shire, 2002)
   The Victorian Domestic Servant (Shire, 2002)

Stuart Menzies, Mrs, *Modern Men of Mark* (Herbert Jenkins, 1921)

Munro, J. Forbes, *Africa and the International Economy, 1800–1960* (J. M. Dent, 1976)

Nevett, T. R., *Advertising in Britain* (Heinemann, 1982)

Nicolson, Nigel, *Lord of the Isles* (Weidenfeld & Nicolson, 1960)

Paxman, Jeremy, *The Political Animal: An Anatomy* (Michael Joseph, 2002)

Poole, Robert, *Popular Leisure and the Music Hall in Nineteenth Century Bolton* (Centre for North-West Regional Studies, 1982)

Port Sunlight Fact Sheets (The Port Sunlight Village Trust, 1999)

Porter, Roy, *Madness: A Brief History* (Oxford University Press, 2002)
   A Social History of Madness (Phoenix, 1987)

Randell, Nigel, *The White Headhunter* (Constable, 2003)

Raymond, E.T., *Portraits of the New Century* (Ernest Benn, 1928)

Reader, W. J., *Fifty Years of Unilever 1930–1980* (Heinemann, 1980)

Readyhough, Gordon, *Bolton Town Centre: A Modern History* (Bolton Archives and Local Studies Service, 1998)

Rubens, Paul, *The Sunshine Girl* (score) (George Edwardes, 1912)

Sackett, Terence, *British Life a Century Ago* (Frith Book Company, 1999)

Scarr, Deryck, *Fragments of Empire: A History of the Western Pacific High Commission* (Australian National University Press, 1967)

Sellers, Sue, *Sunlighters: The Story of a Village* (Unilever, 1988)

Smiles, Samuel, *Self Help* (reprint of 1866 edition, IEA Health and Welfare Unit, 1997)

Smith, M. D., *Leverhulme's Rivington* (Wyre Publishing, 1998)

Stanley, Henry Morton, *The Founding of the Congo Free State* (1895)

The Story of Port Sunlight (Unilever, 1953)

Sutcliffe, Anthony, *The Rise of Modern Urban Planning 1800–1914* (Mansell, 1980)

British Town Planning: The Formative Years (Leicester University Press, 1981)

Sweet, Matthew, *Inventing the Victorians* (Faber & Faber, 2001)

The Thompson Blue Book on Advertising (J. Walter Thompson Co., 1904)

Turner, E. S., *The Shocking History of Advertising* (Penguin, 1965)

Watson, Angus, *My Life* (Ivor Nicholson & Watson, 1937)

Westlake, Ray, *Kitchener's Army* (Spellmount, 1989)

Wheen, Francis, *Karl Marx* (Fourth Estate, 1999)

Williams, Edmund, *Port Sunlight Factory: The First Hundred Years* (Unilever, 1988)

Williams, Harley, *Men of Stress* (Jonathan Cape, 1948)

Wilson, A. N., *The Victorians* (Hutchinson, 2002)

Wilson, Charles, *The History of Unilever* (3 vols, Cassell, 1954)

Wood, Christopher, *Burne-Jones* (Weidenfeld & Nicolson, 1998)

Wood, Lucy (ed.), *The Lady Lever Art Gallery* (Bluecoat Press, 1996)

INDEX

INDEX

INDEX

International Garden Cities congress, 234; James Lever's view, 58, 66, 149; Lady Lever Art Gallery, 144–5, 157, 255–6; Lever memorials, 309; Lever's death, 298; Lever's vision, 58; location, 55; manse, 309; ownership of houses, 302; plans, 60; politics, 175–6; Princess Beatrice's visit, 255; Prize Band, 76; profit-sharing-by-property, 74–5, 128; quay, 57; rents, 68–9; retirements, 259–60; roads, 56; site, 56–7; Social Department, 76; social engineering, 73–4; societies, 69–70; street plan, 61; swimming-pool, 71; Technical Institute, 125; Village Estate Department, 273; Village Society, 71; Village Trust, 302; war memorial, 247; in wartime, 239–40

Port Sunlight News, 297, 307
Port Sunlight Pals, 237–9, 247
Port Sunlight Village Trust, 302
Portable Building Company of Manchester, 166
Porter, Gail, 41
Porter, Roy, 148
Pot Noodle, 305
Progress, 145, 176, 306
Prout, William, 217, 240
Pugin, Augustus, 188

Randell, Nigel, 198
Rankor, N. B., 310
Raymond, E. T., 307
Reckitt family, 62
Reilly, Charles, 141
Renkin, Jules, 210, 212
Rigby, Ethel, 227–8, 231
Rinso, 142
Ripon, George Robinson, first Marquess of, 194
Rivington Hall, 1, 166
Rivington Pike, 1, 3, 10, 21, 161–9
Robinson, Alfred, 86
Rom, Léon, 208
Root, John, 96
Rowntree family, 62
Royal Academy, 46, 158, 250, 256
Royal Court Theatre, Liverpool, 115, 130
Royal Geographical Society, 112, 217
Royal National Lifeboat Institution (RNLI), 45, 51
Rubens, Paul, 114
Russell Islands, 194

Salisbury, Robert Cecil, 3rd Marquess of, 111
Salt, Titus, 59, 124
Samoa, 104, 193

San Francisco, 100–1
Sandwich Islands, 101–3
Scotsman, 274, 289
Scott, Robert, 45
Scott, Sir Samuel, 261
Scottish Board of Agriculture, 273, 275
Scottish Office, 260–1, 271
Seaforth Highlanders, 270
Sealskin, 92
Sellers, Sue, 77, 283
Semple, Chief Fire Officer, 229
Shakespeare, William, 13, 15, 56, 125, 308
Shaw, George Bernard, 75
Siam, 84
Sierra Leone, 217
Silicate of Soda, 33
Simpson, Jonathan: Bungalow fire, 229, 230; education, 11; engagement, 21; friendship with Lever, 11, 27, 29, 167, 251, 259; reading, 13; Scottish holiday, 27; training, 21, 22; work for Lever, 25, 62, 63, 166, 167, 231
Simpson, Mary (Lomax), 21, 27
Sims, George, 58
Smiles, Samuel, 14–15, 306
Smith, F. E., 137
Soap Trust crusade, 134–5
Soapmakers' Association, 53, 132–3
Social Science Congress, 59
Society for the Checking of Abuses in Public Advertising, 41
Sodium Tallowate, 33
Solomon Islands, 194–200, 202–4, 211
Stanley, Henry Morton, 205, 206–7, 211, 217
Stead, William Thomas, 48–9, 75, 254
Stones, John, 16
Stones and Hesketh, 9, 16–19
Stornoway, 262–3, 264, 268
Stornoway Fish Products and Ice Co Ltd, 269
Stuffins, Arthur, 76
suffrage, women's, 224–6
Suffragette, 228
Sullivan, Arthur, 78
Sun, 140
Sunlight Cattle Seed Cake, 91
Sunlight Flakes, 91
Sunlight Soap: advertising, 37, 38–9, 42–6; American market, 86–8; creation, 31–4; *Daily Mail* boycott campaign, 136–7; fakes, 138; formula, 31–4, 73; Frith picture, 46–50; ingredients, 82–3; name, 30–1; packaging, 34; price, 132; production, 34–5, 51–2, 90; promotions, 50–1; sales, 35–7, 52–3, 84–5, 93, 132; size of tablet, 132; uses, 42–3; wartime supplies, 241

327

Sunlight Soap Year Book, 44
Sunshine Girl, The, 114–15, 130
Sutcliffe, Anthony, 62
Switzerland, 85

tallow, 83, 137, 192
Taylor, W. H. S., 54
Terry, Ellen, 91
Thatcher, Margaret, 14, 306
Thoday, E., 215
Thomas Cook & Sons, 79, 111
Thompson, W. P., 30
Thornton Hough: churchyard, 149;
  countryside, 102; history, 151; houses,
  151–2; Lever family homes, 146, 153–4,
  159, 267; Lever's work, 152–3, 224;
  manor house, 63; population, 152–3,
  182
Thornton House, 146, 148, 154
Thys, Albert, 213
Tillotson, John, 260
Tillotson, Mary (Lever, sister), 13–14, 17,
  26, 154
Tillotson, W. F., 14, 26, 86, 154
Times, The, 37, 41, 79, 131, 224, 241, 250,
  260, 289
Titan Soap Company, 138
Titchmarsh, Alan, 168
trade union movement, 126–8, 283
Turner, E. S., 42
Tweedmouth, Dudley Marjoribanks, first
  Baron, 158

Unilever, 305
United States of America, 86–9, 95–101
Unwin, Raymond, 64

Van den Bergh company, 85, 305
Vandervelde, Emile, 216

Velvet Skin, 92
Victoria, Queen, 47, 79, 91, 92, 206
Vienna, 84
Villa, 92
Vim, 92, 124
Vosper, Sydney Curnow, 51

Wagner, Richard, 78
Wainwright, Edward, 32
Walker, Frederick, 157
Wall, T. and Sons, 304
Wallace, Edgar, 135, 140
Warrington, 32–5, 51–4, 61, 124
Watson, Angus, 283–4
Watson, Joseph, 137
Watson and Crosfield, 136, 273, *see also*
  Joseph Crosfield & Sons
Webster, A. L., 235–6
Welch, Raquel, 91
Wellington, Arthur Wellesley, Duke of, 29
Whiteley, George, 185
Wigan, 24–5
Williams, Ethel, 76
Wilson, Charles, 130
Winser, Percy, 32, 52, 121
Wirral constituency, 176–8
Wolfendale, A. J., 86, 87–8
Wolsey, Thomas, 15
Woodford, Charles, 194, 195, 197, 199, 201
World War I: declared, 235; drink policy,
  244–5; female employment, 245–6;
  glycerine supplies, 235–6; hospitals, 239;
  Lever's war work, 240–1; Lewis losses,
  270–1, 272; margarine, 242–4; munitions
  work, 239–40; Port Sunlight Pals, 237–9,
  247; refugees, 239; war memorial, 247

Y-Z Disinfectant Soap Powder, 91–2
Yeadon, Albert, 227